IMAGES
of America

LONG BEACH

On the Cover: Members of the water ballet team of Gulf Park College for Women strike a relaxed pose along a seawall with their physical education director in this 1950 photograph. The students at Gulf Park participated in many water sports, including swimming, diving, and synchronized swimming. The seawall, constructed in 1925, borders the longest man-made beach in the world, stretching for 26 miles along the Mississippi Gulf Coast. (Courtesy of Mississippi Gulf Coast Community College C.C. "Tex" Hamill Down South Magazine Collection.)

IMAGES
of America

LONG BEACH

Allisa L. Beck

ARCADIA
PUBLISHING

ISBN 978-1-4671-1371-7

Published by Arcadia Publishing
Charleston, South Carolina

Printed in the United States of America

Library of Congress Control Number: 2014949591

For all general information, please contact Arcadia Publishing:
Telephone 843-853-2070
Fax 843-853-0044
E-mail sales@arcadiapublishing.com
For customer service and orders:
Toll-Free 1-888-313-2665

Visit us on the Internet at www.arcadiapublishing.com

Contents

ACKNOWLEDGMENTS

I would like to thank everyone who has been gracious enough to share photographs, family stories, and his or her own Long Beach experiences. This includes Paul Jermyn, Betty Shaw, Julia Arceneaux, Eddie Ware, Donald Dana, Mable Skellie, and Rose Donaldson. Special thanks go to Brenda Batey and Beth Hansen for contacting everyone they know to ask for photographs. I would also like to thank Janet Griffin, daughter of Mary Ellen Alexander, who allowed me to use photographs from her mother's extensive research collection. Last, but certainly not least, much appreciation goes to Charles L. Sullivan, who allowed me to use many of the Long Beach photographs from the archives at Mississippi Gulf Coast Community College.

INTRODUCTION

Known as the "Friendly City," Long Beach is situated along the Mississippi Gulf Coast between Gulfport to the east and Pass Christian to the west. Although the city is one of the youngest along the coast, the history of the area can be traced back for hundreds of years before it was incorporated in 1905. The first name given to the area that would become Long Beach was Bear Point, labeled as such on 1774 British maps. At that time, the area was settled by the Choctaw Indians, who made their home along the stream that wound its way through the area. This stream would eventually be called Bear Point Bayou. The Choctaw would have found good soil for farming, the woods full of game, and the waters of the Mississippi Sound plentiful with fish and other seafood. The offshore barrier islands also offered some protection from the damaging storms that would frequently roar in from the Gulf of Mexico.

Long Beach went through several name changes during its history. After the original Bear Point name, it was known as the Chimneys for a time, named after the house built by the original European settlers, the Ladner family (sometimes written as L'Adner). When the John McCaughan family moved to the area, they called it Rosalie. George Scott was responsible for getting the railroad to come through the area by building the first railroad stop. In appreciation for his generosity, the town was renamed Scott's Station. When James Thomas platted the town, Scott wanted to name the town after his wife, Harriet. However, a decision was made to name the town Long Beach after the beautiful beaches along the shore.

As the names for Long Beach changed, so did the town itself. The photographs throughout this book show how the road along the beach went from the unpaved, one-lane, shell Beach Road to a wider Beach Boulevard and then a four-lane Highway 90. Jeff Davis Avenue also grew from a narrow lane with only one or two general stores to a bustling downtown with a center of city government as well as shops and restaurants.

During the early 1900s, Long Beach became a truck farming center because of the rich soil along the coast. Although the Long Beach Long Red radishes were the most well known, farmers also grew other crops such as lettuce, sweet potatoes, beans, corn, and strawberries. There were also citrus groves and fruit and pecan orchards. When the Great Depression put an end to truck farming as an industry, the town then became known for the beautiful beaches and water sports that brought in tourists and summer residents.

The threat of hurricanes has always been in the minds of those who live along the Mississippi Gulf Coast, and locals accept this risk as just a part of living in the region. Nothing is known about the earliest hurricanes that struck the coast, as little to no records were kept. Later, Mississippi Gulf Coast hurricanes were documented in letters, postcards, diaries, and photographs. Some of these photographs are reprinted here, from the relatively mild 1906 hurricane to the devastation of Hurricane Katrina in 2005. The few photographs of Katrina's aftermath are the only contemporary images included, because that devastating hurricane has become a major event in the history of the Mississippi Gulf Coast.

This book offers just a sampling of the stories and photographs that help to tell the story of Long Beach, Mississippi. These photographs serve not only to relate these stories, but to also to document the loss of so many historical buildings and landmarks. The photographs are arranged in chronological order when possible, and it is hoped that this book opens a small window into the rich history of Long Beach and will be appreciated and enjoyed by those who read it.

One

Early Settlers

There were many families who helped settle Long Beach. They moved to the area for the rich soil in which they could grow plentiful crops and the seafood-rich waters of the Mississippi Sound, which would support their families. Some came to the area because their friends and relatives had already settled here and sent encouraging words back home. Not all who moved here were farmers. There were businessmen who helped develop the town, and there were also the summer visitors who sometimes journeyed here for a time and left, but there were many who came to visit and remained.

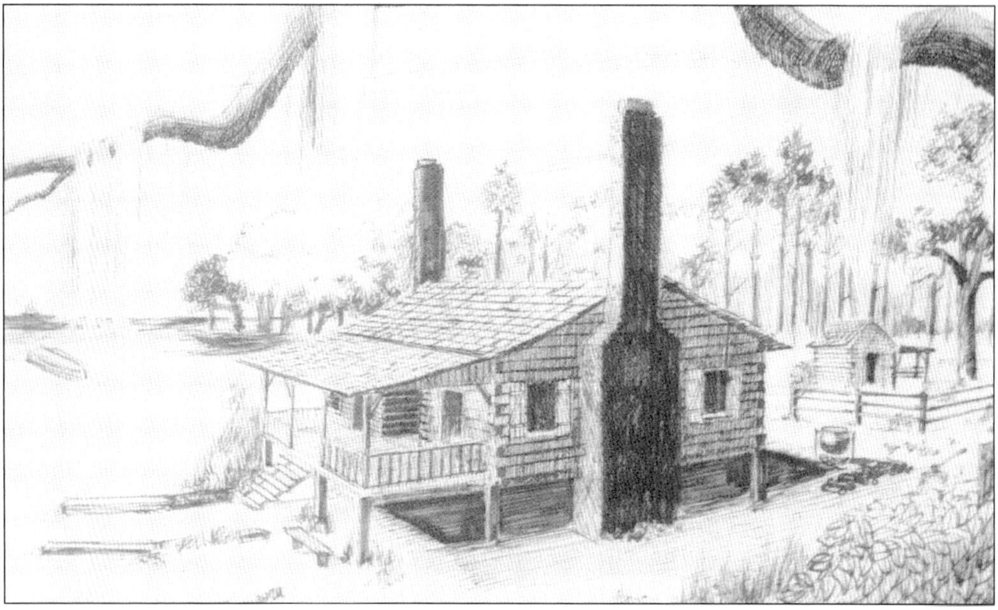

Nicholas and Marianne Ladner were the first to settle in the Long Beach area. This is a modern drawing of the Chimneys, the home that they built. When Nicholas died, his widow was given title to the land, which covered much of present-day Long Beach. It became known as the Widow Ladner Claim. The house later burned, leaving only the two tall chimneys. These were used as navigational landmarks for ships entering the Mississippi Sound. The entire area became known as the Chimneys. (Courtesy of Denise Bourg.)

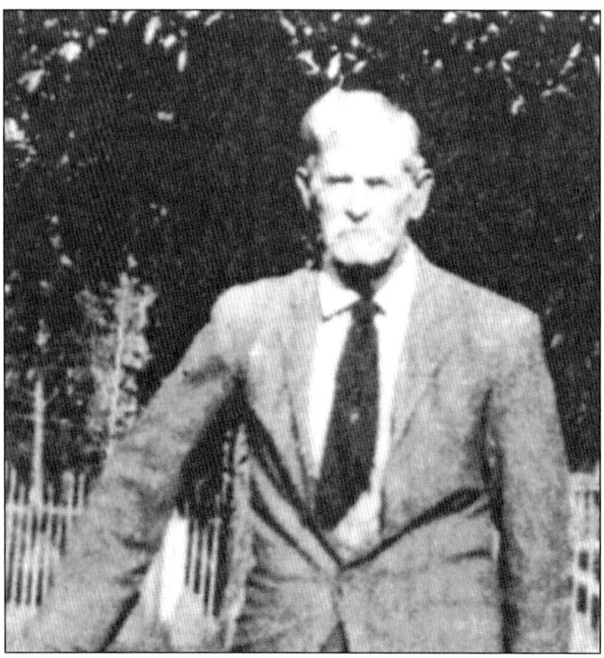

Harper McCaughan was born in 1856 at the site known as Rosalie. His father, John Johnston McCaughan, had come to the area to build the first railroad. He established nearby Mississippi City before moving to the area that had been part of the original Ladner Claim, which he named Rosalie. The former Rosalie site is now the location of the Gulf Coast Campus of the University of Southern Mississippi. Harper later donated much of the family's land for educational use, and the Harper McCaughan Elementary School is named in his honor. This photograph was taken around 1918 in front of his Jeff Davis Avenue home. (Courtesy of Long Beach Historical Society Archives.)

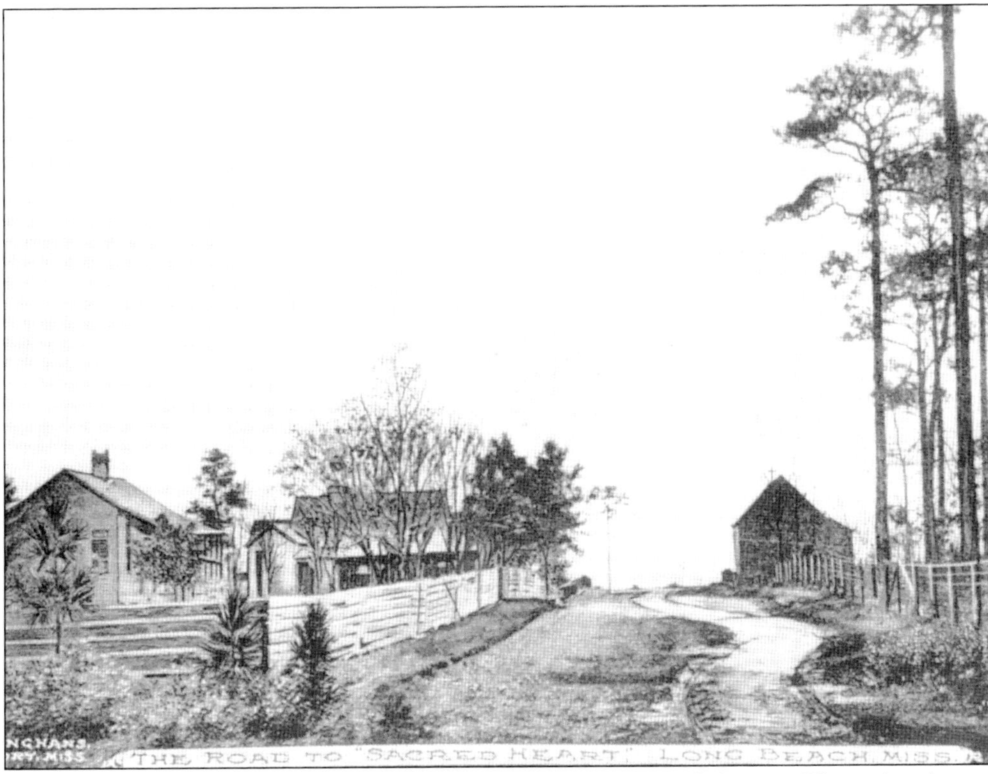

In 1853, George Scott and his family lived on what is now Girard Avenue. The railroad came through in 1870, and a railroad stop was needed. Scott donated land and built the station. As a result of Scott's generosity, the community was renamed Scott's Station. This postcard shows Girard Avenue, then called Scott Avenue, as it looked in the 1880s. The building on the right is the Sacred Heart Orphanage. Scott Avenue was the first street between Pass Christian to Mississippi City to be graded from the railroad to the beachfront. (Courtesy of Beth Hansen.)

Lawyer James O. Thomas came to Long Beach from Tennessee in the 1880s. It was thought that the milder climate would be beneficial to his ailing wife. His brothers, Woods and Caesar, later joined him. The three brothers started a nursery and sold satsuma, pear, pecan, and peach trees. They also planted a pear orchard that extended from the beach north to the railroad tracks. St. Thomas Catholic Church now sits on part of the original Thomas land. James later platted the town and changed the name from Scott's Station to Long Beach. (Courtesy of Long Beach Historical Society Archives.)

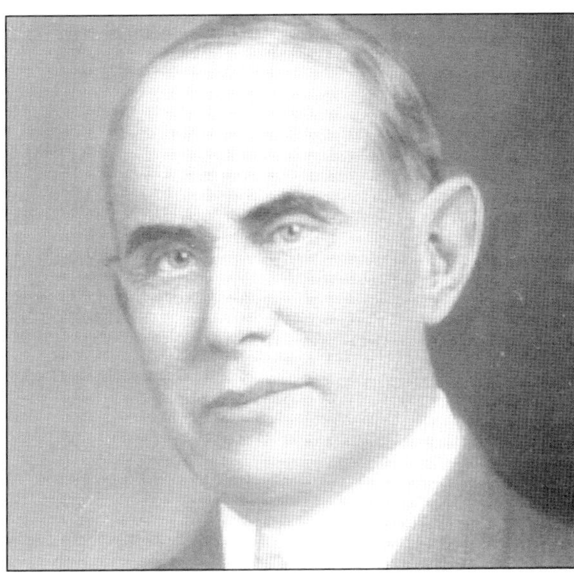

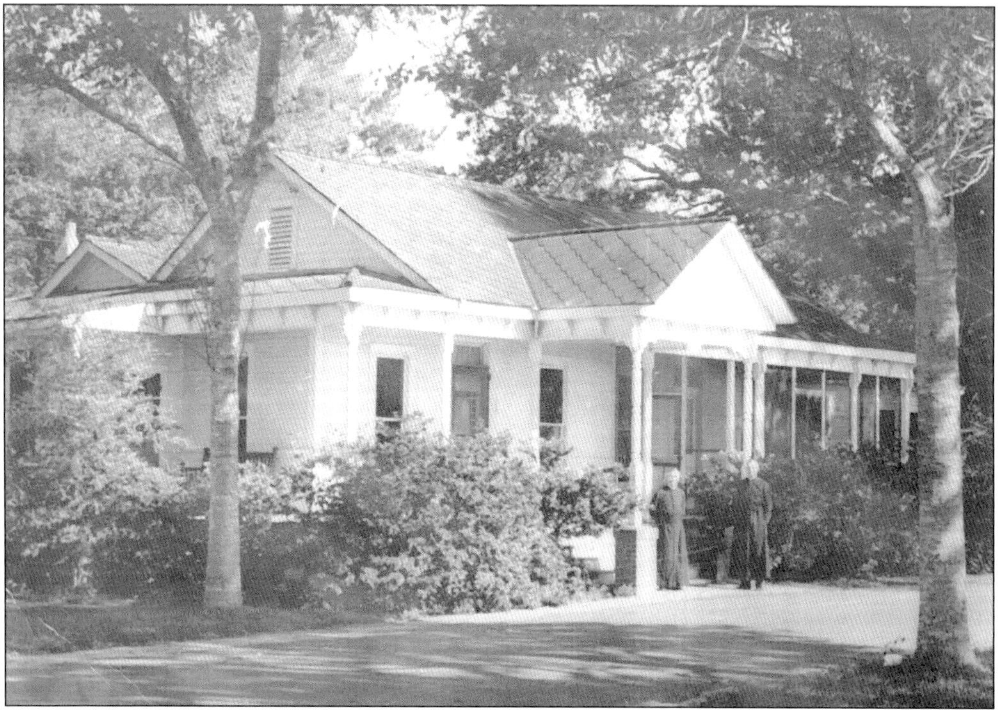

James Thomas built this home in 1881 after arriving in Scott's Station. In 1903, he sold the house and 30 acres of property to the Vincentian Fathers for the development of a retreat for their priests. Until it was torn down and replaced with a new building in 1959, the original Thomas home was used as the priests' home. Pictured in front of the house are Father George O'Malley, CM (left) and Father John Shaughnessy, CM. (Courtesy of Long Beach Historical Society Archives.)

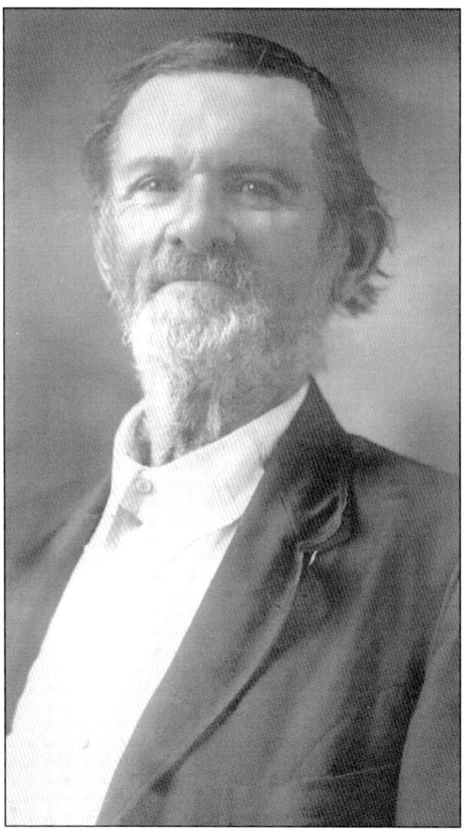

William James Quarles was a schoolteacher, also from Tennessee. He came to Long Beach in 1883 and purchased a large amount of land from his college friend James Thomas. Quarles brought his family to Long Beach in 1884. He taught at Long Beach's first school in the front room of his home and also served as the first postmaster. He opened the first store on property adjoining his homestead. Quarles wanted his children to be able to walk safely to the beach, so he cleared a path that would later become Jeff Davis Avenue. (Courtesy of Long Beach Historical Society Archives.)

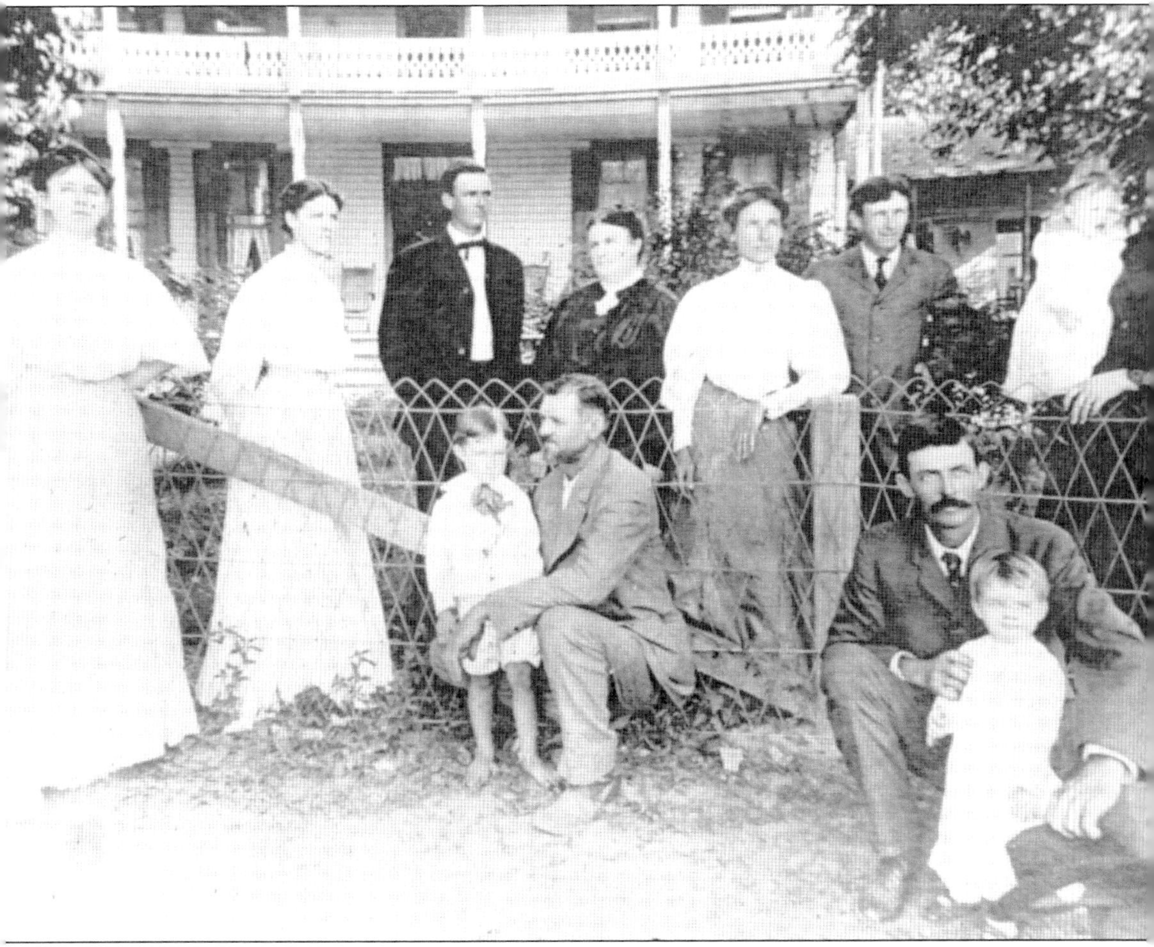

This 1906 photograph shows the W.J. Quarles family posing in front of their home. Pictured are, from left to right, (first row) May (Mrs. G.S. Watrous), grandson Hershel Eugene, W.J Quarles, H.Y. Quarles, and Alice; (second row) Winnie (Mrs. F.Z. Goss), Ben Tarver, Merinda Quarles, Mamie Lou Toomer (Mrs. H.Y. Quarles), I.D. Toomer, and Allie (Mrs. I.D. Toomer) holding daughter Eleanor. (Courtesy of the Mary Ellen Alexander Collection.)

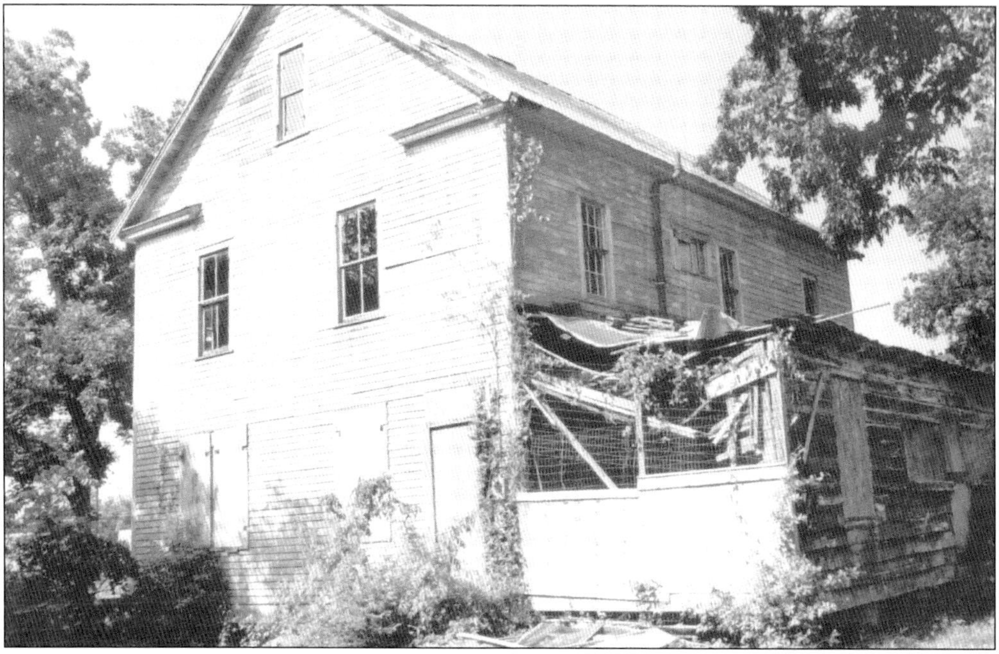

This Quarles home was built in 1892. The house was originally located at 120–122 Railroad Street, but it was moved to the back of the property near the family cemetery and turned to face Old Pass Road. The home is listed in the National Register of Historic Places and is on the Mississippi Heritage Trust's Ten Most Endangered List for 2003. Some exterior restoration has been done on the home, including a new roof, but much interior work has yet to be completed. (Courtesy of Long Beach Historical Society Archives.)

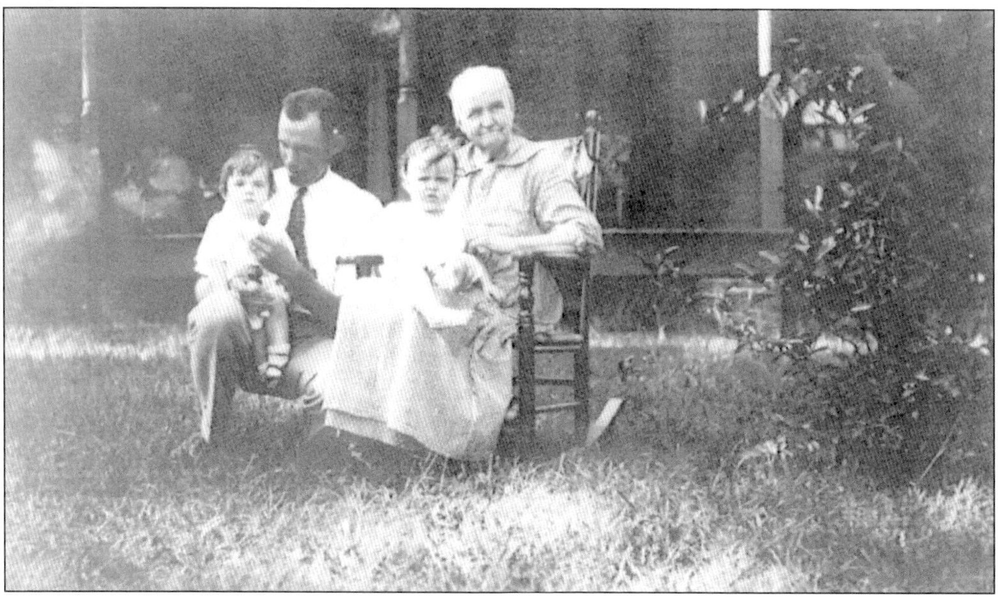

Merinda Quarles, W.J. Quarles's wife, is pictured here posing with her son Herschel and grandchildren Elaine and George. The photograph was taken in 1924 in front of the Quarles home on Railroad Street. Written on the back of the photograph is "Mama is holding Sid's baby George." (Courtesy of the Mary Ellen Alexander Collection.)

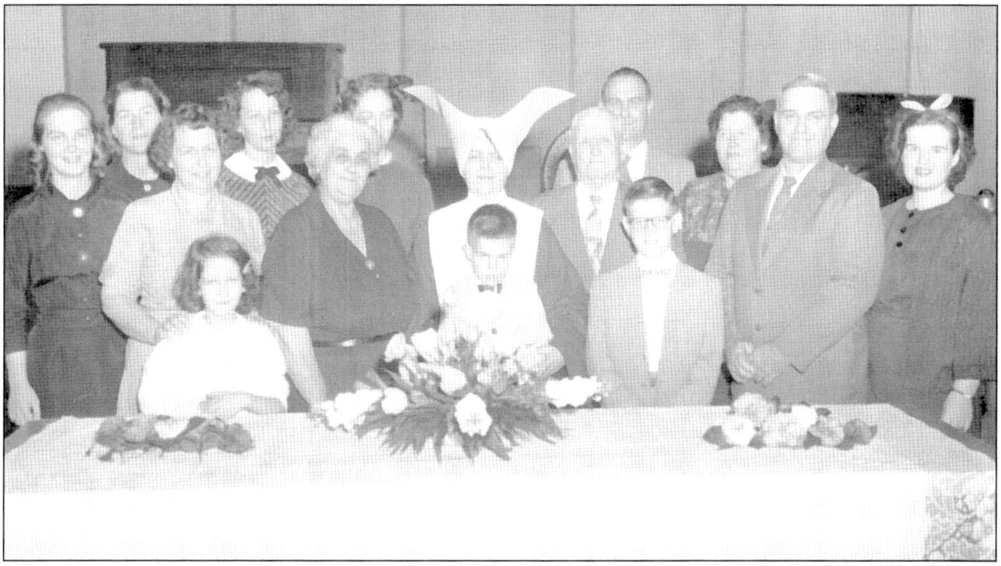

In 1905, a census was taken to see if the population was large enough for the town to be incorporated. The minimum needed was 900, and there were 890 living in town. Several families were persuaded to relocate to Long Beach, including the Dubuissons. Donatien and Anastasia Dubuisson moved their family, including 13 children, to Long Beach. This increased the population to 905, providing more than enough population, and the town was incorporated later that year. The Dubuisson family is pictured here at a family get-together at the St. Thomas Catholic Church Parish Hall in the late 1950s or early 1960s. (Courtesy of Mable Skellie.)

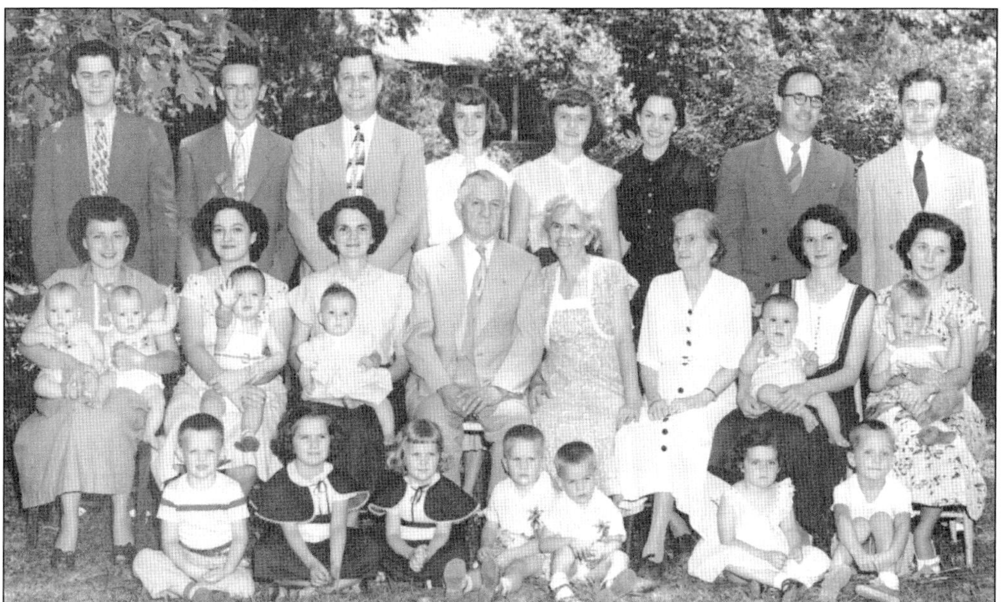

The Skellie family is posing for a portrait at their family reunion in 1951. The reunion was held at the home of Fred A. and Elaine Skellie. Included in the photograph are (top row, second from left) D.G. Skellie, who was mayor from 1962 to 1972 and (bottom row on left, seated) William D.G. "Billy" Skellie Jr., mayor from 2004 to present. (Courtesy of Mississippi Gulf Coast Community College Dixie Press Collection.)

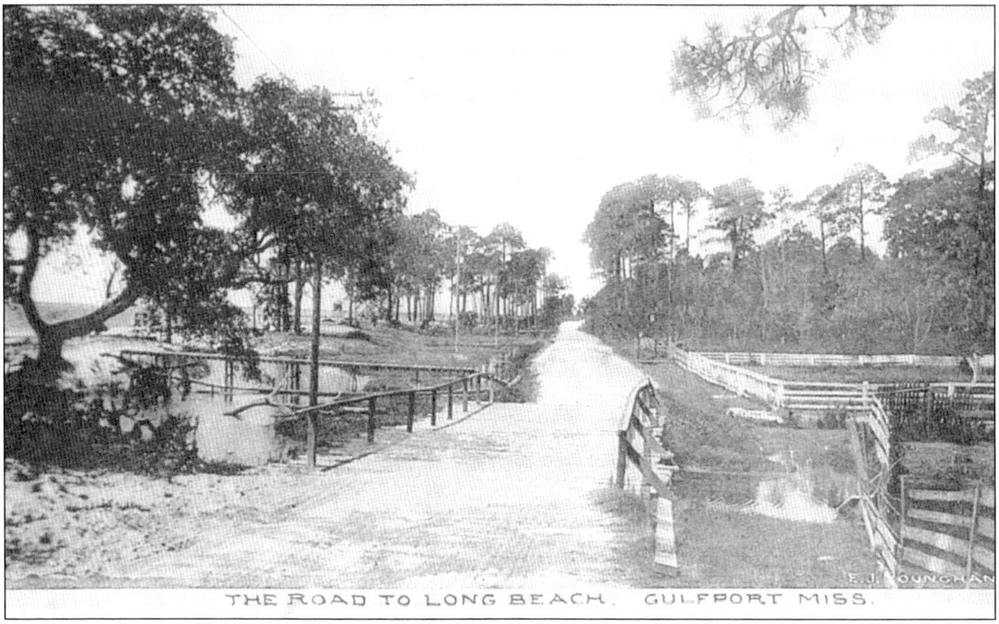

This is a postcard showing how the beachfront road looked in 1909. The road was made of crushed oyster shells and sand, which were plentiful in the area. The wooden bridge allowed passage over Bear Point Bayou, which wound its way through parts of Long Beach until it emptied into the Mississippi Sound. At that time, the bayou was open for most of its length. Today, all but a small section that runs through the University of Southern Mississippi's Gulf Park Campus has been covered. This view looks west from a site between Douglas Avenue and Nicholson Avenue. (Courtesy of the Mary Ellen Alexander Collection.)

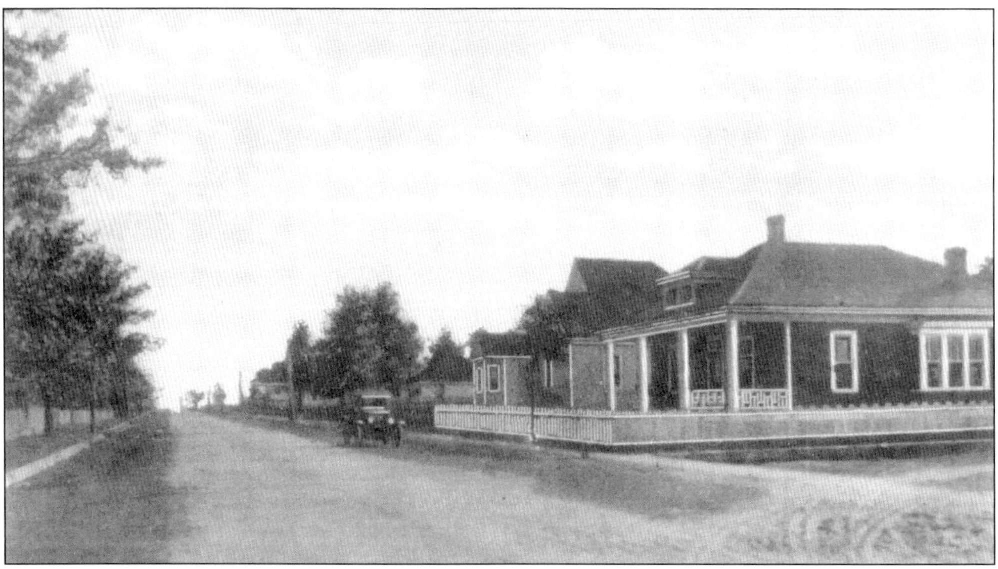

This 1910 view looks south on Jeff Davis Avenue from Fourth Street. At that time, the road was also made of crushed shell. Businesses and the school were located on the north part of the avenue (on the last three blocks to the railroad), and homes were located nearest the beach. The First Baptist Church, which was located at the corner of Jeff Davis Avenue and West Fifth Street, can barely been seen behind a tree. (Courtesy of Paul Jermyn.)

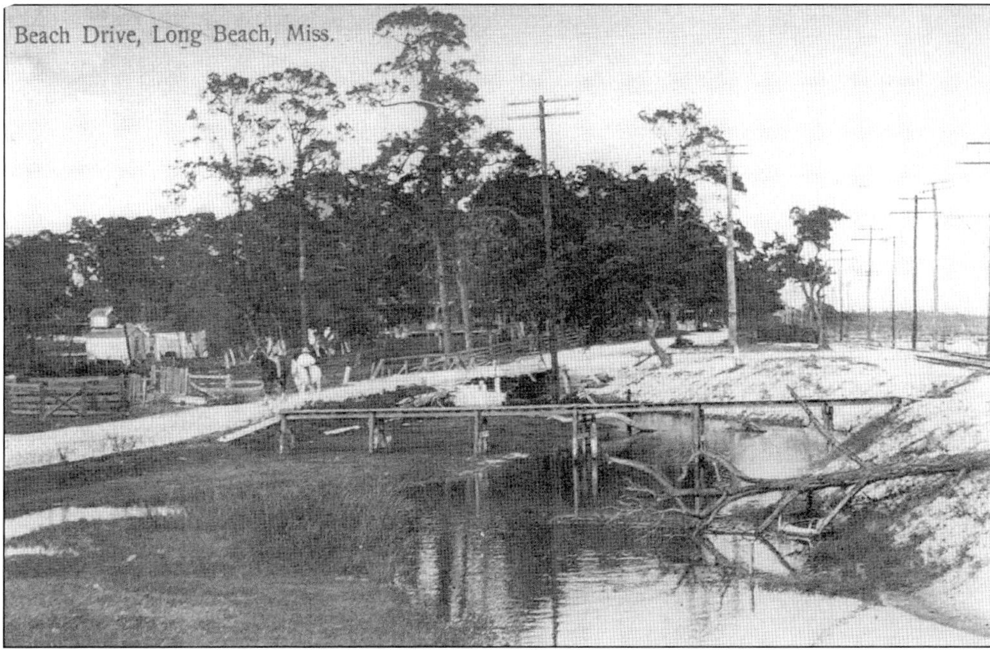

This is an early 1900s view of Bear Point Bayou as it nears the Mississippi Sound. The area was basically in a wild state at that time, and the large homes with their manicured lawns did not exist—at least in this part of Long Beach. The main mode of travel was by foot or on horseback. Landowners likely constructed wooden bridges to cross Bear Point Bayou as needed, without following any official building codes. (Courtesy of Paul Jermyn.)

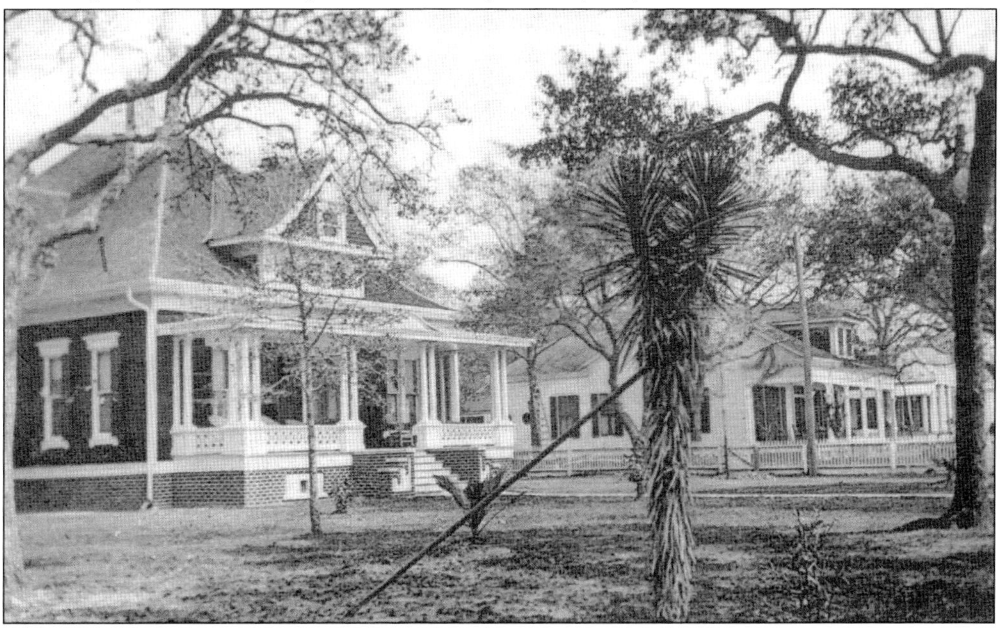

This postcard shows some of the magnificent homes along the beachfront. Some were occupied by permanent residents of Long Beach, while others were owned by families who lived elsewhere—usually New Orleans—and came to the beach for weekends or summer vacations in order to enjoy the mild sea breezes. (Courtesy of Paul Jermyn.)

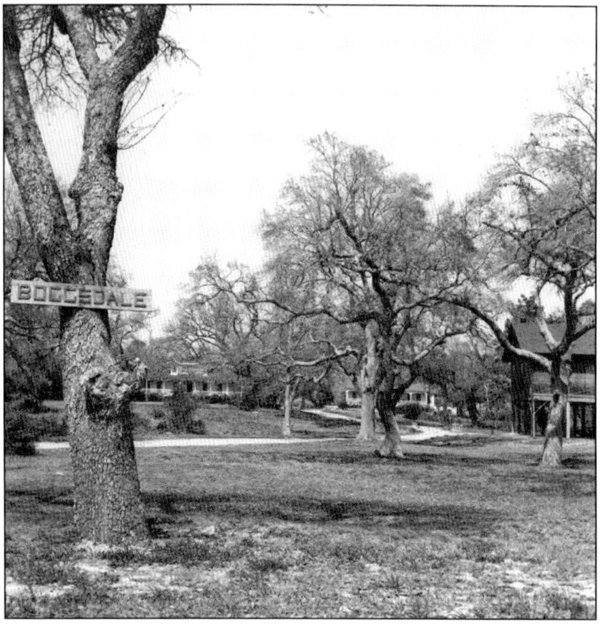

In 1875, artist and writer Robert Boggs brought his family to the Mississippi Gulf Coast. The most well-known story is that he built his home Breezydale close to the water, even though local Indians advised him not to because of storms. Eventually, several other families built on the property, and Boggsdale was born. The original homes were destroyed during the 1947 hurricane and were rebuilt farther away from the water. However, those homes were destroyed by Hurricane Camille in 1969. US Congressman Thomas Hale Boggs (1914–1972) was born at Boggsdale. (Courtesy of Mississippi Gulf Coast Community College C.C. "Tex" Hamill Down South Magazine Collection.)

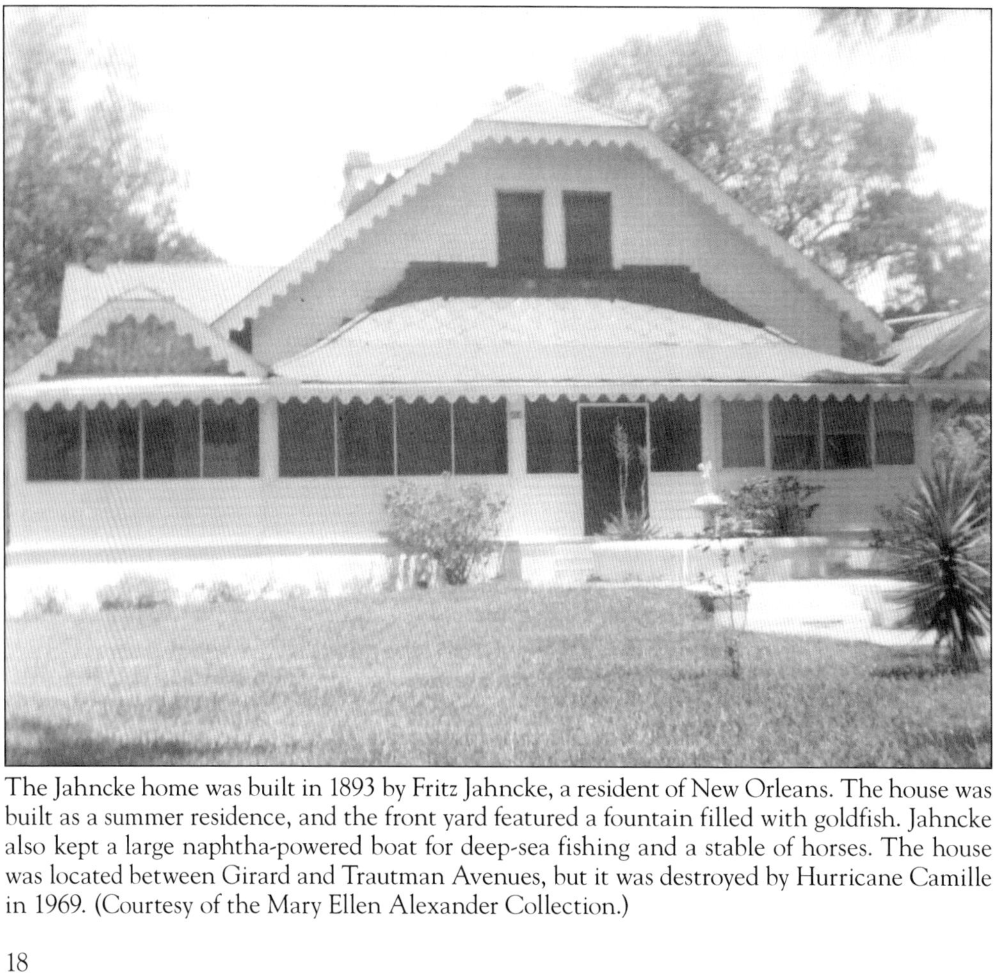

The Jahncke home was built in 1893 by Fritz Jahncke, a resident of New Orleans. The house was built as a summer residence, and the front yard featured a fountain filled with goldfish. Jahncke also kept a large naphtha-powered boat for deep-sea fishing and a stable of horses. The house was located between Girard and Trautman Avenues, but it was destroyed by Hurricane Camille in 1969. (Courtesy of the Mary Ellen Alexander Collection.)

The Pierre Michel home was constructed in 1893. Like many of the other beachfront homeowners, Michel was a New Orleans resident. The home was constructed on pillars that allowed for a ground-floor basement. Many people would come to watch the construction, as most had never seen such a tall house before. The home was later demolished to make way for an apartment complex. In turn, the apartments were destroyed by Hurricane Katrina in 2005. (Courtesy of Mississippi Gulf Coast Community College C.C. "Tex" Hamill Down South Magazine Collection.)

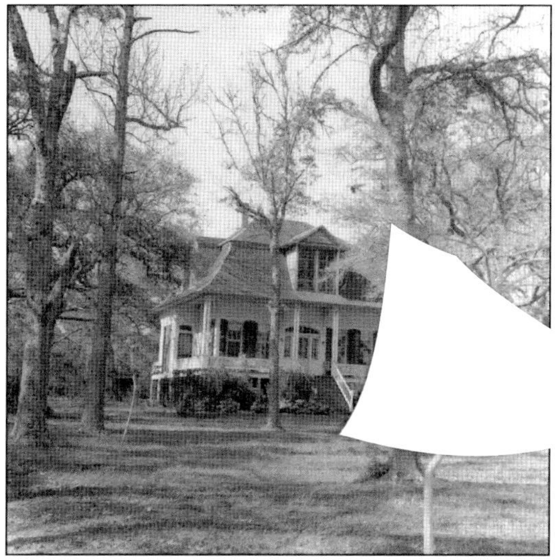

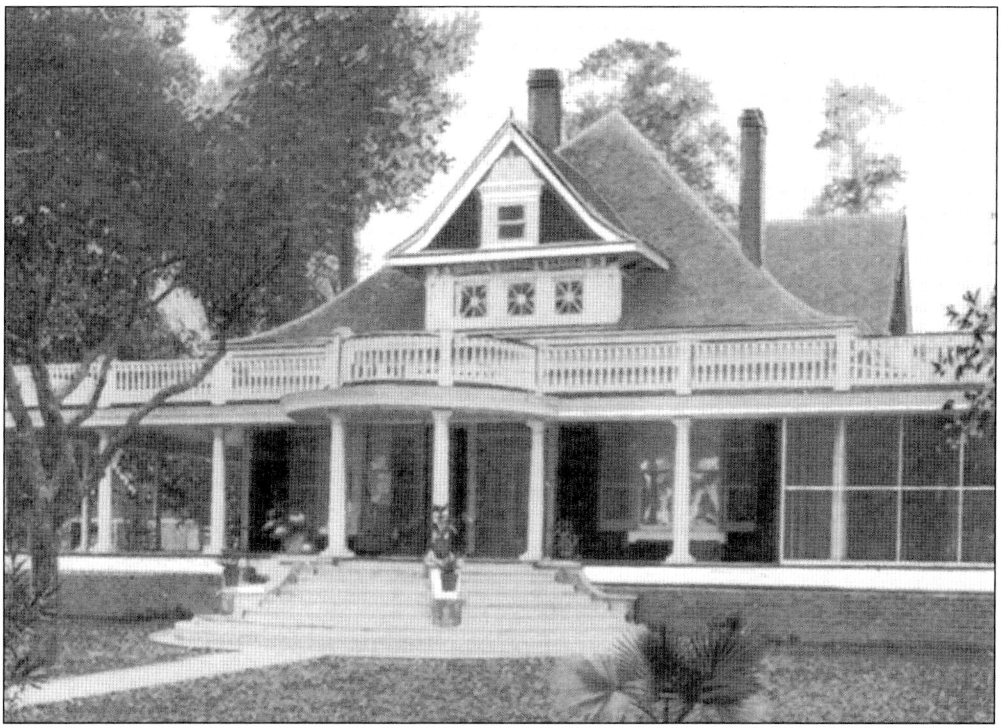

Joseph Van Cloostere was a banker from Illinois who became a stockholder in Gulfport and Mississippi Coast Traction Company (which later became Mississippi Power). His beautiful beachfront home had no heating installed when it was constructed in 1900, because Van Cloostere underestimated the Mississippi winter temperatures—radiators were later added. The home was sold in 1947 to the Future Farmers of America and destroyed by Hurricane Camille in 1969. When the FFA was in residence, there were coastal activities for youth members throughout the summer. The director lived in the main house, and there were cottages on the property, which stretched north to Magnolia Street. During the late summer and non-summer months, the property was used for football camps and as extra classrooms for the local schools. (Courtesy of Long Beach Historical Society Archives.)

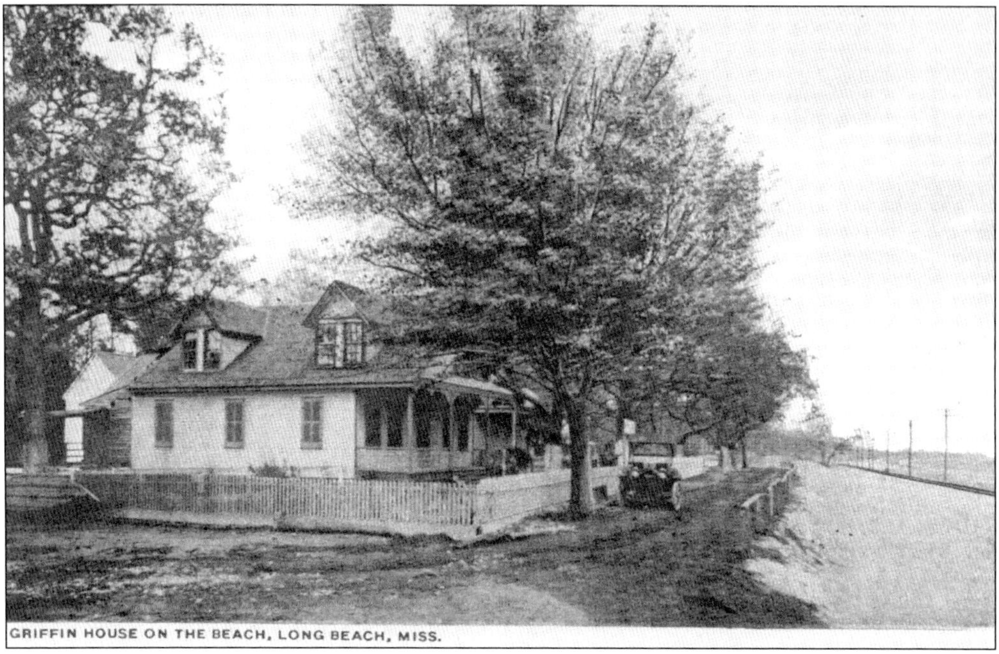

The Griffin house was located on the corner of Highway 90 and Nicholson Avenue. At the time, Nicholson was known as Griffin Lane. Mary Griffin operated the house as a boardinghouse for a time. The road along the shore was a narrow one-lane dirt road. Notice the expanse of sand between the road and the trolley tracks to the right. This photograph dates back long before the seawall was constructed. (Courtesy of Paul Jermyn.)

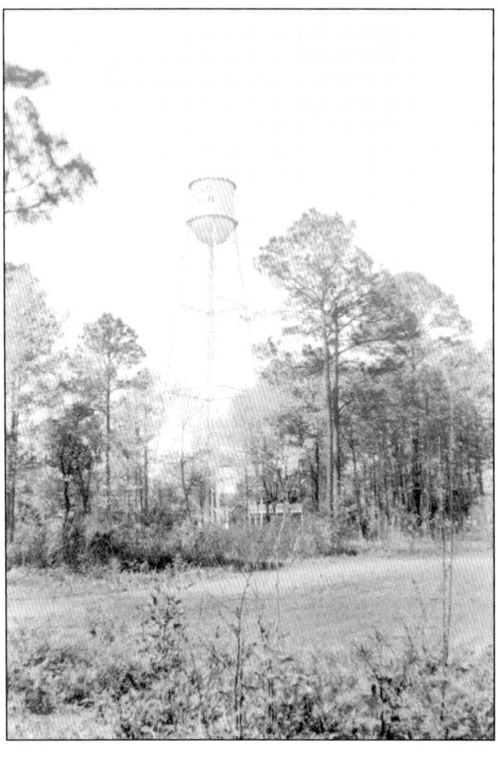

The original water tower in Long Beach stood for many years until a more modern one was built. The replacement tower was under construction when Hurricane Camille struck in 1969, and the completion of repairs on the system and a new tower was seen as a sign of recovery from the storm. This photograph dates from 1938. (Courtesy of the Mary Ellen Alexander Collection.)

Two

The Beach

The busy highway that today runs the four-mile length of Long Beach is very different than the original one-lane unpaved shell road that used to wind its way through the town. As the photographs in this chapter will show, the beachfront in early Long Beach ranged from elegant waterfront homes to rural areas of land where rustic footbridges crossed Bear Point Bayou. There were few cars along Beach Road at first, as most people got around by walking, on horseback, or by horse and cart. Before the seawall was built in 1925, some homes were constructed as close to the natural beach as possible. Later, as motor traffic became more common and more homes were built, the road was widened and became known as Beach Boulevard. Tourists began to learn about the Mississippi Gulf Coast, and the influx of visitors and increase in population lead to the creation of multilane Highway 90 (although it is still commonly called Beach Boulevard). The beach has always been a magnet for locals and tourists. Sand was pumped in during 1951 to create the longest man-made beach in the world—26 miles.

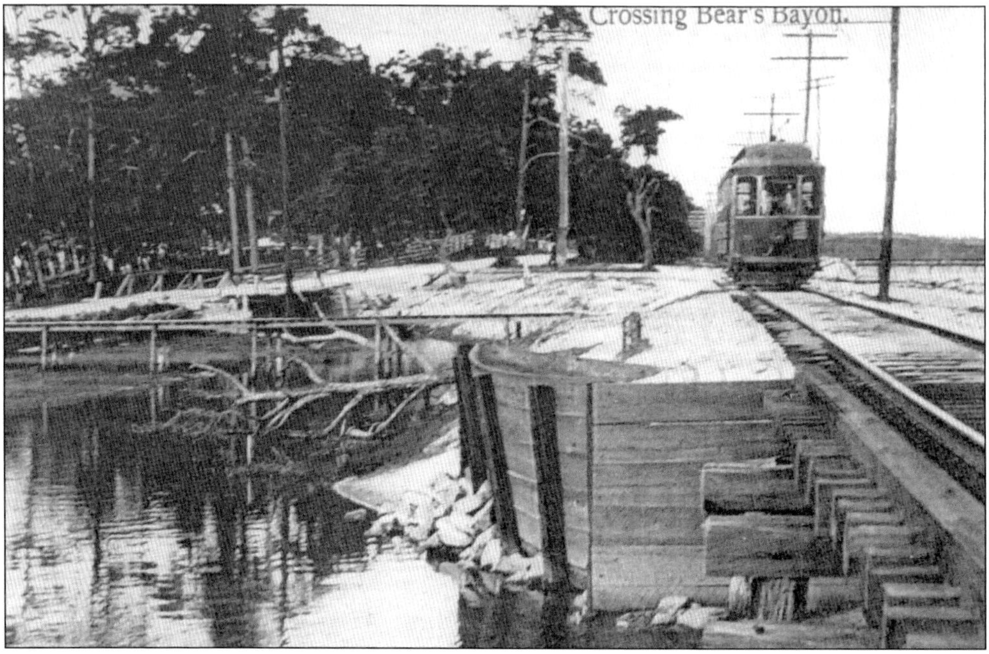

Bear's Bayou (actually named Bear Point Bayou) was first mentioned on a British map in 1774. It flowed from a spring near what is now Wright Avenue all the way south to the Mississippi Sound. Most of the bayou is covered today, but this photograph shows it flowing freely into the sound, probably around Douglas Avenue. There were many wooden bridges that spanned the bayou at various places along its length, including the sturdy bridge for the trolley tracks. (Courtesy of Paul Jermyn.)

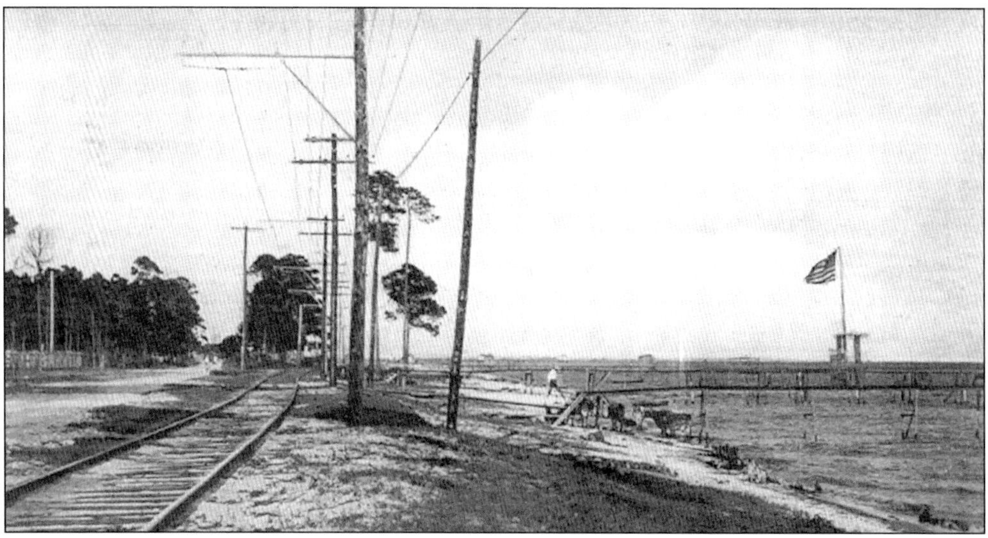

This is a view looking east along the waterfront towards Gulfport. The photograph is undated, but it likely is from the very early 1900s. The trolley tracks cut through the sandy beachfront, and the way is lined with telephone poles. When the hurricane of 1915 struck, 20 miles of trolley tracks were washed out. At that time, there were many piers along the beach, which can be faintly seen here. These too were destroyed by the storm. Note the cattle right at the water's edge. (Courtesy of the Mary Ellen Alexander Collection.)

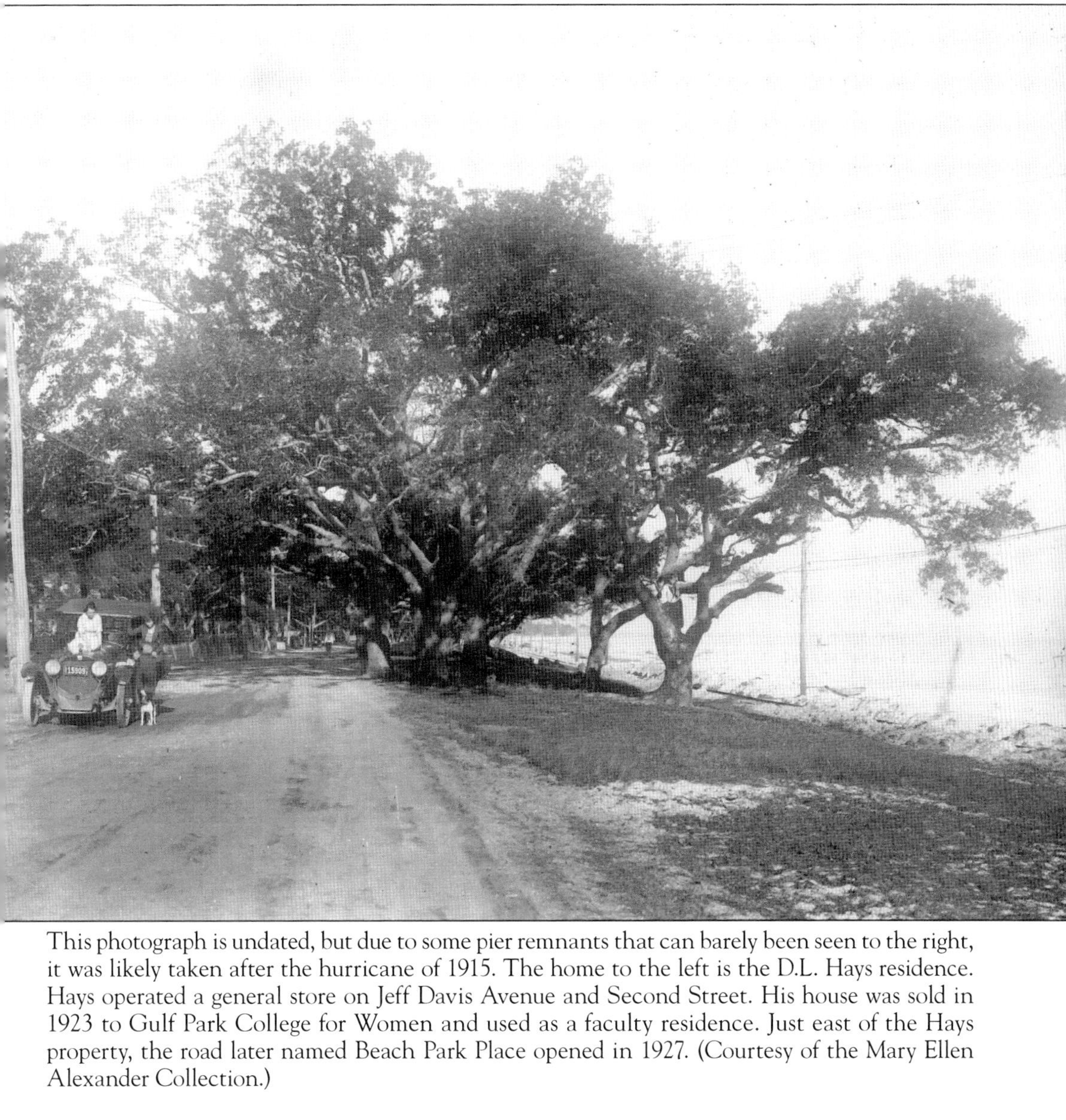

This photograph is undated, but due to some pier remnants that can barely been seen to the right, it was likely taken after the hurricane of 1915. The home to the left is the D.L. Hays residence. Hays operated a general store on Jeff Davis Avenue and Second Street. His house was sold in 1923 to Gulf Park College for Women and used as a faculty residence. Just east of the Hays property, the road later named Beach Park Place opened in 1927. (Courtesy of the Mary Ellen Alexander Collection.)

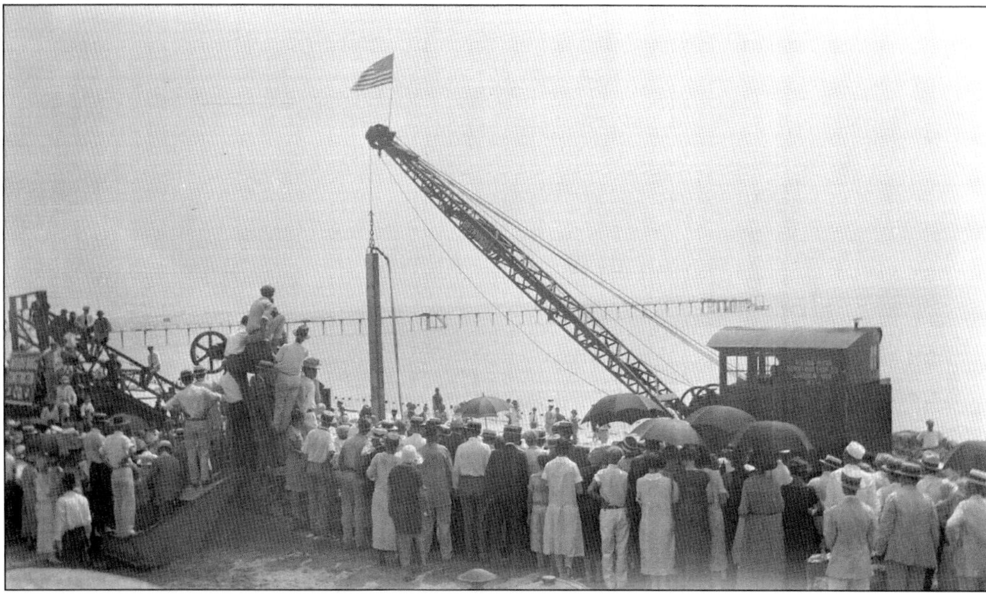

On September 4, 1925, the first piling of the seawall that would eventually stretch along the entire Mississippi Gulf Coast was set in place in Long Beach. This photograph was taken in front of St. Thomas Catholic Church. The work was done by Woods Brothers Construction of Lincoln, Nebraska. The steel crane raised the first concrete pillar at 9:00 a.m. and let it drop. Sen. Pat Harrison spoke during the ground-breaking ceremony. (Courtesy of Mississippi Gulf Coast Community College Dixie Press Collection.)

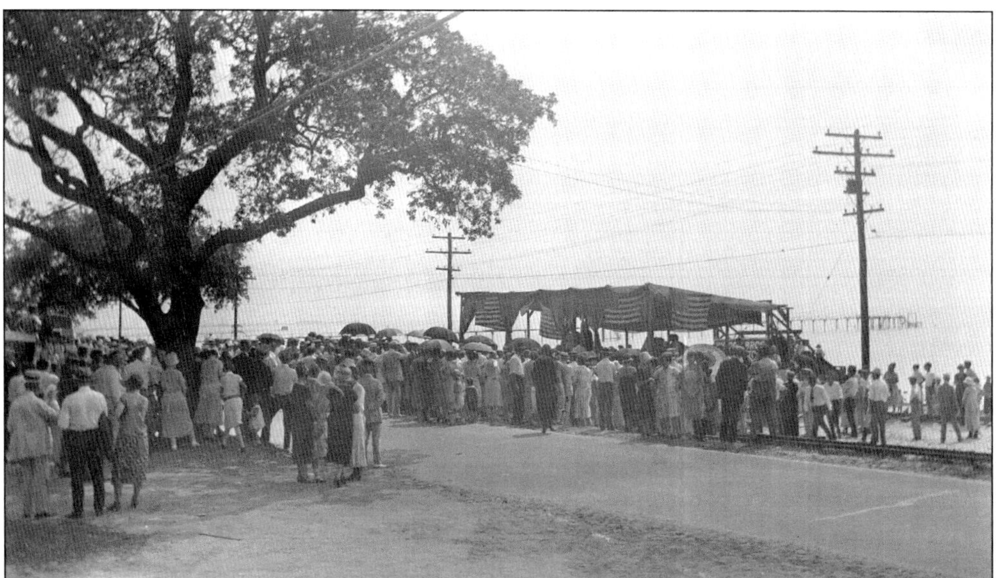

This is another view of the September 1925 seawall ceremony. The ceremony was well attended, and the numerous umbrellas on what looks to have been a sunny day were probably being used as protection against the late summer sun. (Courtesy of Mississippi Gulf Coast Community College Dixie Press Collection.)

After the initial ceremony marking the beginning of the seawall construction, the project moved forward. The construction of the concrete step seawall was a huge undertaking, as shown in this photograph taken in front of St. Thomas Catholic Church. (Courtesy of Eddie Ware.)

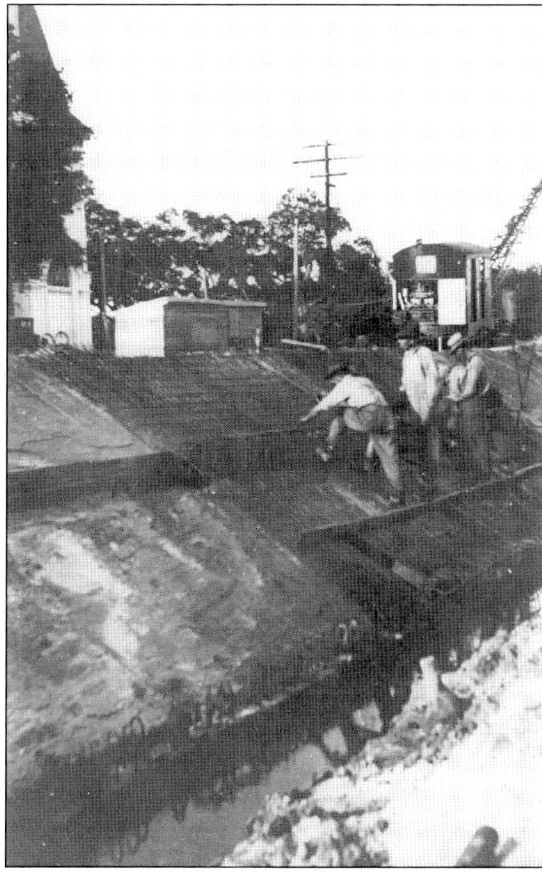

When the seawall was finally finished in 1928, it was the longest concrete seawall in the world at the time, stretching 26 miles along the shore. It helped to protect Highway 90 from the ravages of storms. The steps leading down to the beach were gradually covered by the sand that was later pumped in for further protection and to create a beautiful beach for locals and tourists. (Courtesy of Eddie Ware.)

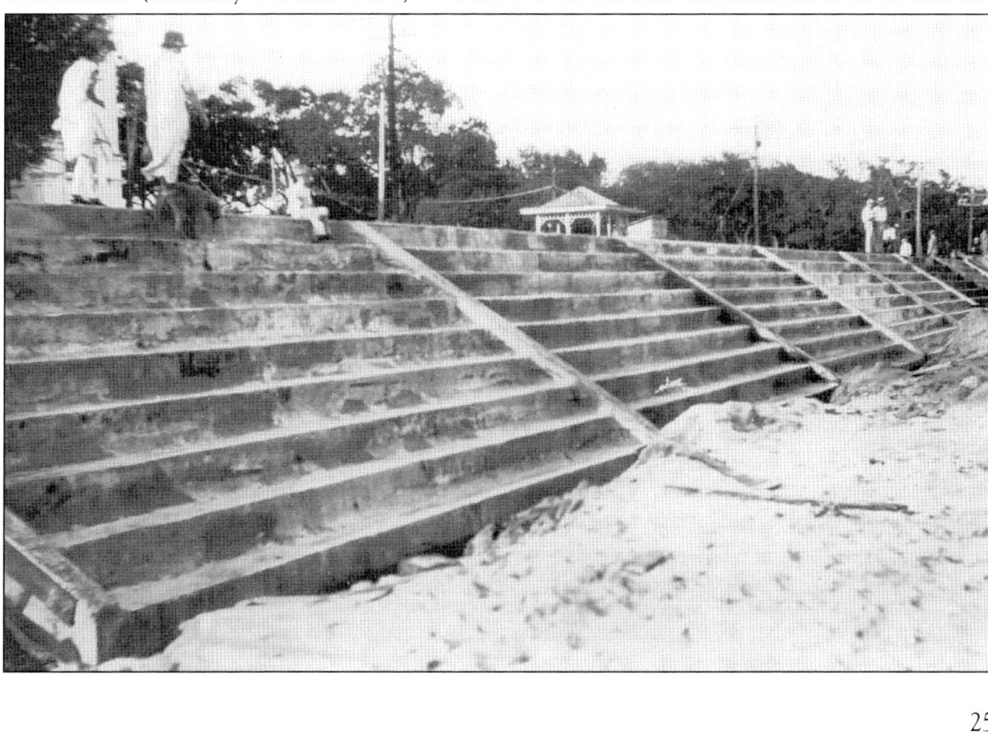

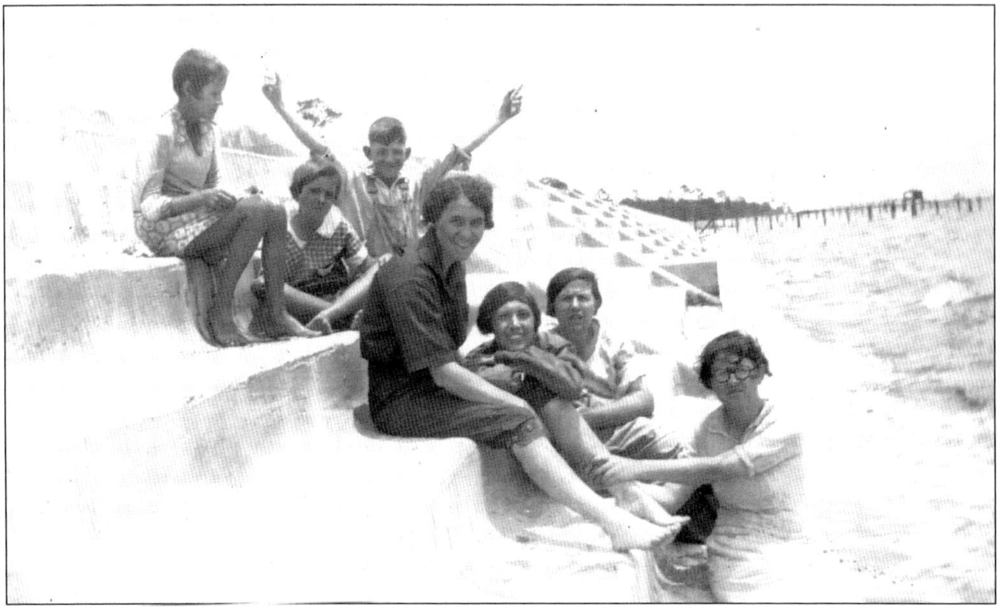

Even before the sand beach was created, families enjoyed outings at the shore. This photograph from 1928 shows the Werner family and friends enjoying a day at the waterside. The seawall steps made a great place to sit and watch the water. The note on the back of the photograph identifies the group as, from left to right, Gaynel ?, Barbara Werner, Charles Werner, Jewel ?, Mrs. Strain, Gertrude Werner, and Agnes Werner. (Courtesy of Rose Donaldson.)

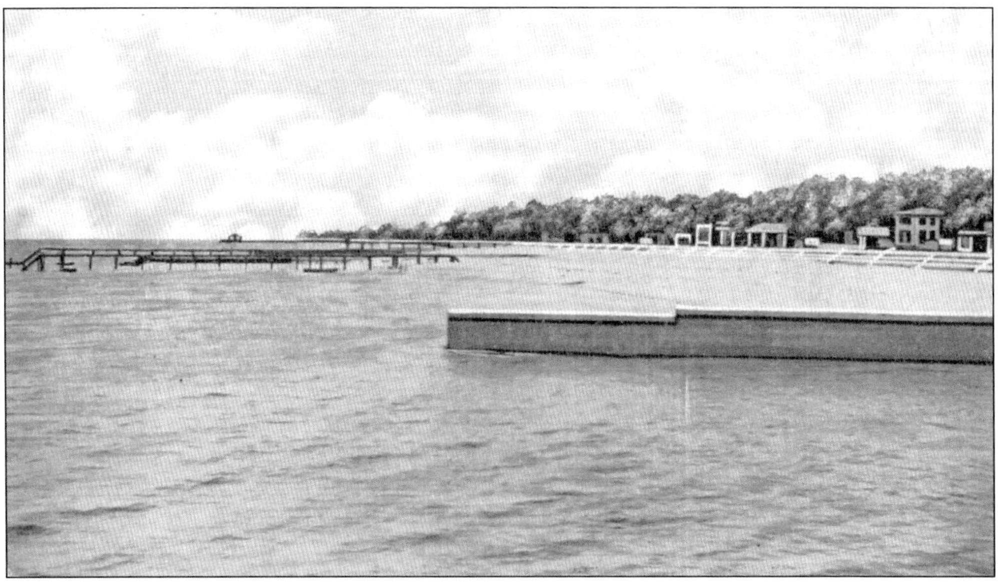

Prior to 1951, the natural sand beach varied from place to place along the seawall. In some areas, it was several hundred feet wide, but in other areas there was no sand and waters of the sound lapped against the seawall. In 1951, sand was pumped in to create a 26-mile stretch of beach, the longest man-made beach in the world. This postcard shows some of the concrete groins that were constructed before the artificial beach existed. These groins helped catch any drifting sand in order to sustain the natural beach. (Courtesy of Long Beach Historical Society Archives.)

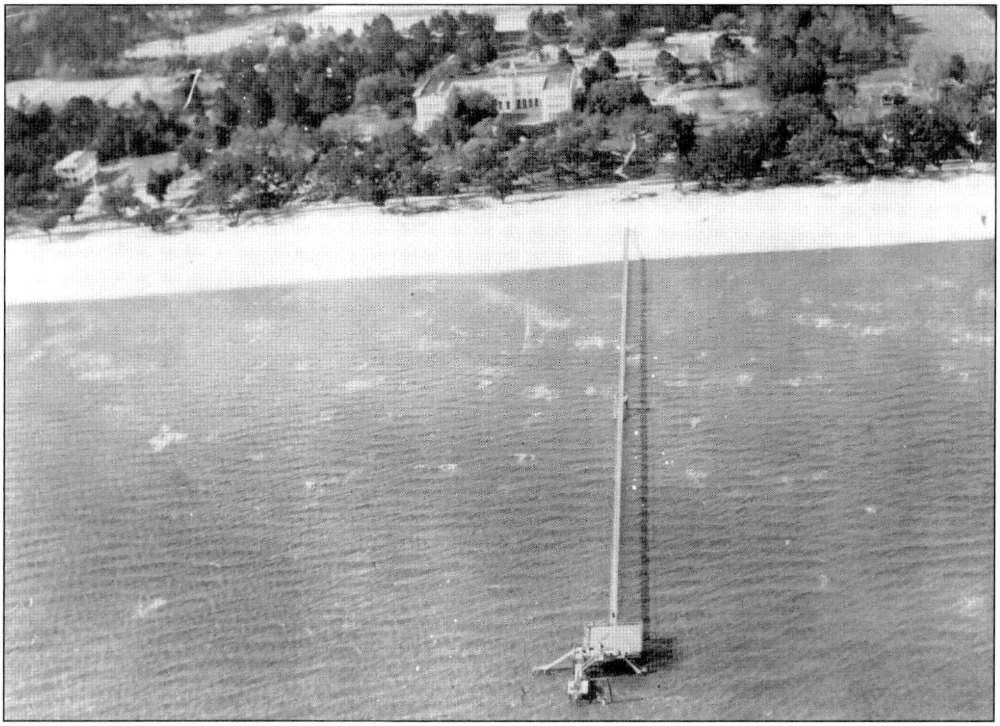

This is an aerial shot showing the long pier in front of Gulf Park College for Women. This pier stretched for over a thousand feet into the Mississippi Sound during the 1930s, and it was extended an additional 800 feet during the 1940s. It contained a lower platform for tying up boats and easy access for swimmers; there were rope swings, a slide, and stairs leading right down to the water. (Courtesy of Mississippi Gulf Coast Community College Dixie Press Collection.)

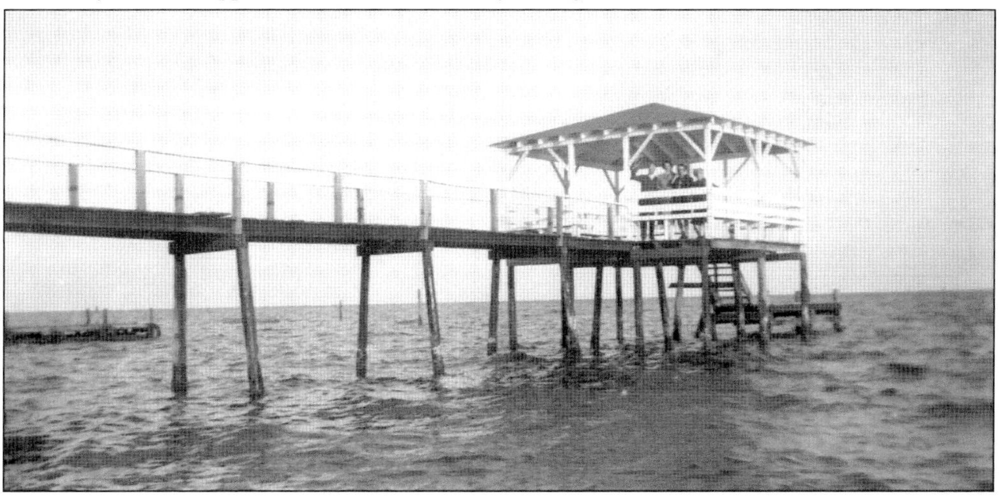

This photograph shows a typical pier with a covered area at the end as protection from the elements, particularly the harsh sun. Pier design was generally at the whim of the builder. Some were simple wooden walkways close to the water, with only crude handrails for guidance, but others were constructed high above the water and had covered areas at the end, built-in benches, steps leading to boat landings, and lower platforms for swimmers. (Courtesy of the Mary Ellen Alexander Collection.)

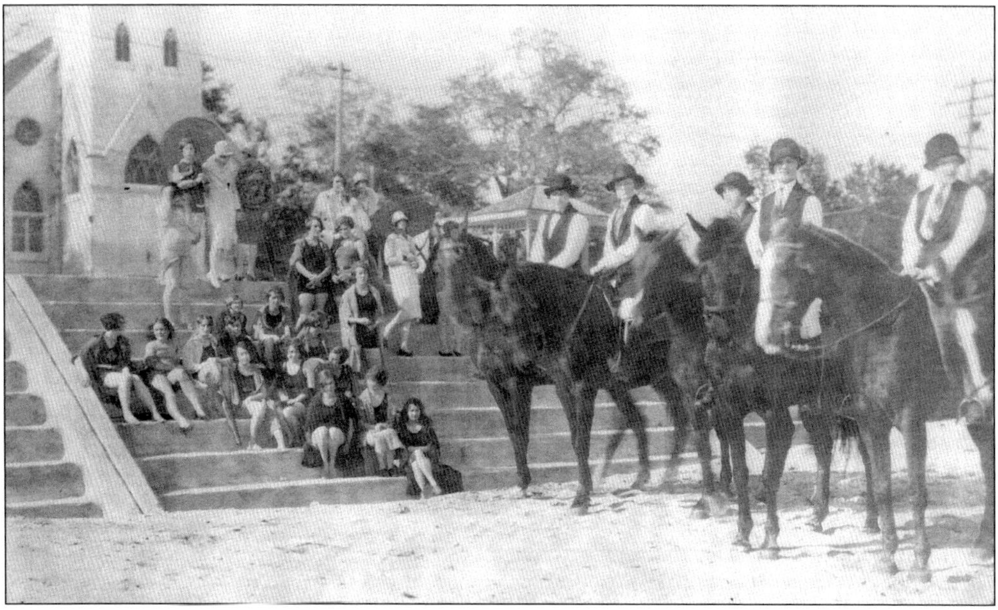

The girls who attended Gulf Park College for Women frequently exercised their horses by riding along the beach. This practice is one that has not been seen along the public beach in many years. During the early days of the college, when automobile traffic was almost nonexistent on Beach Boulevard, the girls would also ride their horses along the road. This photograph probably dates from the late 1920s and was taken in front of St. Thomas Catholic Church. (Courtesy of Paul Jermyn.)

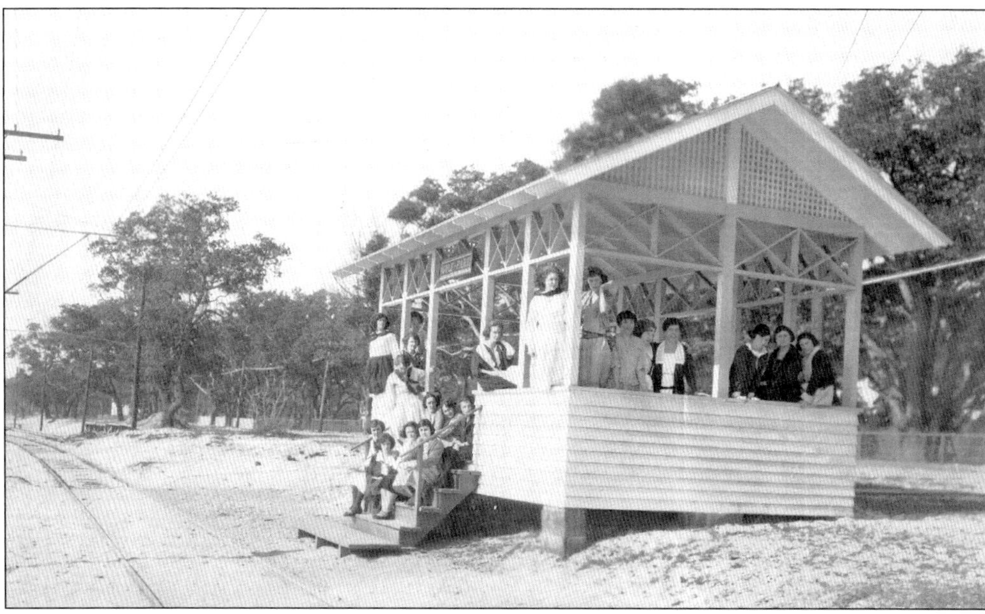

This photograph shows one of the many trolley car stops along the coast. This one was located across the Beach Road from Gulf Park College for Women and allowed the girls to travel to and from downtown Gulfport, about four miles to the east. The attractive car stops provided shade during the hot summers and protection from inclement weather. (Courtesy of Mississippi Gulf Coast Community College Dixie Press Collection.)

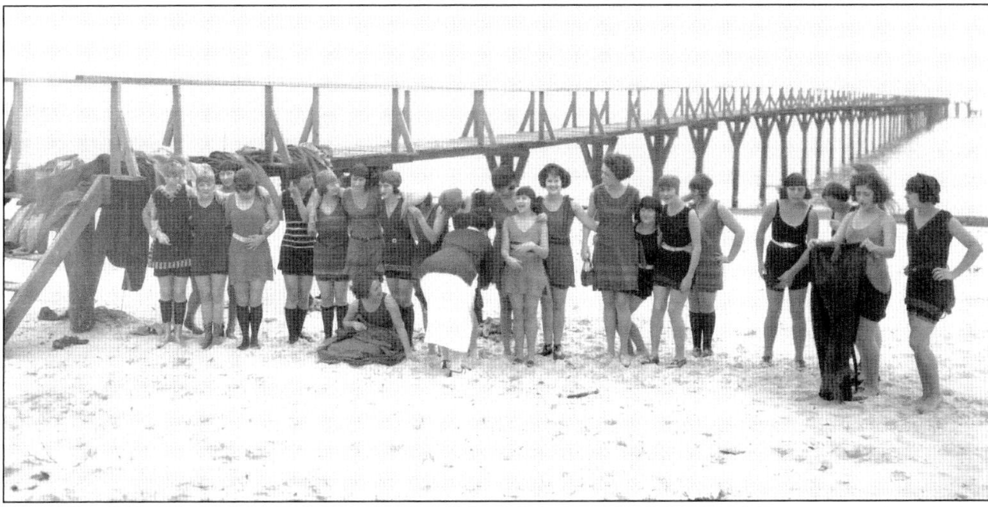

Gulf Park College for Women faced the Mississippi Sound, so the students spent a lot of their leisure time on the beach. Water activities included sailing, swimming, and diving off the school's long pier, and the girls went horseback riding along the shore. This photograph is undated, but judging from the swimsuit styles, was probably taken in the 1920s. One source claims that the girls are actually standing on the beach during a rare snowfall and posed in swimsuits just for the photograph. This story could be true, especially with the coats piled on the pier to the left. (Courtesy of Mississippi Gulf Coast Community College Dixie Press Collection.)

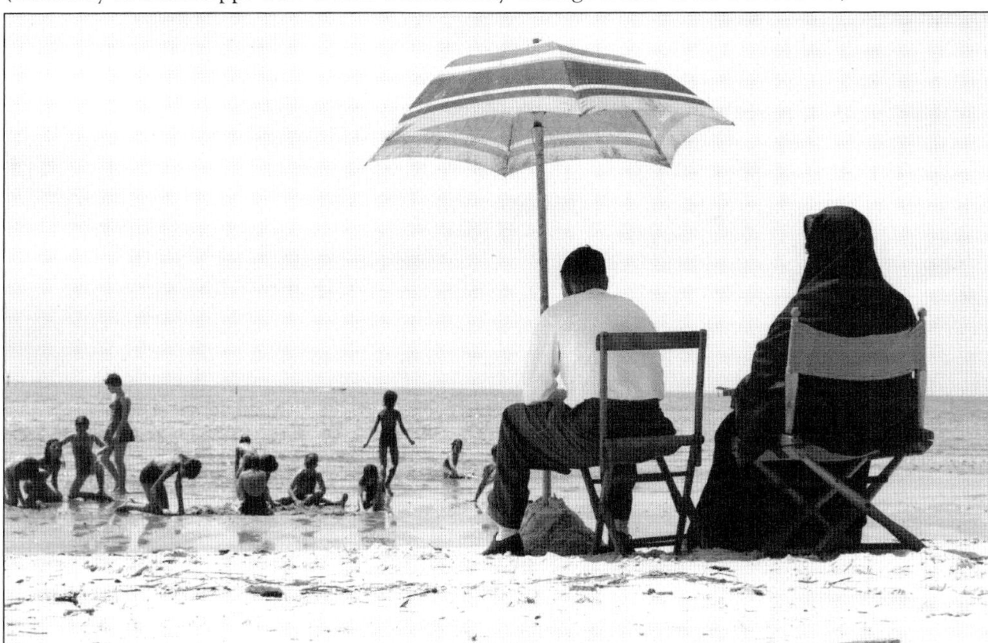

For many decades, the children of the Sacred Heart Orphanage in New Orleans came to the Mississippi Gulf Coast to attend the St. Frances Cabrini Summer Camp (formerly called Sacred Heart Convent), located at the corner of Highway 90 and Girard Avenue. This gave the children the opportunity to swim and play on the beach under the watchful gaze of one of the sisters. (Courtesy of Mississippi Gulf Coast Community College C.C. "Tex" Hamill Down South Magazine Collection.)

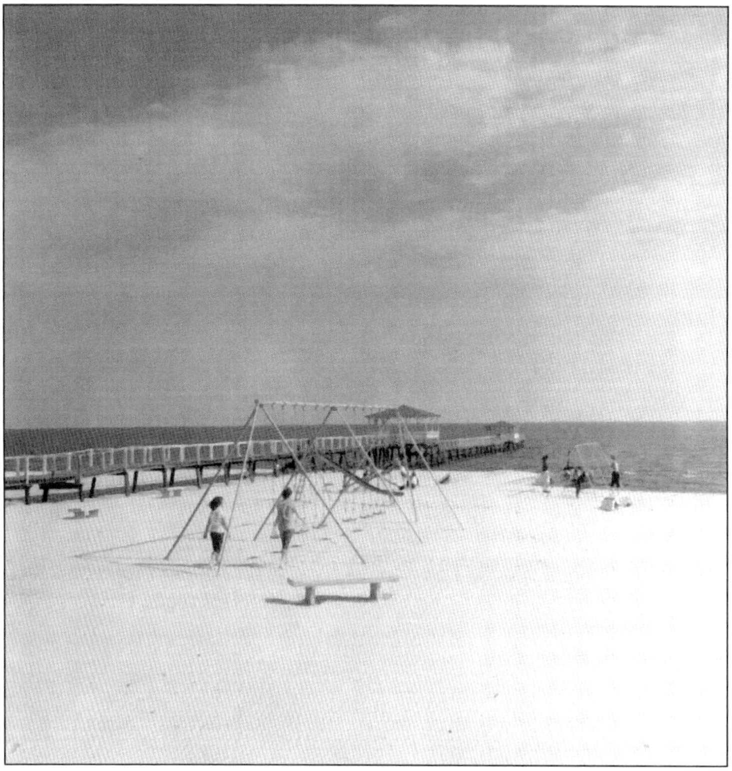

At onetime, playground equipment dotted the beach. This 1952 photograph shows swings, a slide, and seesaws. Although they are long gone, they were very popular at the time. The sand also provided a soft landing. (Courtesy of Mississippi Gulf Coast Community College C.C. "Tex" Hamill Down South Magazine Collection.)

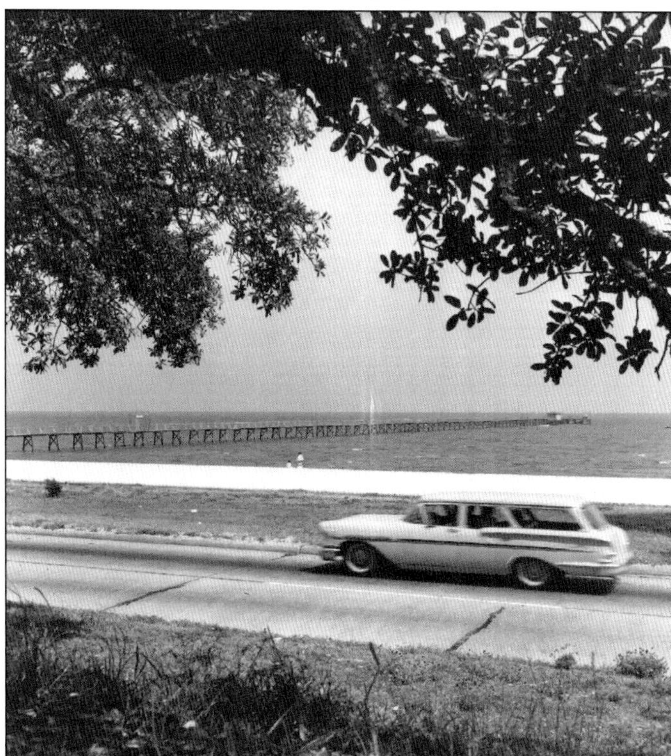

By the 1940s, Highway 90, locally known as Beach Boulevard, was developed into a four-lane road across all three coastal counties. This 1962 photograph shows the beautiful views that visitors saw as they traveled the length of the beachfront. The smooth straight highway seen here is in stark contrast to the unpaved single lane that meandered through Long Beach in earlier years. (Courtesy of Mississippi Gulf Coast Community College C.C. "Tex" Hamill Down South Magazine Collection.)

Three

EDUCATION

In 1884, William James Quarles started the first school in Long Beach. He taught basic subjects to 11 children in a small room at his family's home. As Long Beach grew, so did the need for a school building. Two years after the first classes were taught, a one-room wooden schoolhouse was built on Jeff Davis Avenue on land that was donated by Harper McCaughan to be used "forever for school purposes." Over the years, several school buildings have stood on that site, including a new high school and two elementary schools. Today, the number of schools has expanded as the population has grown, and now includes a high school, middle school, Catholic school, and several elementary schools.

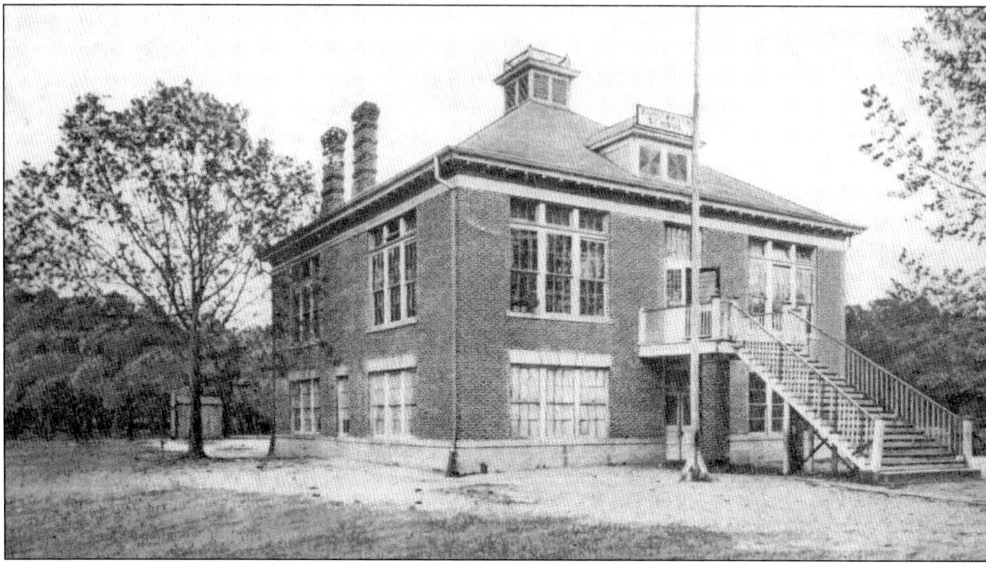

The first public school building was constructed in 1906 at a cost of $7,000 on land donated by Harper McCaughan. It replaced a one-room wooden building constructed in 1886. The school taught up to 10th grade, and students who wanted to complete their high school education attended 11th and 12th grades at nearby Gulfport High School. The first class to complete all 12 grades in this building graduated in 1923. The bell from the first wooden school still exists today at the Tennessee home of the Presley family. (Courtesy of the Mary Ellen Alexander Collection.)

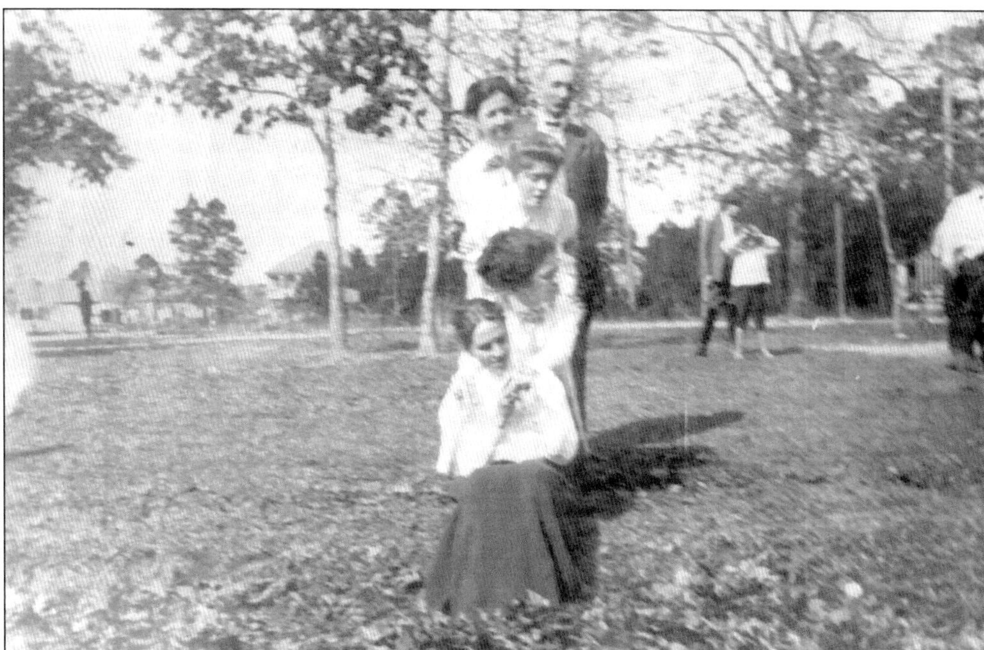

The faculty poses in front of the Long Beach School in 1910. Pictured here, from front to back, are May Quarles, Ethel Backus, Ruth Eisele, Annie Lee McLean, and principal O. Harman. The four faculty members taught the 10 grades that were offered. (Courtesy of the Mary Ellen Alexander Collection.)

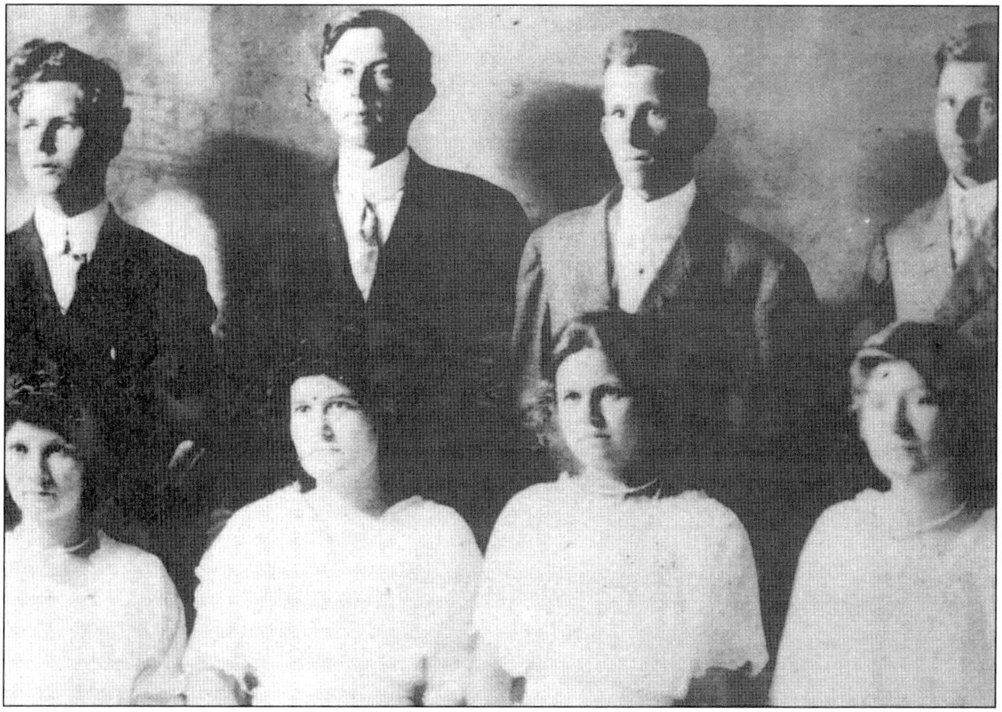

Member of the graduating class of 1914 are, from left to right, (first row) Novita Dossett, Feltie McManus, Alma Simmons, and Hazel Lindsey; (second row) Marshall Allen, Cleveland Hodge, John Prados, and Julian Watrous. (Courtesy of the Mary Ellen Alexander Collection.)

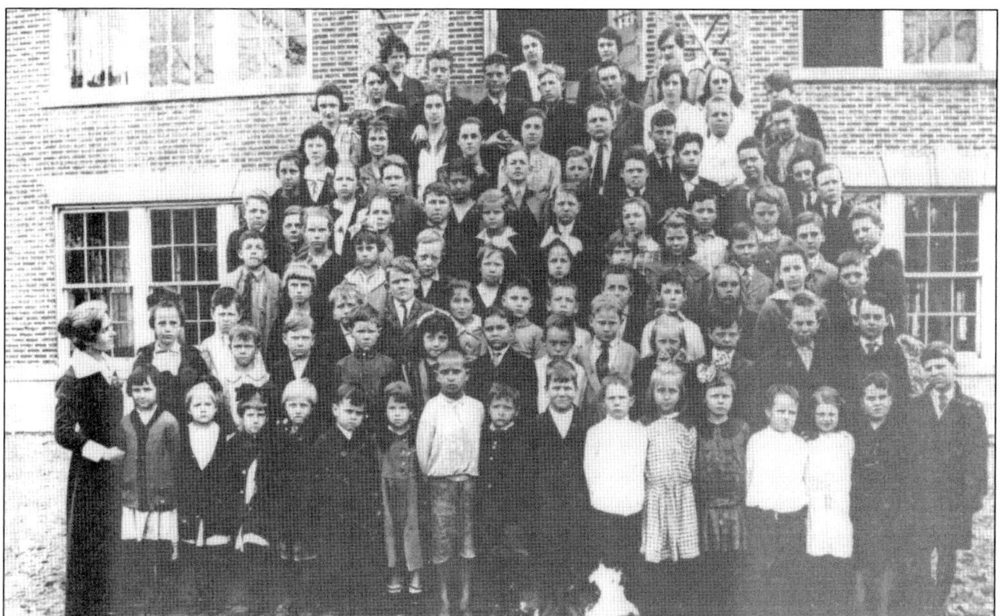

This is a photograph of the entire class on the steps of the brick school in 1916. At the bottom left is the principal, Annie Bethel. The teachers shown in the back row are, from left to right, Cristine Ziz, Grace Quarles, and Anne Sugden. (Courtesy of the Mary Ellen Alexander Collection.)

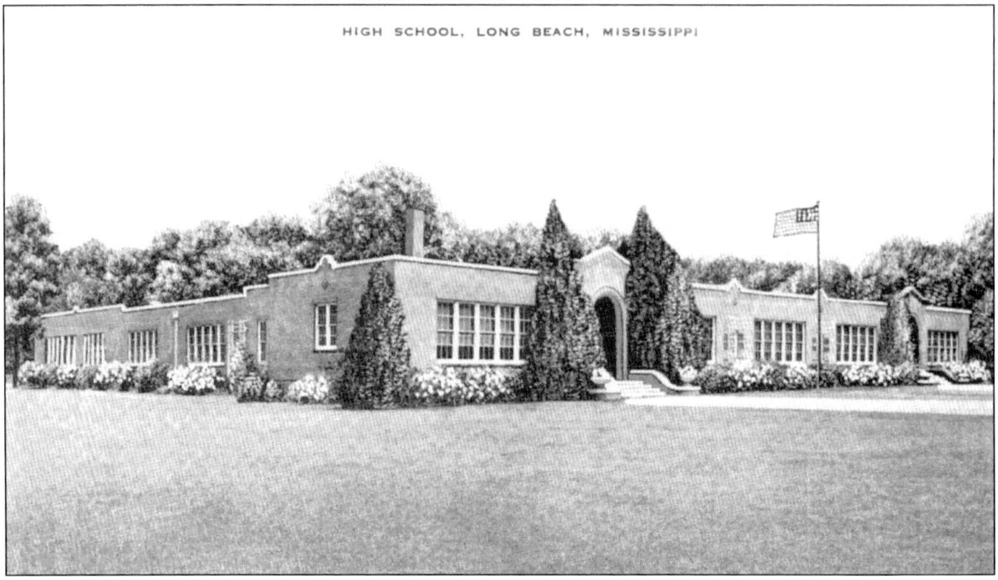

The first high school was built on Jeff Davis Avenue in 1925. It served as the high school until 1956, when a new school was built on the corner of Old Pass Road and Cleveland Avenue. It then became Jeff Davis Elementary School until 1978. Additions were made to the building during its years of operation as a high school, including classrooms, a cafeteria, a band hall, and a home economics department. (Courtesy of the Mary Ellen Alexander Collection.)

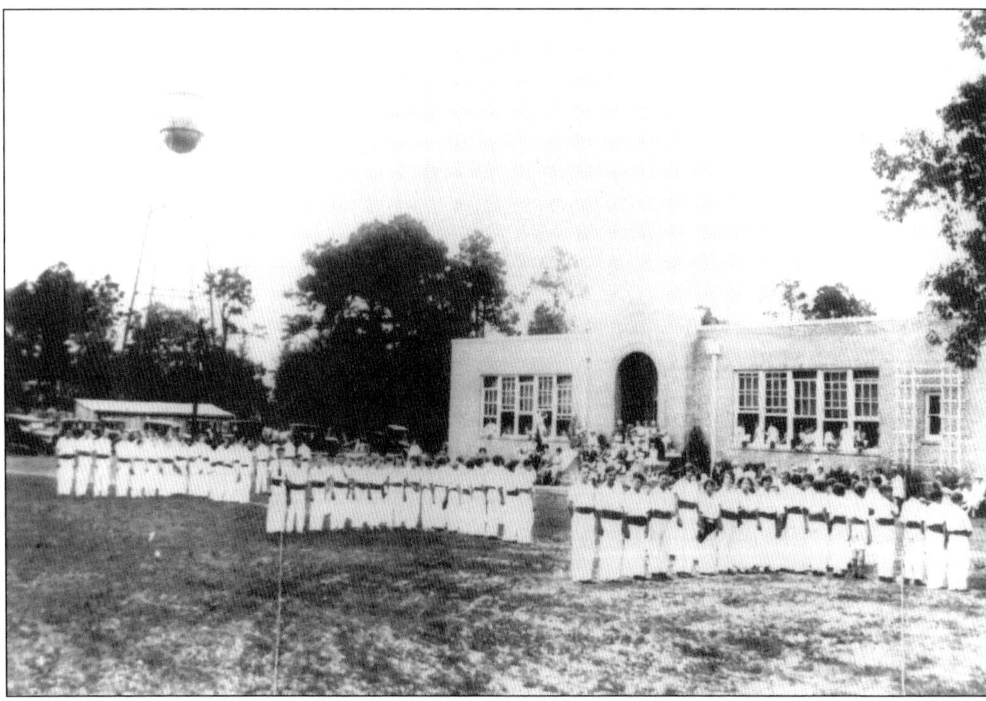

May Day activities are being celebrated in this 1930 photograph. This celebration was held at the high school, and the entire student body attended the festivities. The May Queen that year was Mary Boggs, and the captain was Robert Maxwell. Ed Fillingim owned the home at the far left, at what is now the site of the public library. (Courtesy of the Mary Ellen Alexander Collection.)

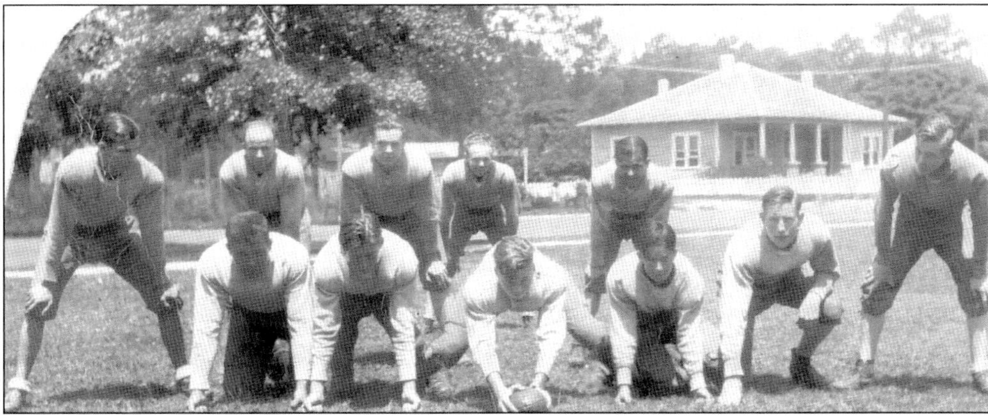

The first football team at the high school poses on the school ground in 1930. Pictured are, from left to right, (first row) Mobley Cox, Pete Bass, Joe Parker, Karlson Thomas, and Dwight Allen; (second row) J.T. Hooker, Tom Napier, Knox Jones, Aubrey Alexander, Randall Genung, and Robo Maxwell. (Courtesy of the Mary Ellen Alexander Collection.)

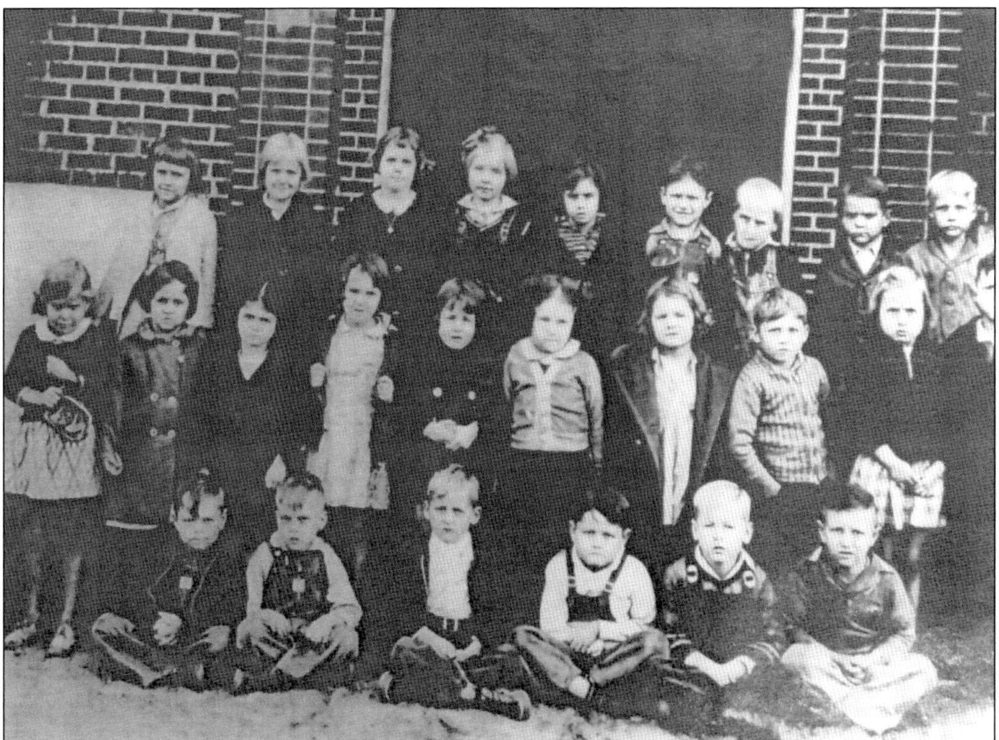

This is the primer (later called kindergarten) class of 1938, taught by Margaret Murphy. Among those pictured are Leroy Woodcock, Gilbert Collins, Durwood Suber, Margie Scarborough Gentile, Joyce Ward McCauley, Margaret Skellie, Dorothy Lakey, Lois Armstrong, and Otis Beech. (Courtesy of Otis Beech.)

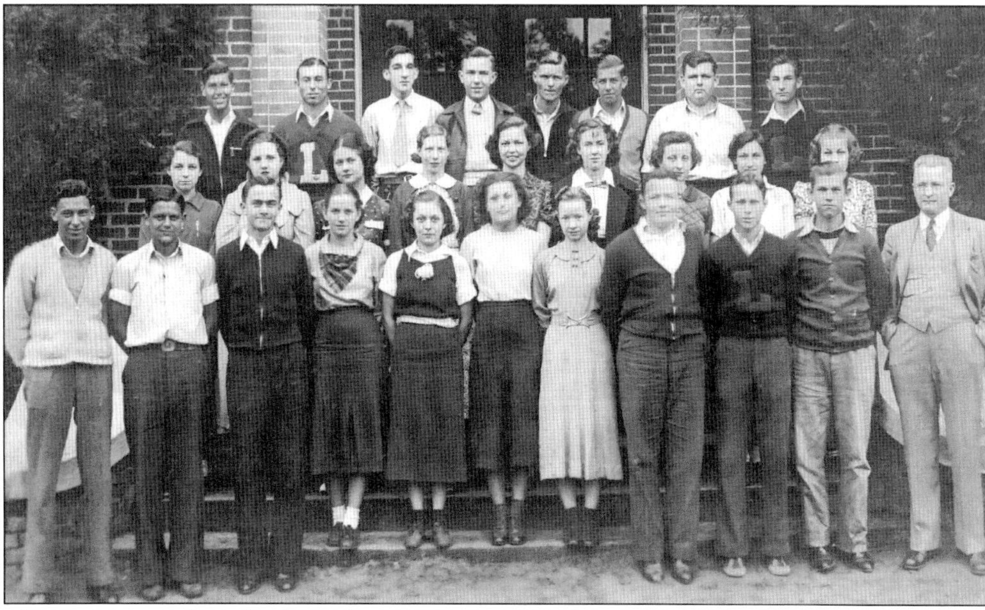

The graduating class of 1938 is shown here. Among the graduates are Pete Carrubba, Claude Miller, William Seal, Eugene Murphy III, Virta Mae Head, Barbara Werner, Mary Ellen Watrous, Louise Hodges, Fred Skellie Jr., Lois Meek, Marianne Stokes, Felicia Guiffria, Warren Lassiere, Wilfred Clark, and R.P. White. (Courtesy of the Mary Ellen Alexander Collection.)

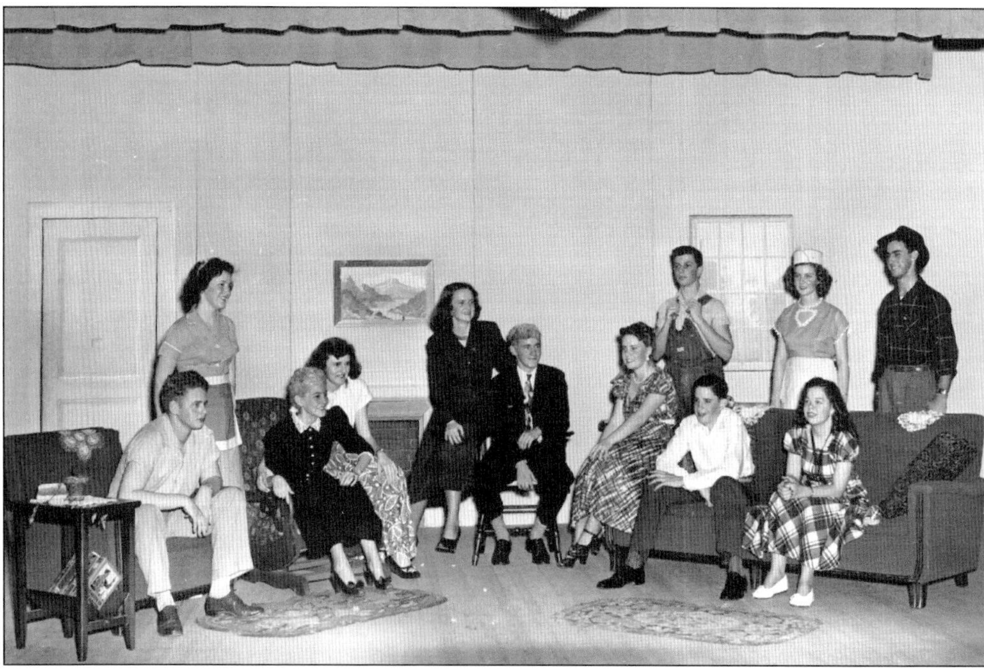

In 1949, one of the plays presented by the Long Beach High School juniors was the exciting mystery *Betty Mason, Detective*. The cast included Sue Kilpatrick, Jim Allen, Joanne Quarles, Margaret Skellie, Edwina Stossel, Kenneth Worth, Betty Jean Jordan, Robert Vogt, Doris Parker, Donald Bosarge, Joyce Ward, and Gilbert Meek. The play was directed by Josephine P. Imig. (Courtesy of Mississippi Gulf Coast Community College Dixie Press Collection.)

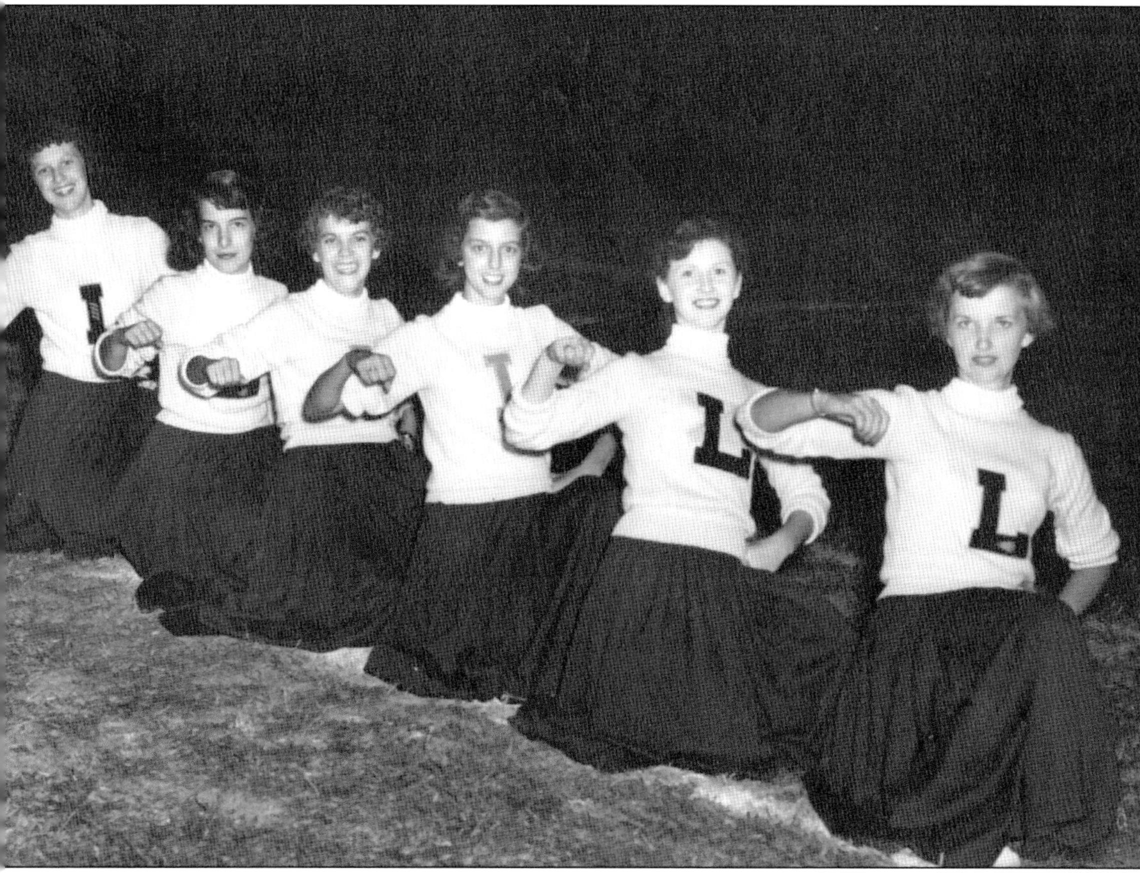

The Long Beach High School cheerleaders of 1953 are cheering on the Bearcats. Pictured here, from left to right, are Barbara Parker, Ann Dauro, Adele Allen, Elaine Vogt, Betty Reinike, and Beth Davis. (Courtesy of Rose Donaldson.)

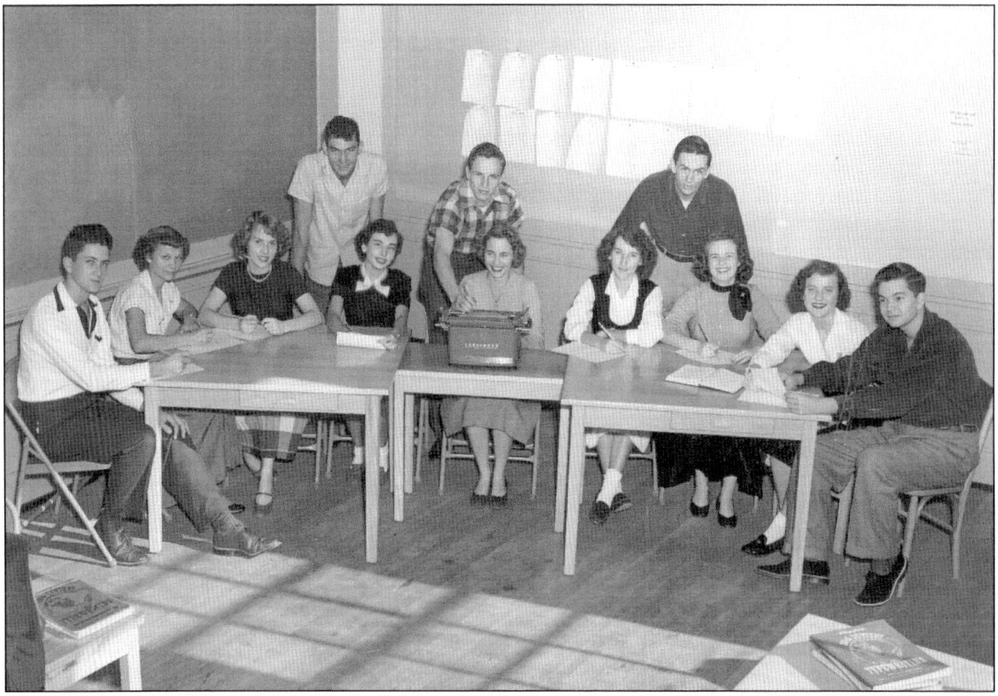

The annual staff in 1953 is shown working diligently on the high school's yearbook, *The Sea Gull*. Pictured here are, from left to right, Darby Gilmer, Julia Taylor, Sharon Ford, Pat Switzer, Syble O'Connor, Faye Johnson, Freddie Mincher, Pete Wren, Newton Hews, and Jimmy Johnson. (Courtesy of Rose Donaldson.)

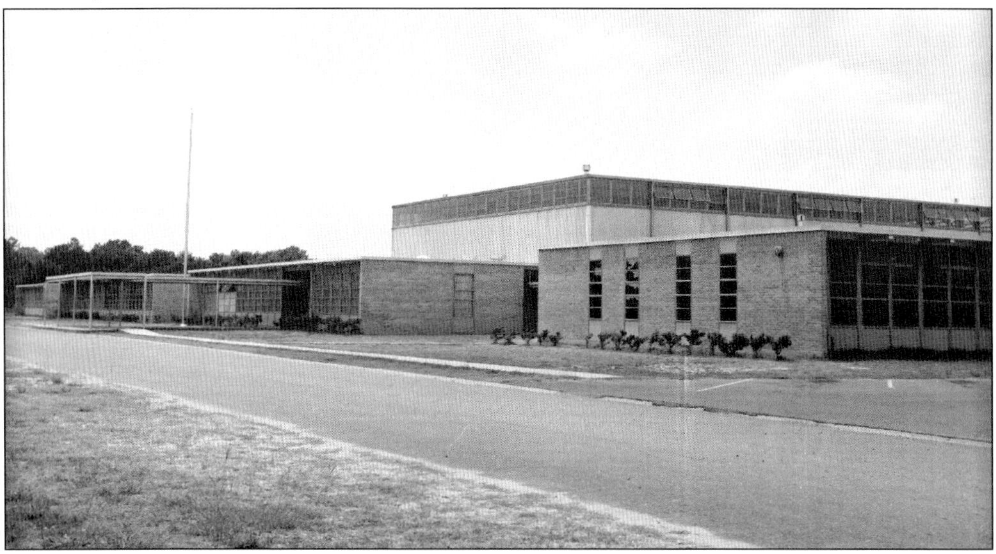

A new high school was built in 1957, when the student population outgrew the old school. The initial construction cost was $500,000. Additional classrooms were added in 1960 as enrollment continued to increase. At the time this photograph was taken in 1962, the enrollment was 1,385. This building is still in use as the high school and is located at the corner of Old Pass Road and Cleveland Avenue. (Courtesy of Mississippi Gulf Coast Community College C.C. "Tex" Hamill Down South Magazine Collection.)

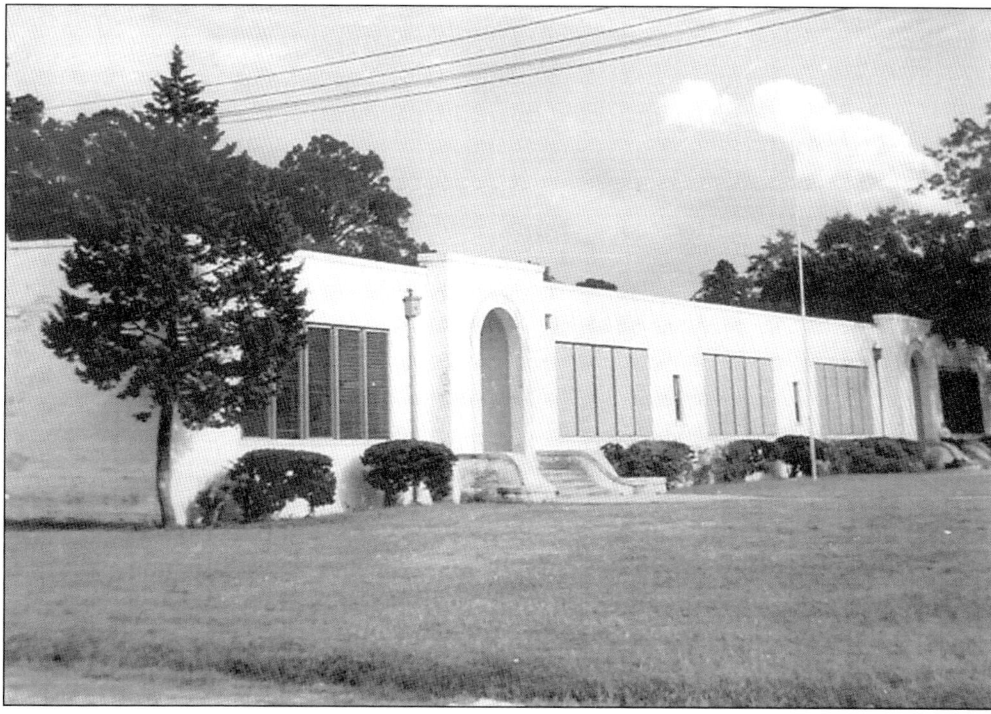

When the new high school opened, the former high school on Jeff Davis Avenue became Jeff Davis Elementary. The building served as an elementary school until 1978 when it was condemned. When a new elementary school was constructed on the site, it was later named Harper McCaughan Elementary School. That school was destroyed by Hurricane Katrina and was rebuilt farther north on Pineville Road. (Courtesy of the Mary Ellen Alexander Collection.)

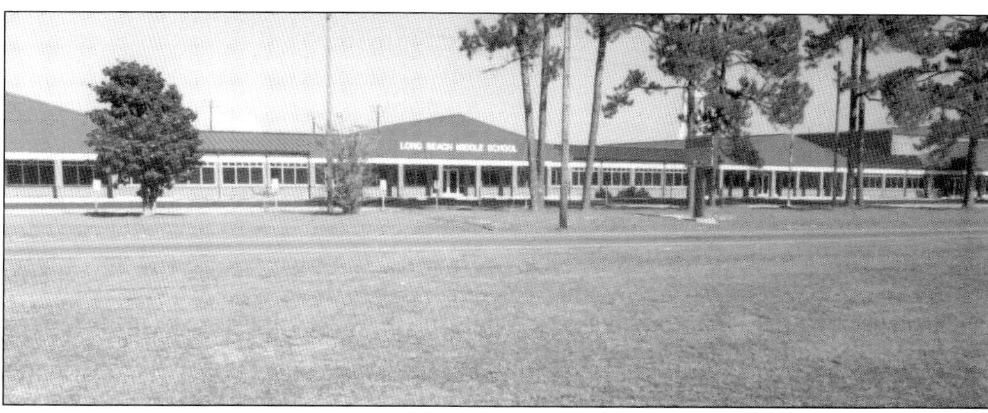

Long Beach Junior High (now called Long Beach Middle School) was constructed in 1963, when the high school became too small to house all of the students. All students in grades seven through nine moved to the new junior high, which was located next door to the high school on Cleveland Avenue. (Courtesy of the Mary Ellen Alexander Collection.)

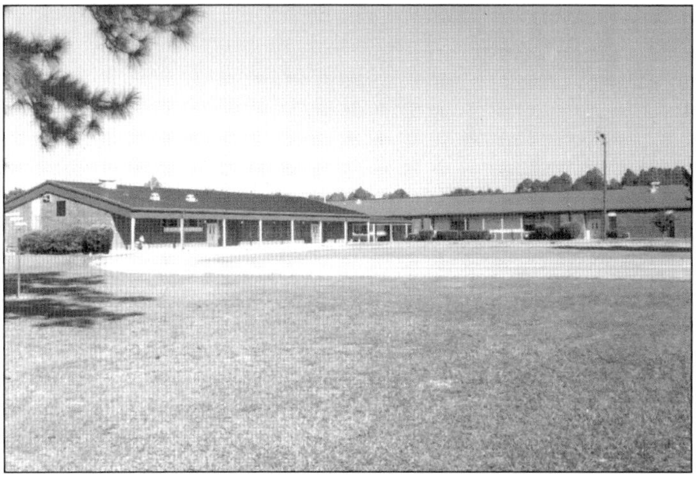

Green Acres Elementary School was built in 1966. The other two elementary schools that were in operation at the time were Quarles Elementary, built in 1963, and Harper McCaughan Elementary. Green Acres and Quarles Elementary Schools are still open today at their original locations. (Courtesy of the Mary Ellen Alexander Collection.)

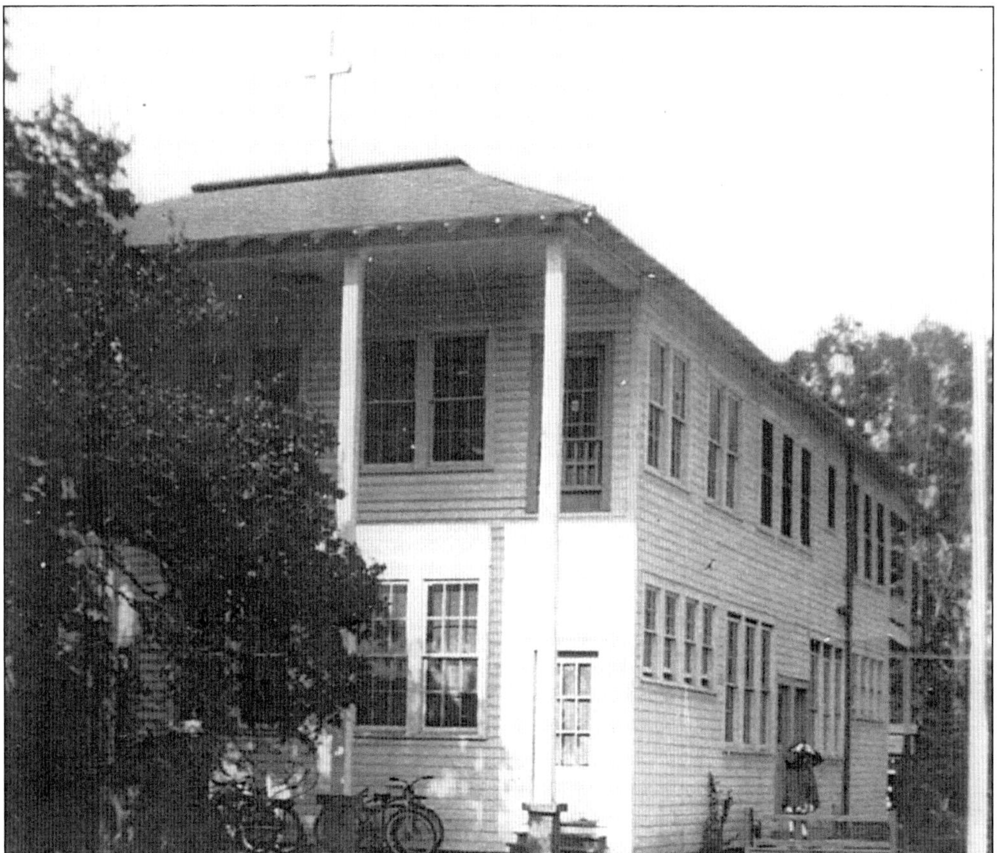

St. Thomas Catholic School opened in 1924. Before this building was constructed, all coursework offered by the school took place in the home of Ben Maceri on East Railroad—from 1921 until the school was built. There were four members of the first graduating class in 1925. This first building (which also housed a convent—the sisters' living quarters were converted into classrooms in 1925) was replaced by a newer, larger school in 1955. That structure was destroyed by Hurricane Katrina in 2005 and not rebuilt. (Courtesy of Long Beach Historical Society Archives.)

Four

Gulf Park College for Women

Gulf Park College for Women opened in 1921 on the former site of Rosalie. The college was also known by the nickname "Gulf Park By-The-Sea." It was founded by Col. J.C. Hardy, the founder of the Gulf Coast Military Academy, and Richard G. Cox, who became the first president of the college. The last two years of high school and the first two years of college were offered, although in the early years, all four years of high school were offered. The girls who attended Gulf Park enrolled in the usual academic subjects, but there was also emphasis on sports such as horsemanship, water sports, archery, golf, and volleyball. There was also an annual Caribbean cruise and social events such as dances at the local military academy and nearby Keesler Air Force Base. The college opened with only two buildings—Hardy Hall, which was a dormitory, and an administration building. By 1940, there were 12 buildings on campus: two dormitories, an administrative building, a music building, a faculty hut, an art studio, a theater workshop, two residences, a YWCA hut, an infirmary, and a heating plant. Although Gulf Park operated successfully for many decades, it never quite recovered from the devastating effects of Hurricane Camille in 1969 and from declining enrollment and closed in 1971. In 1972, the University of Southern Mississippi opened its Gulf Park Campus on the site, which continues to operate today.

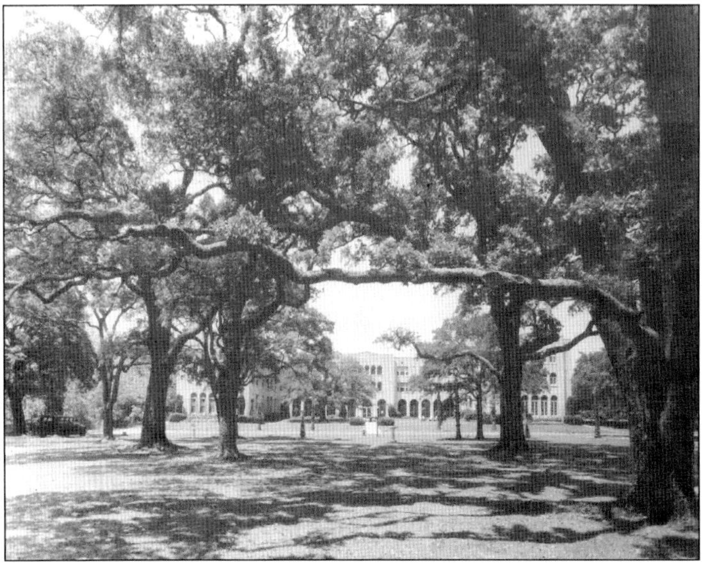

Hardy Hall was a dormitory during the Gulf Park College for Women years, and it overlooks the Mississippi Sound. The building was heavily damaged during Hurricane Katrina, but it has been restored to its original historic appearance. (Courtesy of the University of Southern Mississippi Gulf Coast Library, Gulf Park College for Women Archives.)

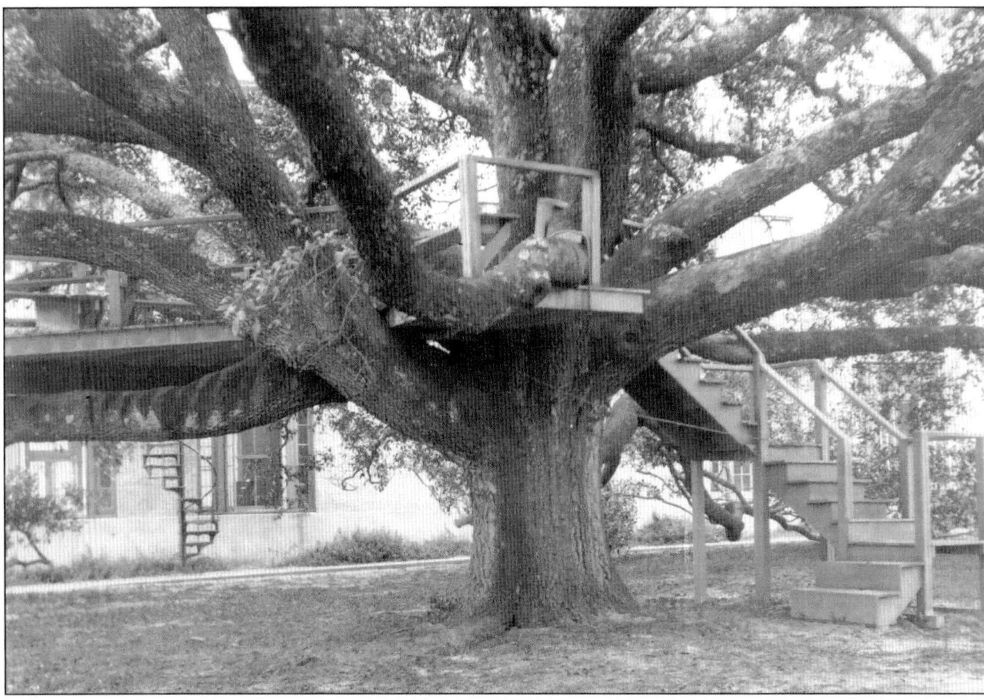

The Friendship Oak dominates the other trees on the Gulf Park Campus. The oak is estimated to be well over 500 years old. When early settler John J. McCaughan lived on the site at Rosalie, he buried sharks at its roots to fertilize it. A plaque at the base of the tree reads, "I am called the Friendship Oak; those who enter my shadow will remain friends through all of their lifetimes." Classes were sometimes held in the tree's platform, and many Gulf Park girls had their photographs taken there. The platform was destroyed by Hurricane Katrina in 2005 and has not been rebuilt. (Courtesy of Mississippi Gulf Coast Community College Dixie Press Collection.)

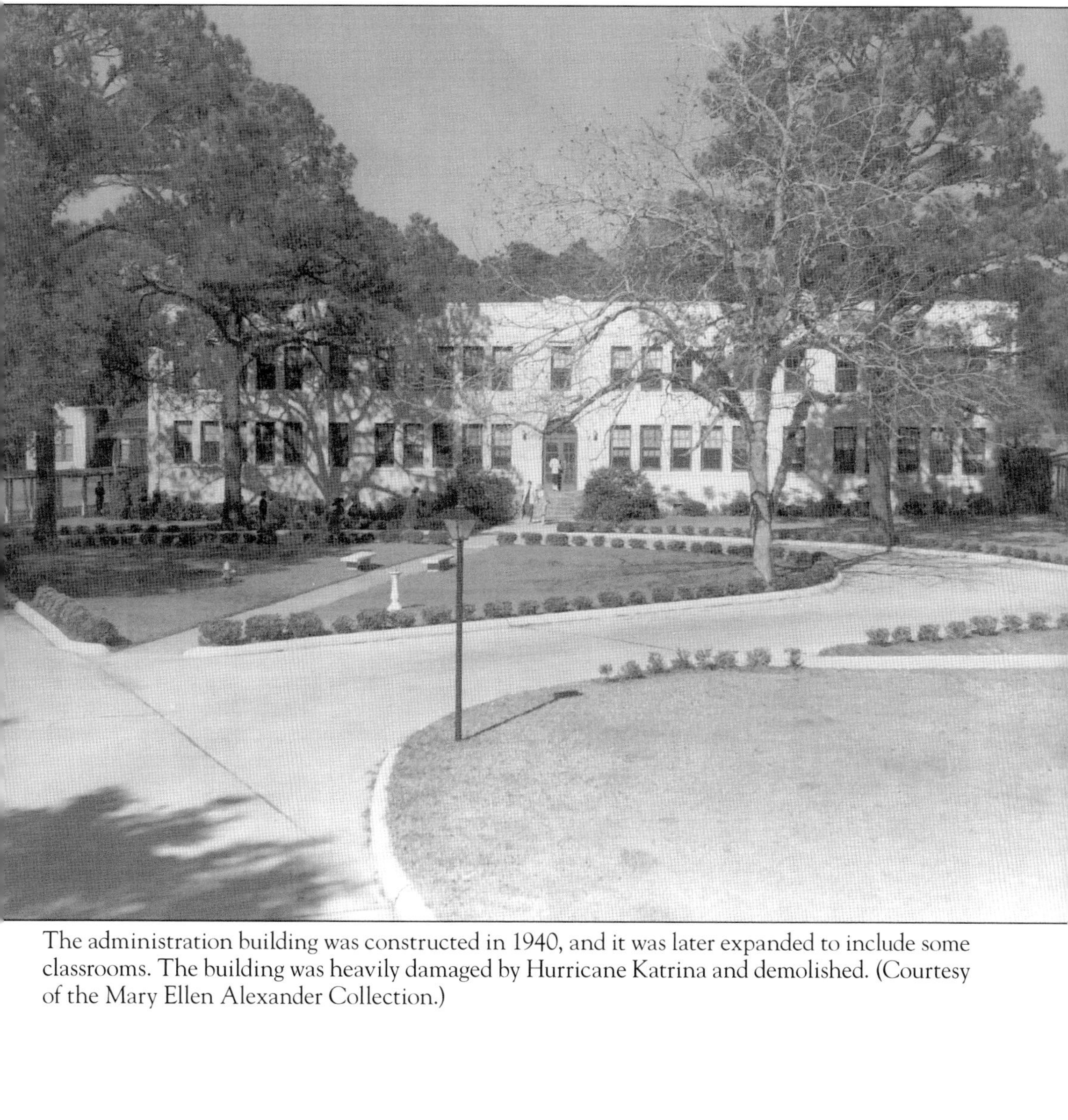

The administration building was constructed in 1940, and it was later expanded to include some classrooms. The building was heavily damaged by Hurricane Katrina and demolished. (Courtesy of the Mary Ellen Alexander Collection.)

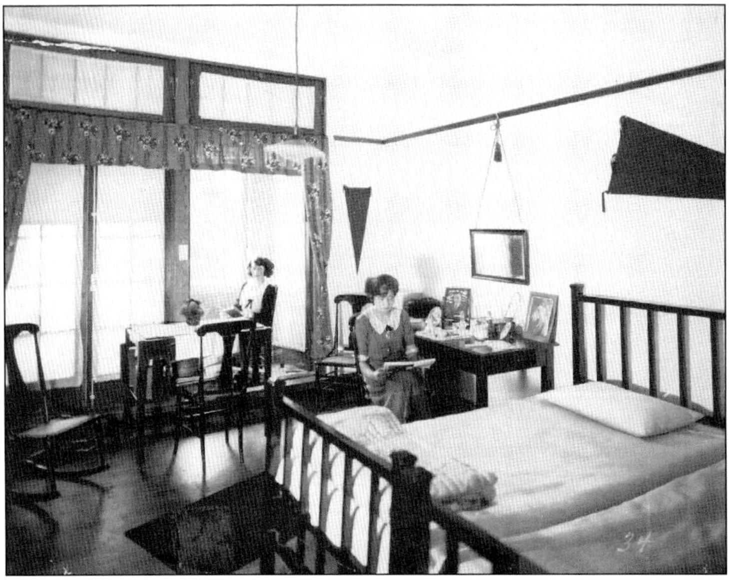

Pictured here is a typical dormitory room of the 1920s and 1930s. Girls were encouraged to personalize the rooms to make them more homelike. Each dormitory also had sun parlors for reading and recreation and also provided smoking rooms. (Courtesy of Mississippi Gulf Coast Community College Dixie Press Collection.)

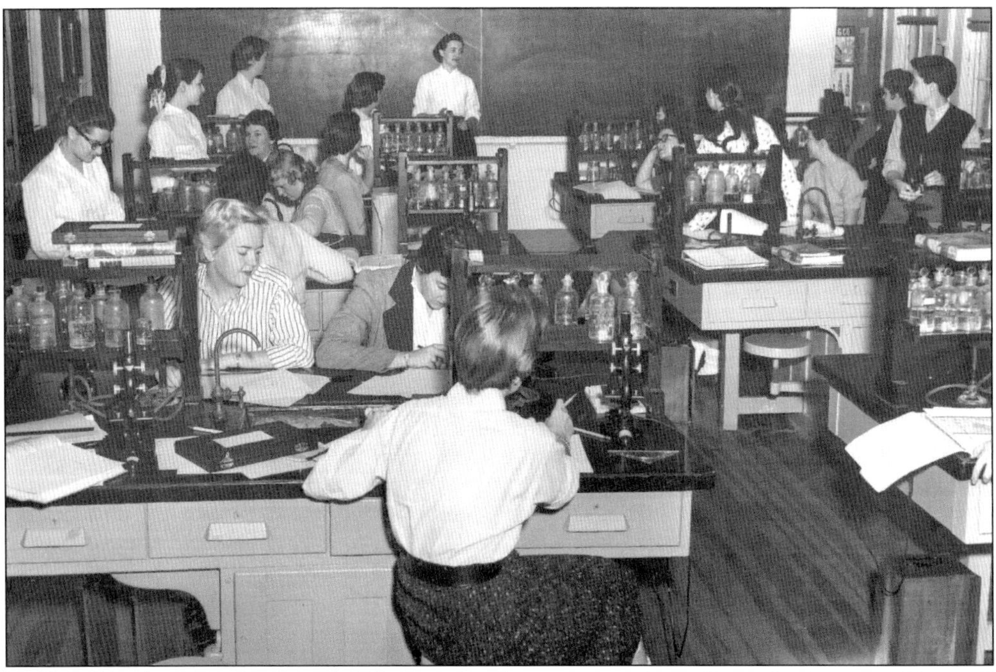

Gulf Park girls are busy in one of the science classrooms at the college. Students could enroll in chemistry, physics, biology, and physiology classes as well as other academic subjects such as history, language arts, mathematics, and foreign languages. Courses in secretarial work and home economics were also offered. (Courtesy of the University of Southern Mississippi Gulf Coast Library, Gulf Park College for Women Archives.)

American poet Vachel Lindsay (1879–1931) was considered the father of singing poetry—poetry meant not to be just read, but to be chanted. His best-known poem is "The Congo." He was a guest lecturer at Gulf Park College in the early 1920s and frequently held lectures on the platform of the Friendship Oak. He is pictured here on campus with two unidentified young women. (Courtesy of Damon Franke.)

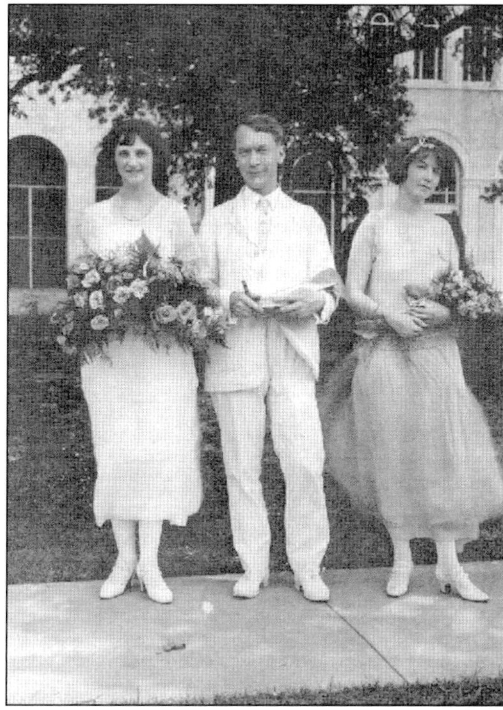

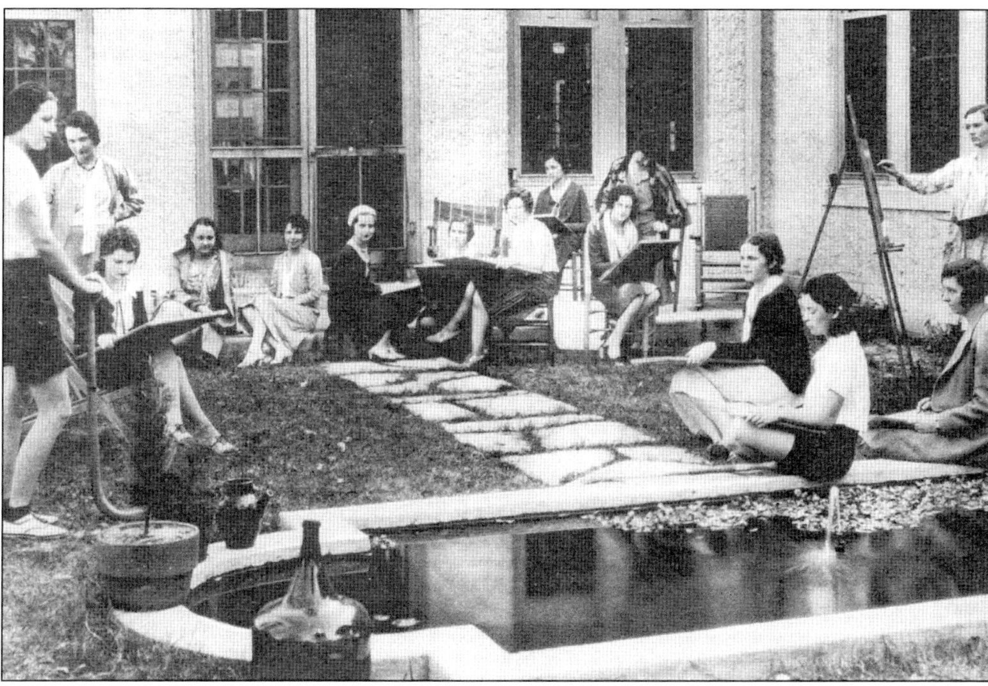

These Gulf Park students are enjoying the fresh air while working outside the art studio in the late 1920s. The courtyard area of this U-shaped structure was later enclosed when the University of Southern Mississippi converted the building into a library, but the original windows were left intact. This created an interesting look to the building's interior, but it was destroyed by Hurricane Katrina. (Courtesy of Long Beach Historical Society Archives.)

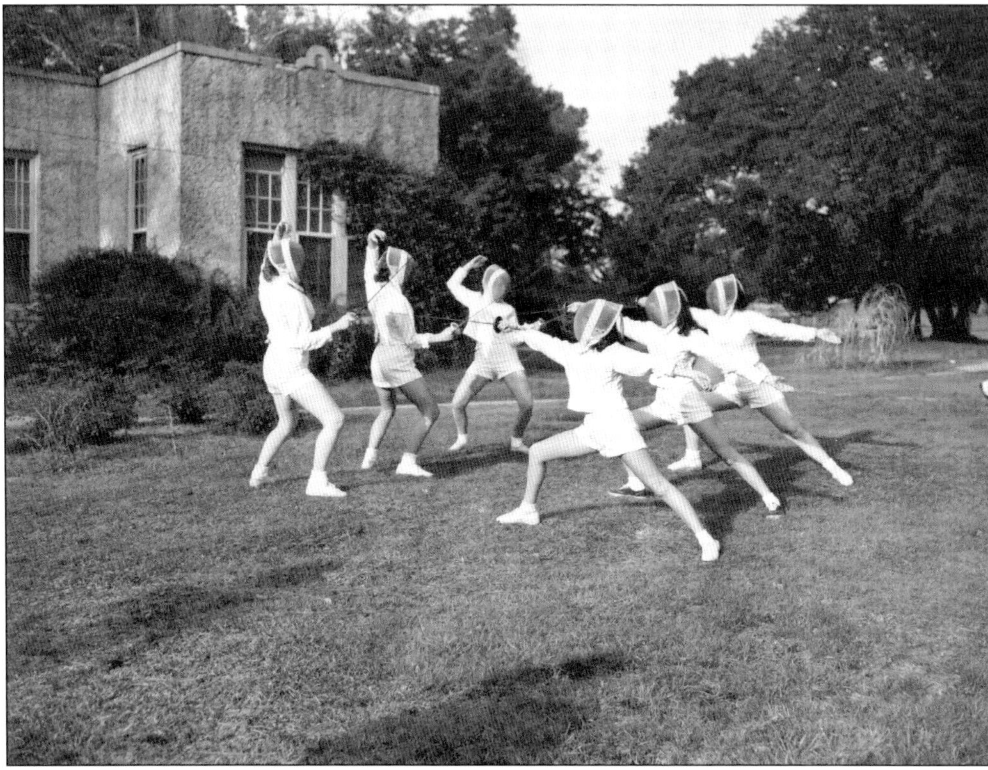

Members of the Gulf Park fencing team take imposing stances in this photograph from 1952. The girls were able to take part in many athletic activities that might not have been offered at other schools. In addition to fencing, they played volleyball, golf, lacrosse, softball, archery, and water sports. Many of the students also won awards for horsemanship. This photograph was taken in front of the art studio. (Courtesy of Mississippi Gulf Coast Community College C.C. "Tex" Hamill Down South Magazine Collection.)

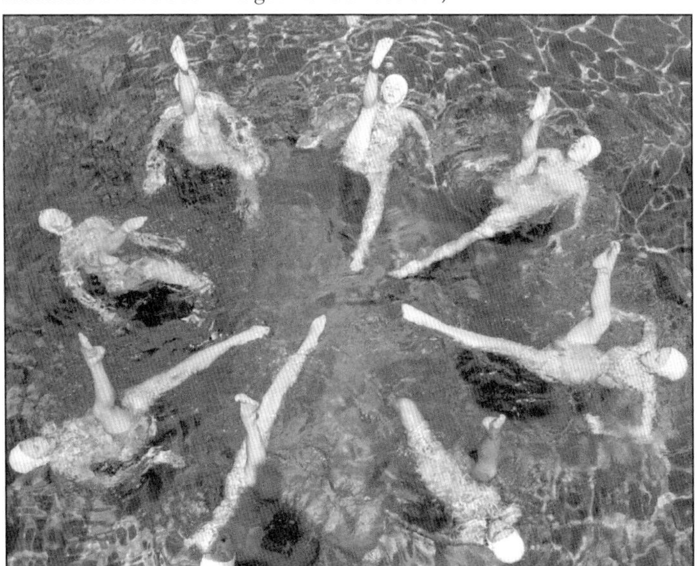

Synchronized swimming was an important aspect of the water sports at Gulf Park. The team performed at the Gulf Park pool as well as at other venues along the coast. There was also a regular swim team and a diving team. (Courtesy of the University of Southern Mississippi Gulf Coast Library, Gulf Park College for Women Archives.)

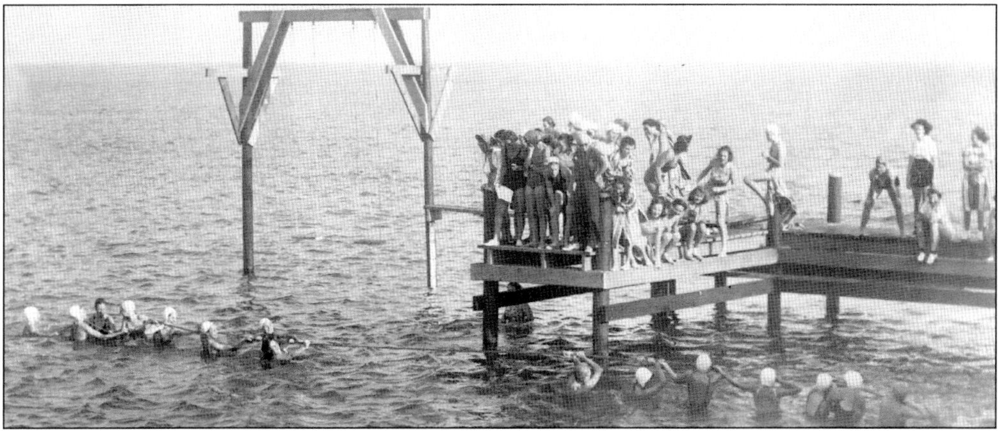

Some of the Gulf Park girls on the pier are cheering on their classmates in a game of water tug-of-war. The thousand-foot-long pier was used as a base for many of the water activities, including swimming, skiing, and sailing. Note the swings to the left of the pier. (Courtesy of Mississippi Gulf Coast Community College Dixie Press Collection.)

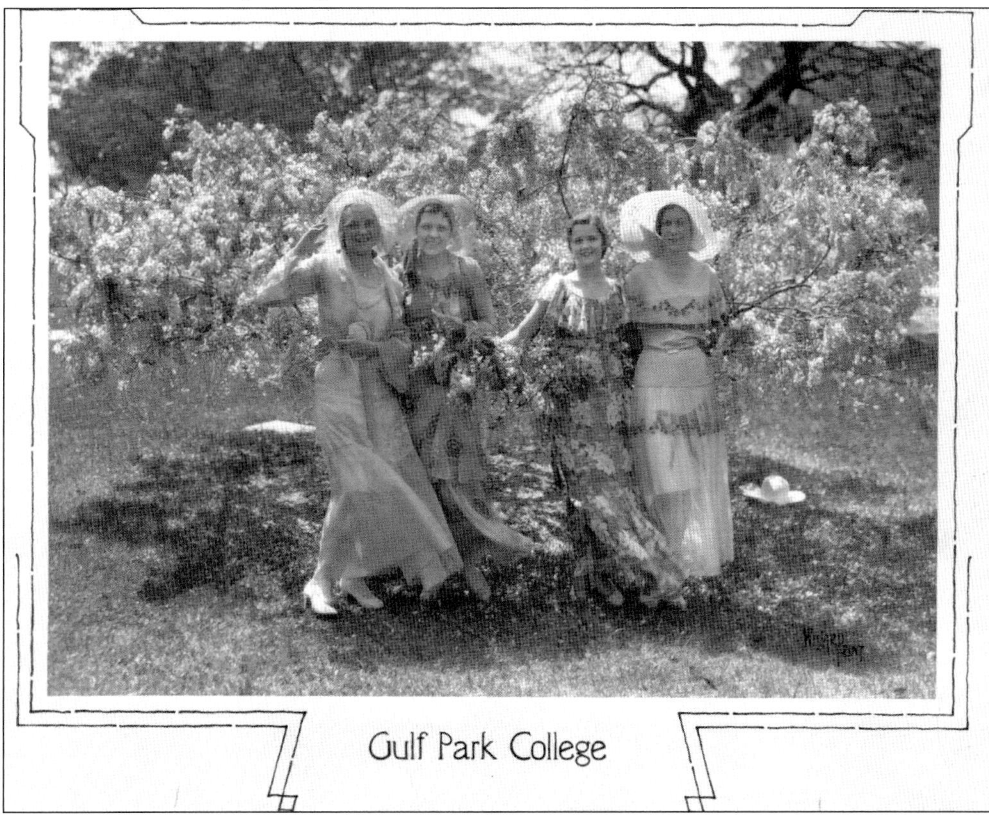

Except for when they were involved in sports activities, the girls who attended Gulf Park College were expected to represent the college well in their dress and deportment. Girls could not leave campus without being dressed in proper attire, including a hat and gloves. Before they could date a Gulf Park girl, young gentlemen had to present letters of reference. This photograph, probably dating from the 1920s, shows some of the girls in their finest spring outfits. (Courtesy of Mississippi Gulf Coast Community College Dixie Press Collection.)

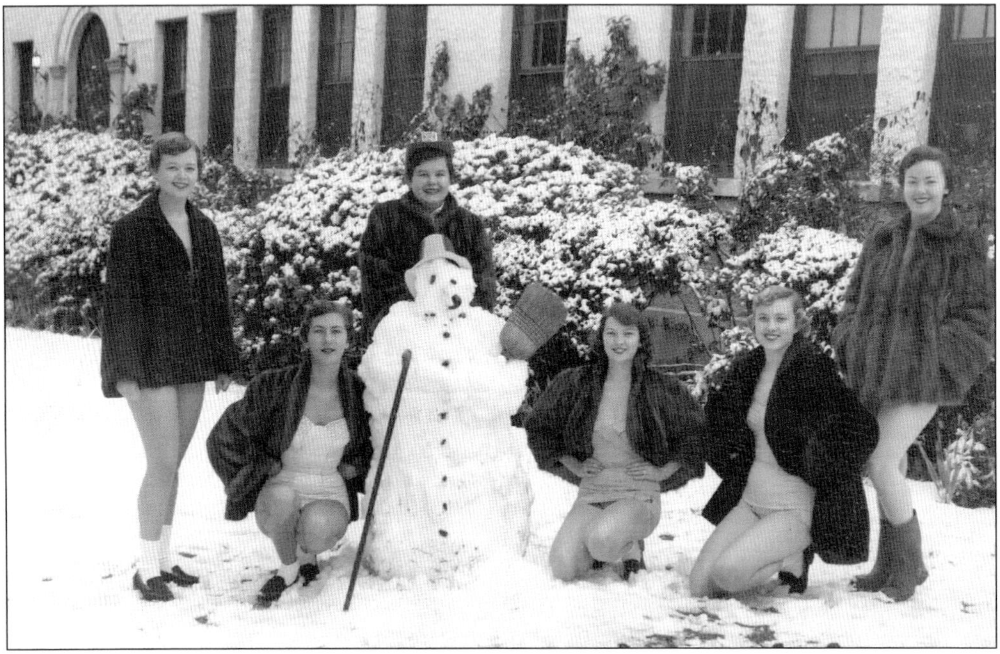

Snowfall in southern Mississippi was and still is a fairly rare event. When the occasional snow fell, the students took advantage of the situation to take many fun photographs. Here, unidentified girls pose in their bathing suits and mink coats. (Courtesy of Mississippi Gulf Coast Community College Dixie Press Collection.)

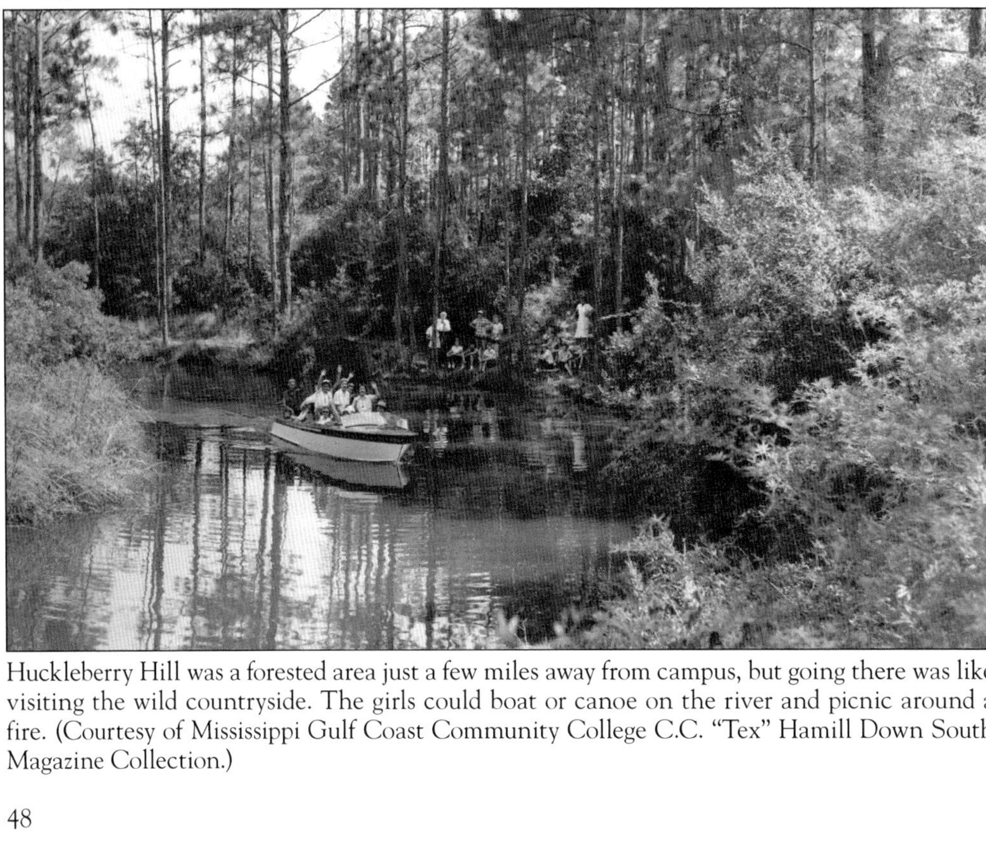

Huckleberry Hill was a forested area just a few miles away from campus, but going there was like visiting the wild countryside. The girls could boat or canoe on the river and picnic around a fire. (Courtesy of Mississippi Gulf Coast Community College C.C. "Tex" Hamill Down South Magazine Collection.)

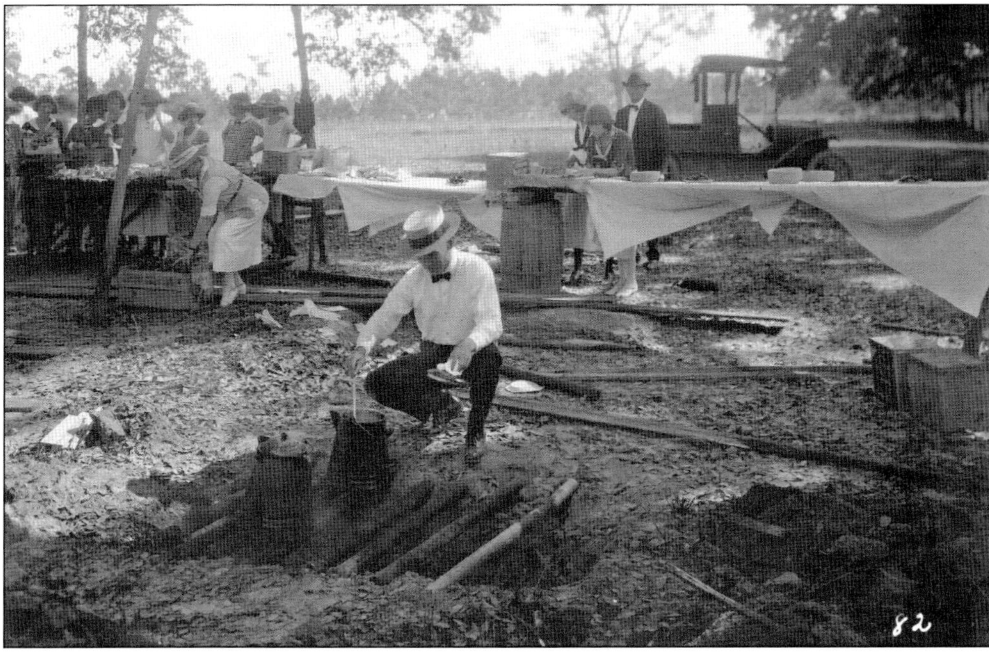

Here is a typical picnic at Gulf Park, probably from the late 1920s. Outdoor activities were offered as much as possible. In this photograph, the president of the college, Dr. Richard G. Cox, is stirring the coffee while Elizabeth Cox helps set out food. The photograph may have been taken on campus, but it could also have been taken at Huckleberry Hill. (Courtesy of Mississippi Gulf Coast Community College Dixie Press Collection.)

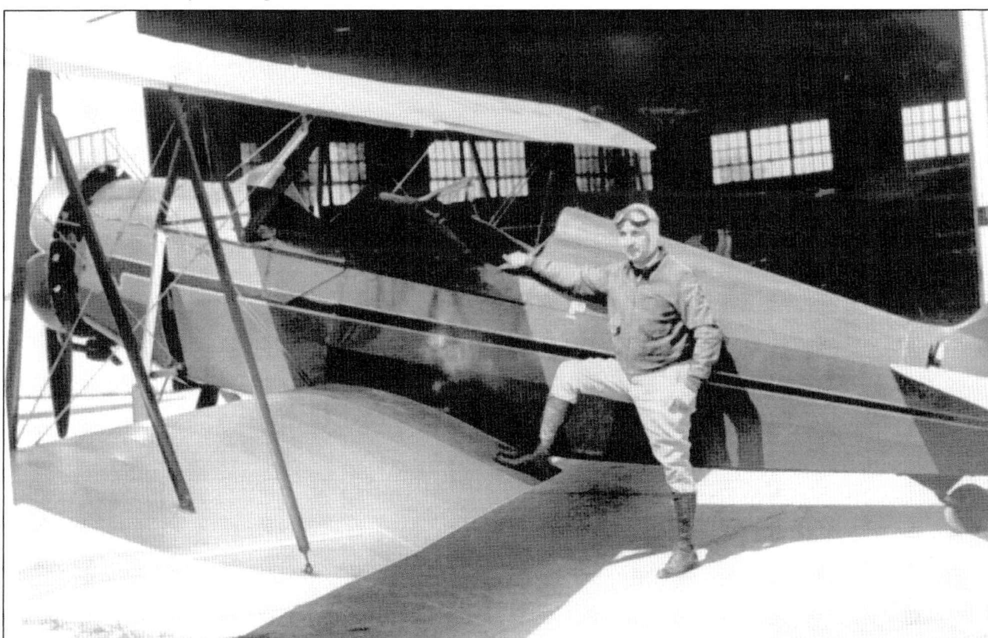

President Cox was an aviation enthusiast. He frequently piloted his own plane around the coast, buzzing the campus as he flew past. (Courtesy of the University of Southern Mississippi Gulf Coast Library, Gulf Park College for Women Archives.)

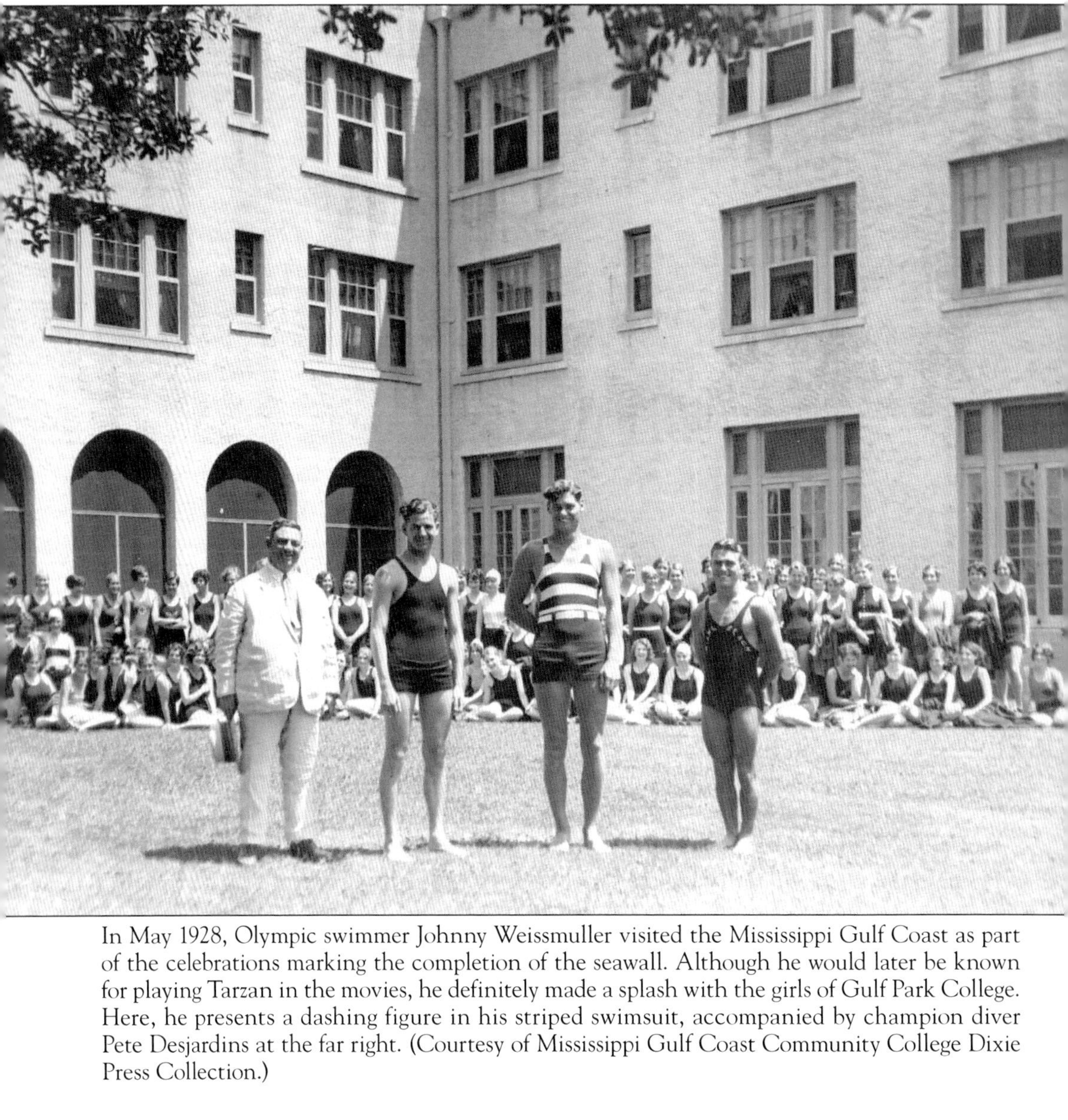

In May 1928, Olympic swimmer Johnny Weissmuller visited the Mississippi Gulf Coast as part of the celebrations marking the completion of the seawall. Although he would later be known for playing Tarzan in the movies, he definitely made a splash with the girls of Gulf Park College. Here, he presents a dashing figure in his striped swimsuit, accompanied by champion diver Pete Desjardins at the far right. (Courtesy of Mississippi Gulf Coast Community College Dixie Press Collection.)

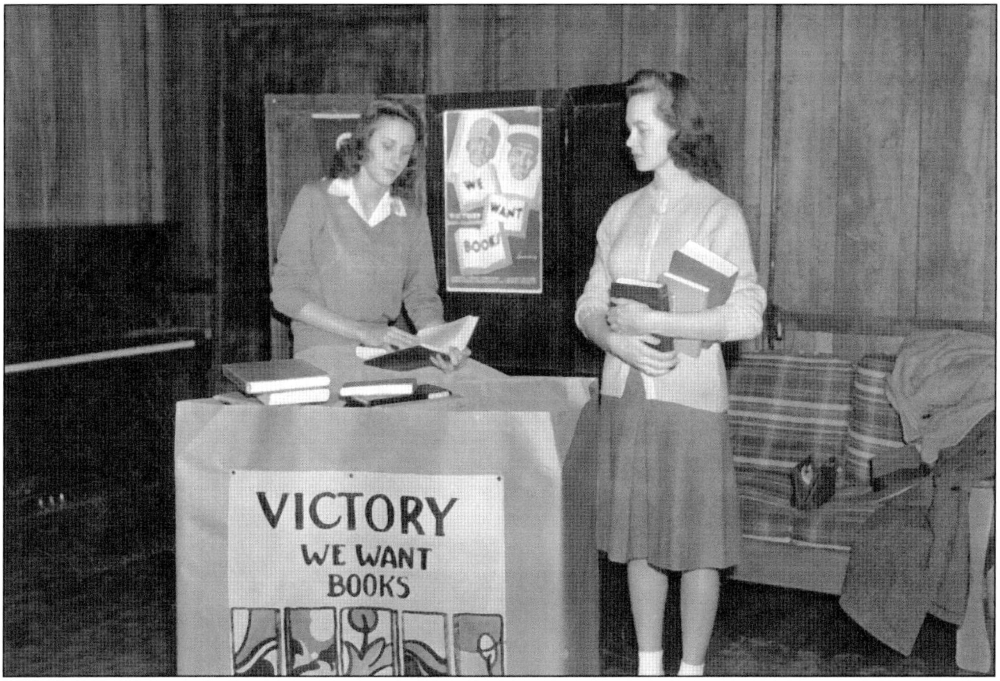

During World War II, the Gulf Park girls did their part to support the soldiers. In 1942, they held a book drive and collected 465 books for the enlisted men. (Courtesy of Mississippi Gulf Coast Community College Dixie Press Collection.)

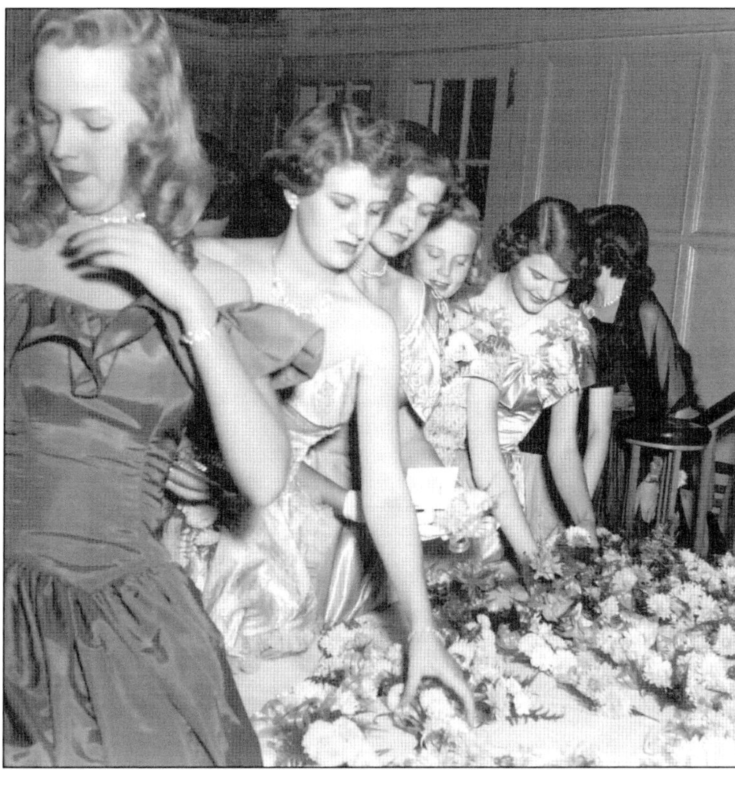

There was also plenty of time for social events. Here, the girls are picking up their corsages before a dance. Dances were held at Gulf Park, as well as at the local Gulf Coast Military Academy and Keesler Air Force Base. (Courtesy of the University of Southern Mississippi Gulf Coast Library, Gulf Park College for Women Archives.)

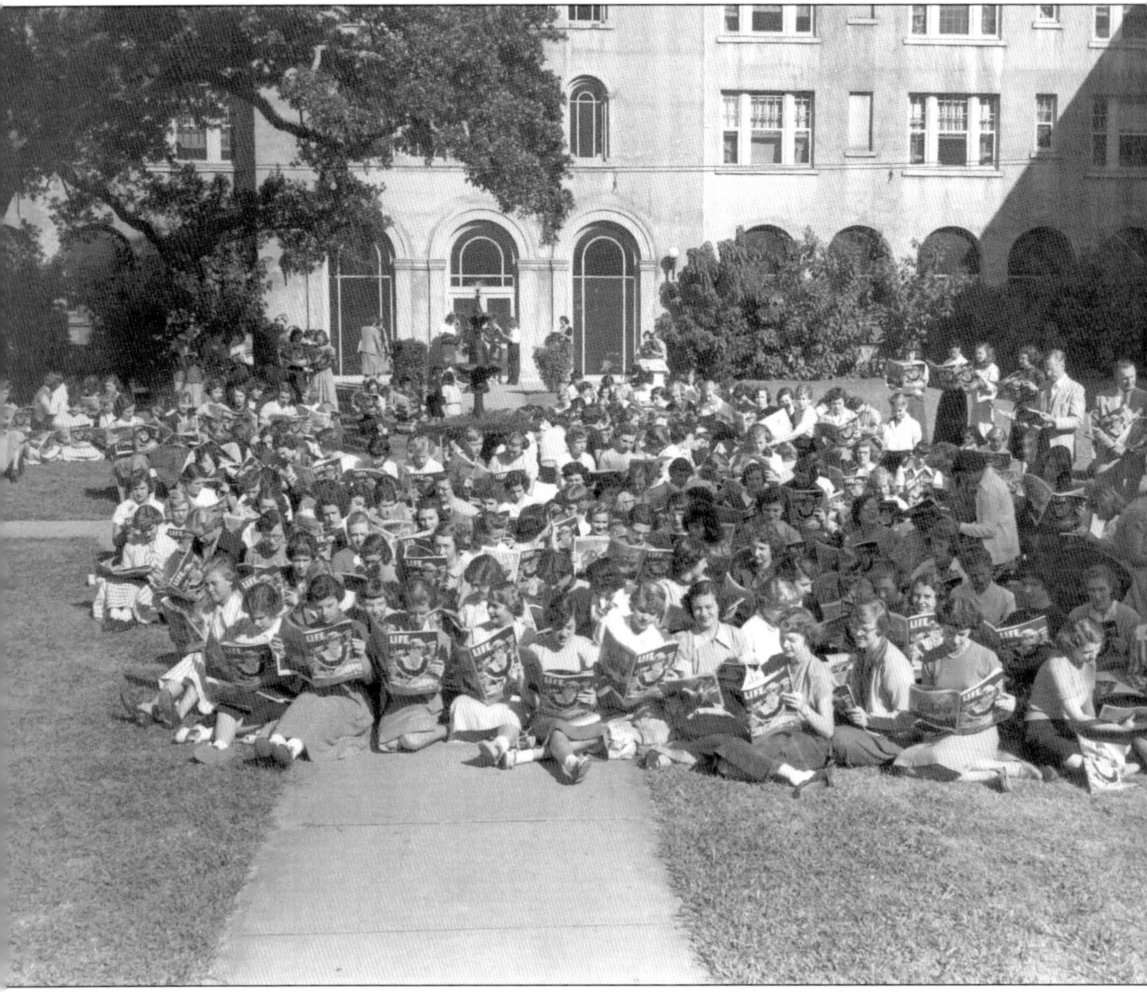

In 1950, *Life* magazine ran a story about Gulf Park College in the October issue. *Life* followed up that story with this photograph in the November 6 issue of the girls reading about themselves. (Courtesy of Mississippi Gulf Coast Community College Dixie Press Collection.)

Five

Agriculture and Business

Although Long Beach was famous for truck farming, there were many other thriving businesses in town. As the truck farming boom burst during the Great Depression, Long Beach turned to other ways to survive. The tourist trade has been the mainstay for many years. The downtown area has expanded from a single general store in 1890 to several grocery stores, specialty shops, diners, and restaurants. Now, as in the past, locals and visitors alike can get great food and products at locally owned restaurants and stores.

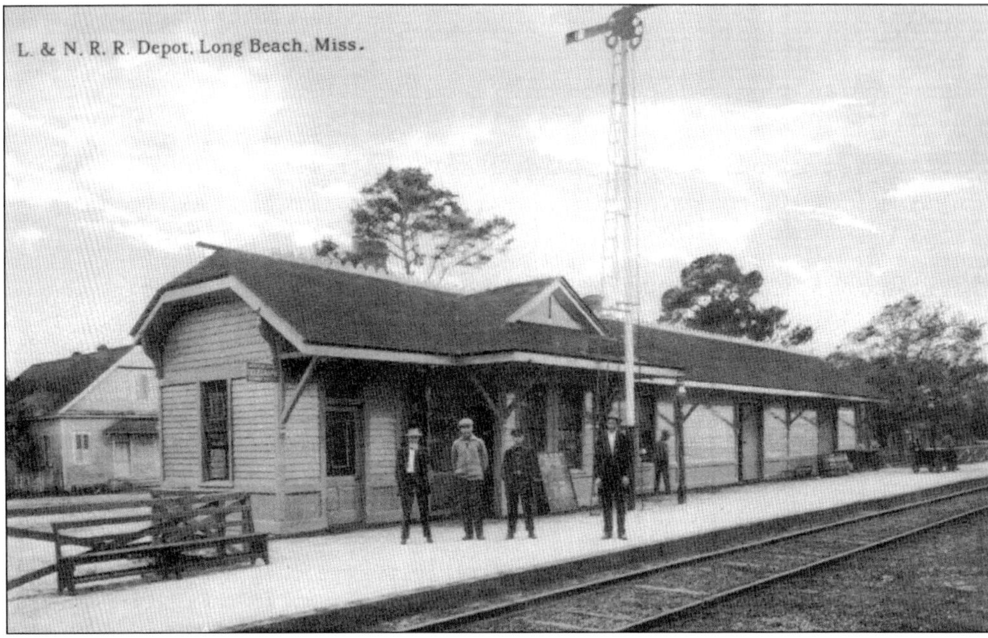

The Louisville & Nashville Railroad depot was built in 1890. The railroad line extending through Long Beach was a boon to the local truck farmers, and soon there was even a daily commuter service between Ocean Springs to the east of Long Beach and New Orleans to the west. The depot closed in 1955 after passenger service was discontinued in the area, and the building was torn down a few years later. Agent Ben Simmons is on the left, in the white shirt, and E.E. Klein is on the right. (Courtesy of Paul Jermyn.)

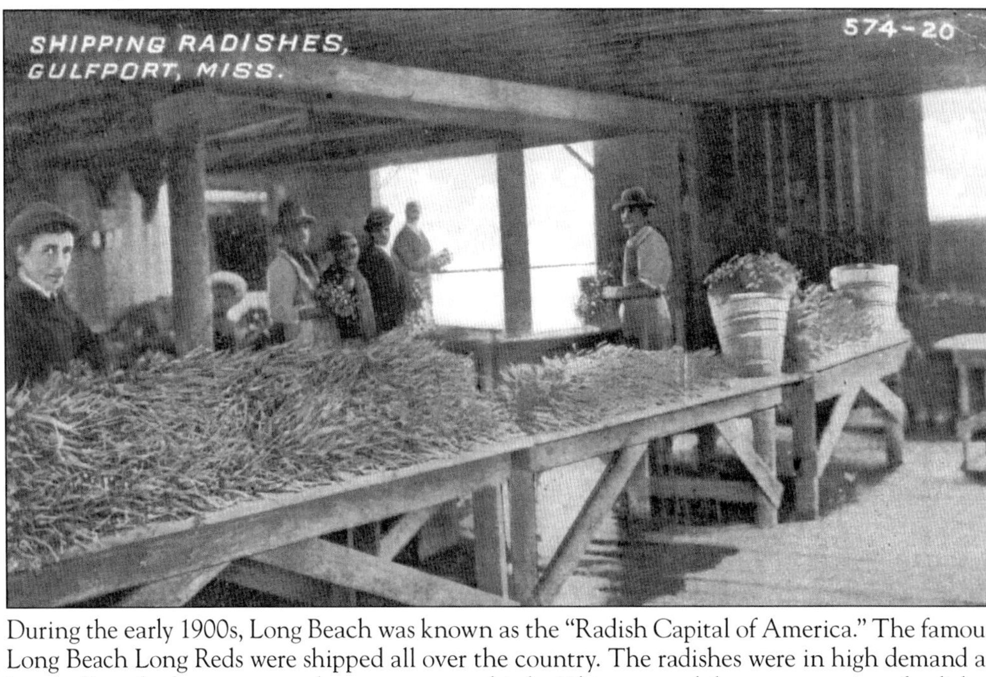

During the early 1900s, Long Beach was known as the "Radish Capital of America." The famous Long Beach Long Reds were shipped all over the country. The radishes were in high demand at beer halls and saloons as a snack to accompany drinks. This postcard shows mountains of radishes being sorted for packing. (Courtesy of Paul Jermyn.)

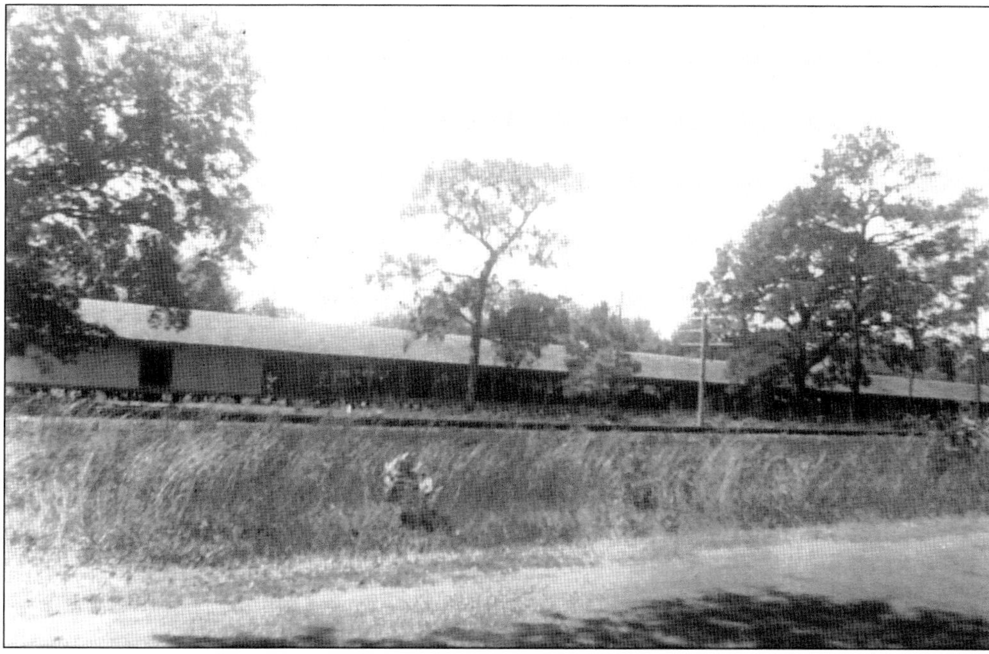

A large packing shed was constructed in 1923 just south of the railroad tracks at what is now the site of Hancock Bank. The packinghouse is where the Long Reds were washed, sorted, and packed for shipping to the northern states. (Courtesy of the Mary Ellen Alexander Collection.)

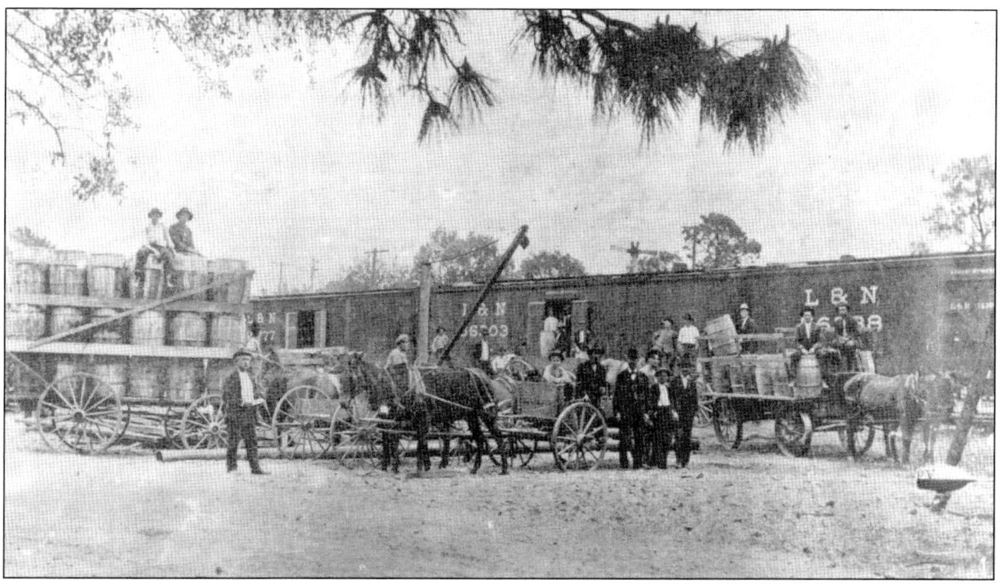

Barrels of Long Beach Long Red radishes are being loaded into these refrigerated railcars near the Jeff Davis Avenue crossing in this 1909 photograph. The chute was used to load ice into the cars to keep the radishes (and other produce) fresh during the long journey to the North. (Courtesy of Mississippi Gulf Coast Community College C.C. "Tex" Hamill Down South Magazine Collection.)

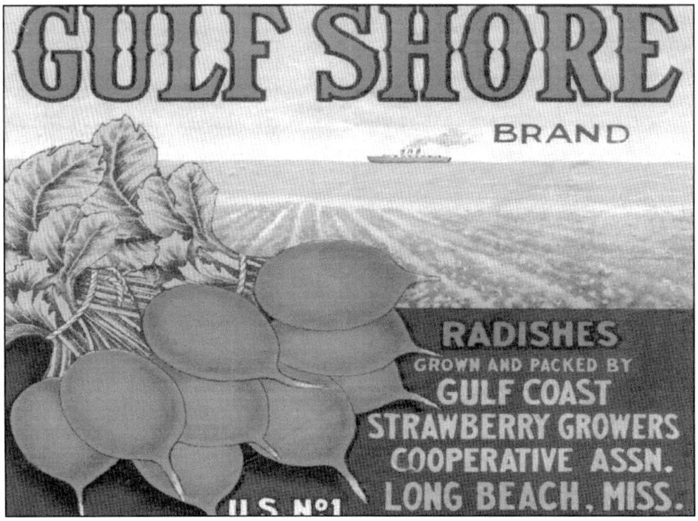

This is a reproduction of the actual label used for the shipping barrels of radishes. There is an error on the label, because the radishes shipped from Long Beach were of the Long Beach Long Red variety, which were shaped more like small red carrots than the round variety depicted. (Courtesy of Long Beach Historical Society Archives.)

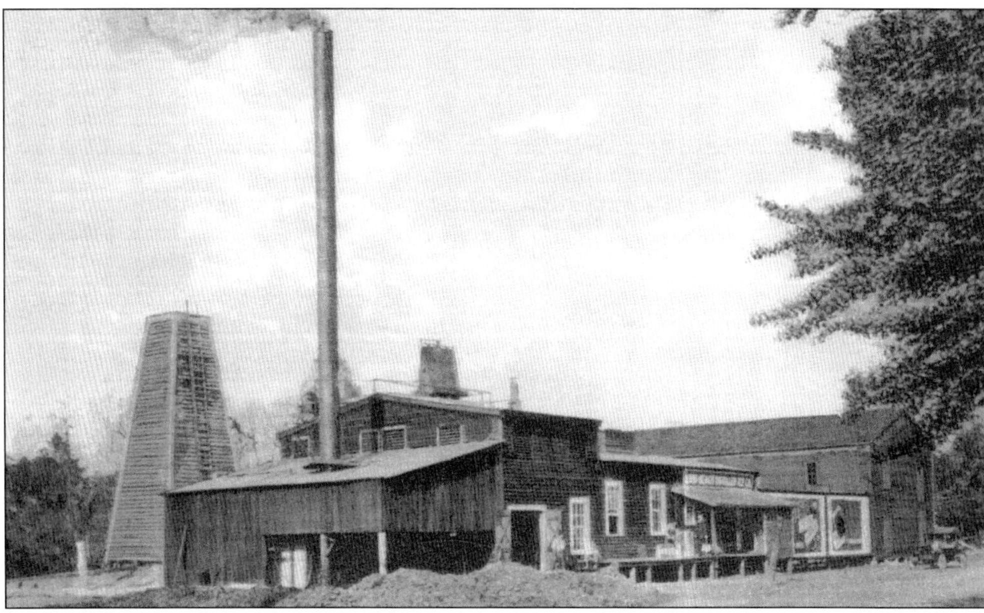

The Long Beach Distilled Ice and Barrel Factory is pictured here in 1916. This was a much-needed industry because barrels were used for packing radishes, and the ice was necessary for the refrigerated train cars used for shipping. The factory was located on the corner of Railroad Street and Pineville Road, where a drugstore stands today. This was near the shed where the radishes and other produce were packed for loading on the nearby railroad cars. The factory was originally owned by William Smith. It was later sold to Pasquale Guiffria, Felice Bertucci, and Paola Gulotta, who operated it for another three years. A cold-storage facility was later added to the icehouse and operated for a number of years. (Courtesy of Paul Jermyn.)

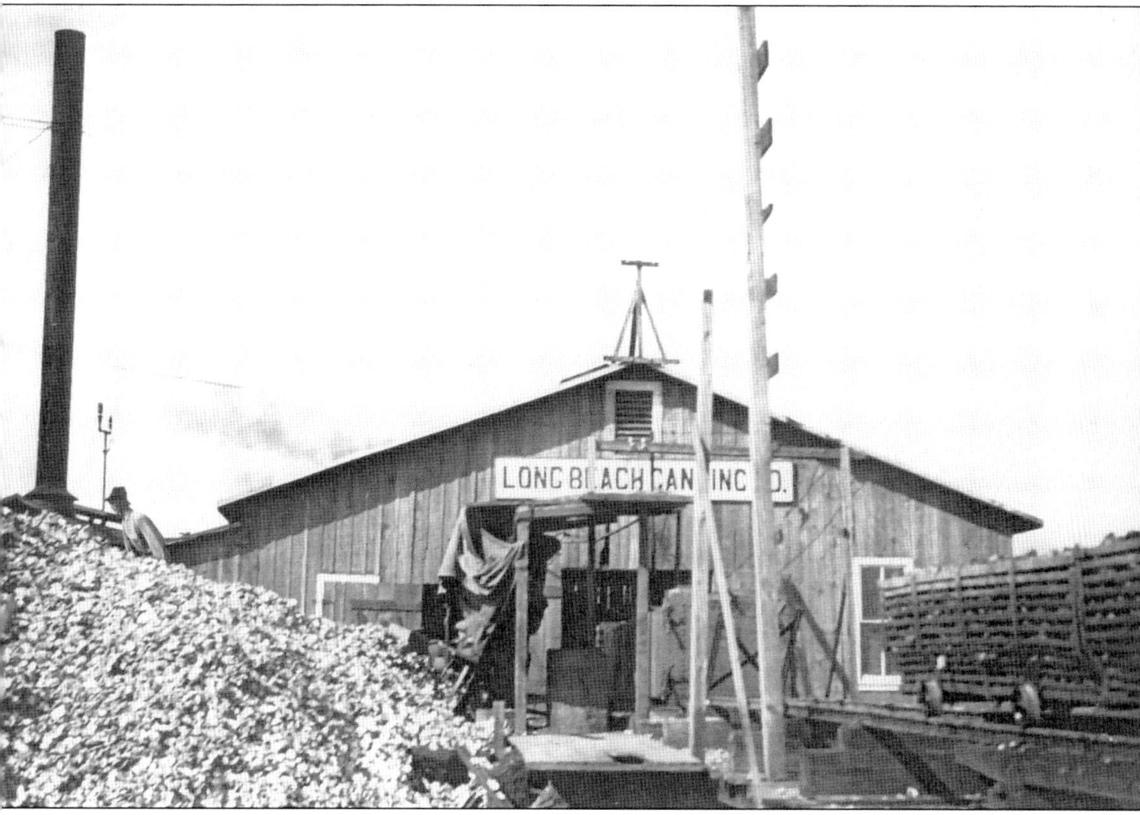

The Long Beach Canning Company was built after 1915, when C.H. Castanera worked with local truck farmers to establish a facility for canning their surplus vegetables during the slump times in shipping. A newspaper article from 1920 reported that oysters and shrimp were being canned as well as up to 400 bushels of sweet potatoes per day. Another article in 1923 reported that the factory was concentrating on canning shrimp, which were "small, but plentiful." There is some confusion about the location. Some sources place it in Long Beach, others on the West Pier in Gulfport. The factory may have been moved from an original Long Beach site at some point, or a second factory may have opened in Gulfport and kept the Long Beach name. (Courtesy of Paul Jermyn.)

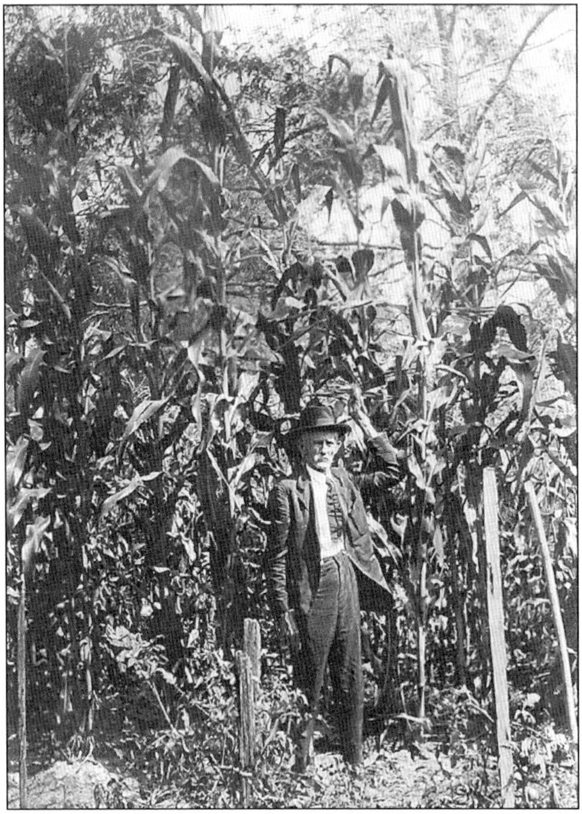

Frank P. Watrous is surrounded by tall cornstalks in one of his fields. There were many other crops grown in Long Beach besides the radishes, including corn, beans, lettuce, sweet potatoes, and strawberries. There were also citrus groves and other fruit orchards. The pear orchard planted by the Thomas brothers on the site of present-day St. Thomas Catholic Church stretched from the beachfront back to the railroad. Some of the other truck farmers in Long Beach included the families of Frank LaRosa, Ben Maceri, Vincent Dauro, R. Inglis, and August Werner. (Courtesy of Paul Jermyn.)

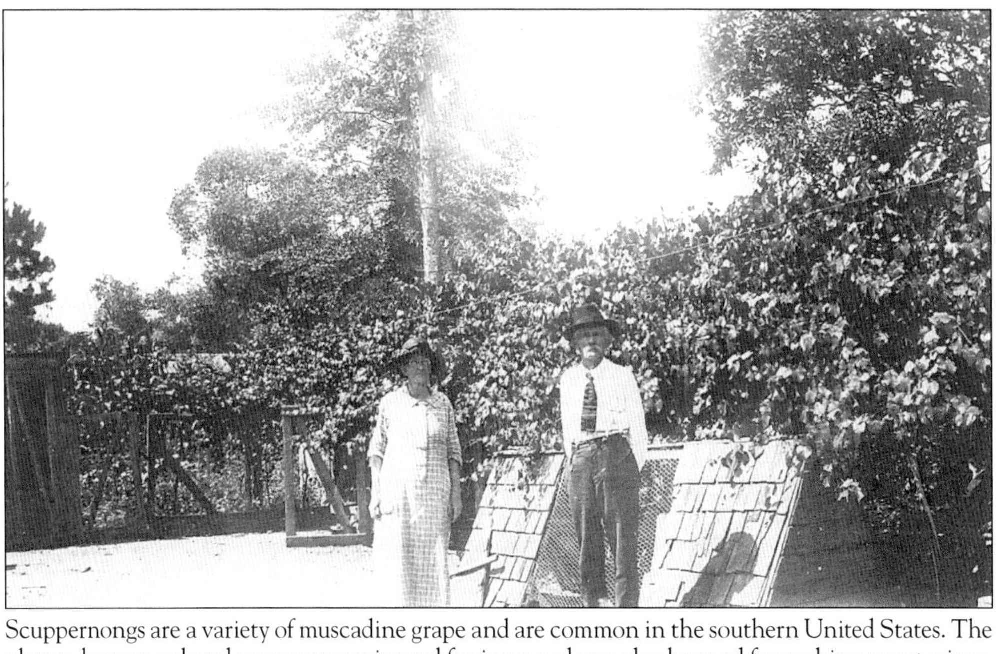

Scuppernongs are a variety of muscadine grape and are common in the southern United States. The plump, bronze-colored scuppernong is used for jams and can also be used for making sweet wines. Pictured here are Frank P. and Ninna (Steele) Watrous in front of their numerous scuppernong vines. (Courtesy of Paul Jermyn.)

May Quarles is pictured with her horse Lady in 1904. In 1912, Quarles was appointed the first Canning Club agent in Harrison County, which at that time included what later became Stone County. Quarles and her horse and buggy traveled throughout her territory of 21 counties as the first district extension agent, which she was appointed in 1917. (Courtesy of the Mary Ellen Alexander Collection.)

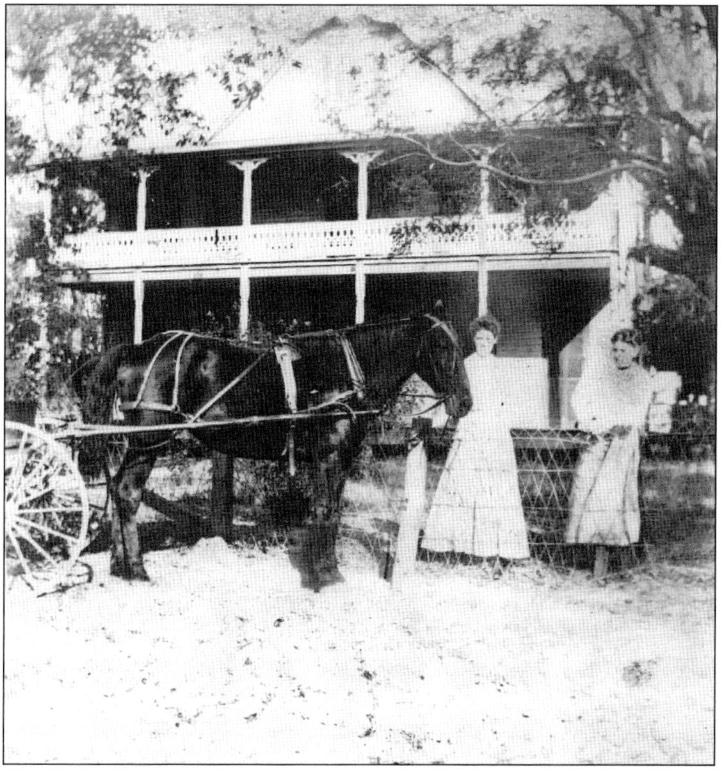

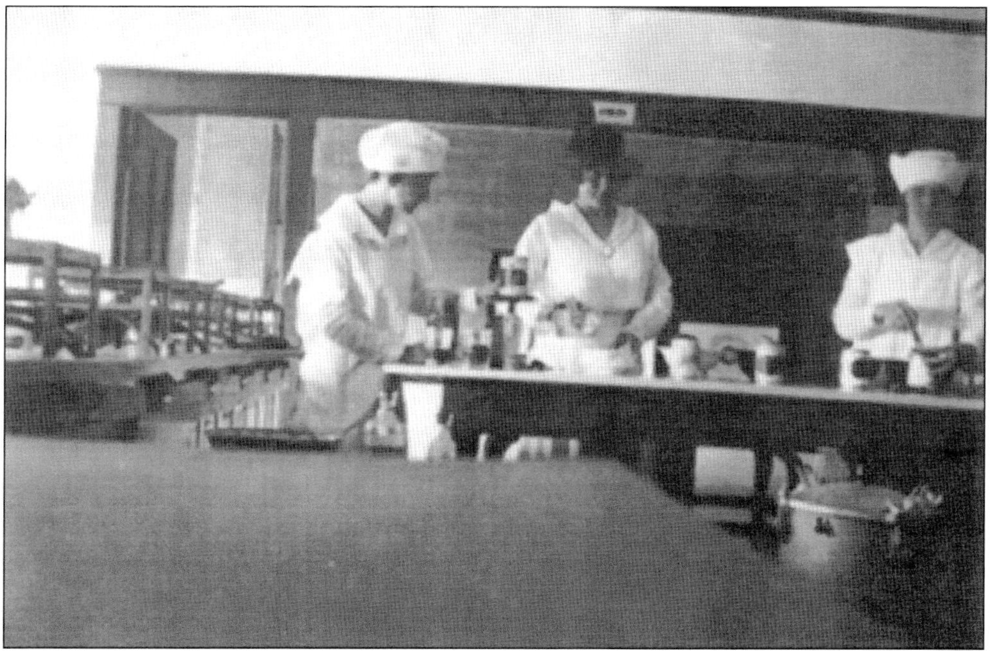

During the 1920s and 1930s, there were tomato canning clubs all over Mississippi, part of the 4-H Clubs. May Quarles (center) began working with the Long Beach group through the Works Progress Administration. Any girl in the state who had access to at least one-tenth of an acre of land could join the club. (Courtesy of the Mary Ellen Alexander Collection.)

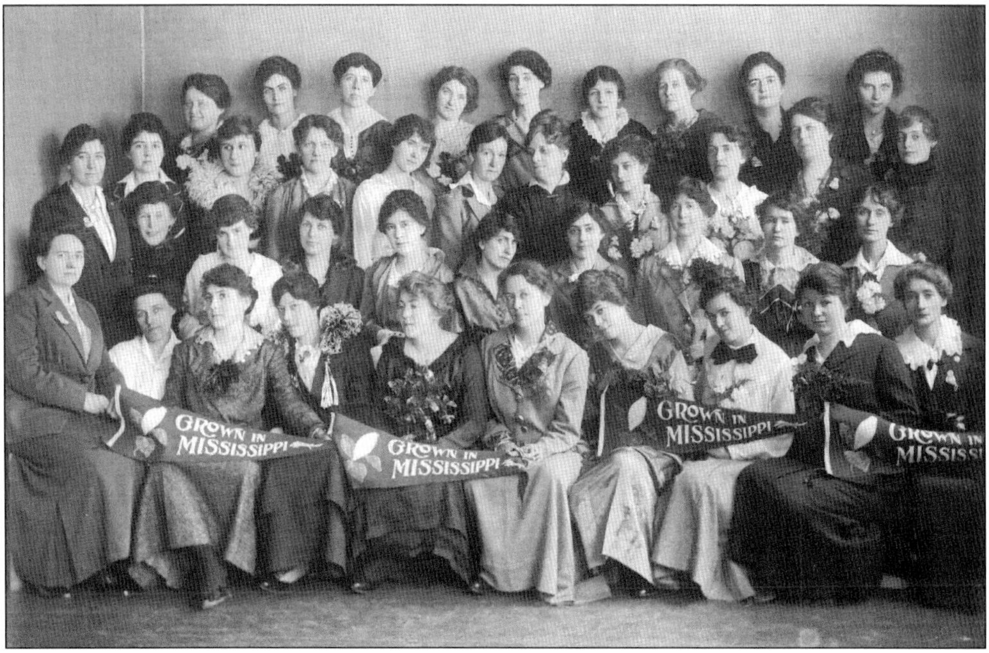

One of the groups that went to the Panama-Pacific Exposition in San Francisco in 1915 was the "Grown in Mississippi" delegation. The delegation's purpose was to demonstrate the varied agricultural products available in Mississippi. May Quarles Watrous was one of the representatives. She is third from the left in the back row. (Courtesy of the Mary Ellen Alexander Collection.)

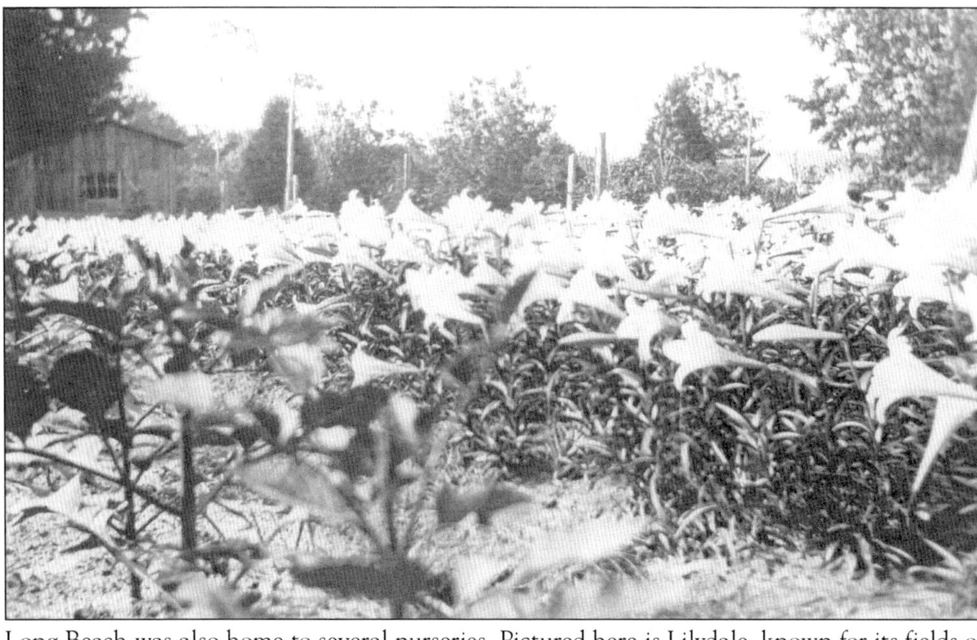

Long Beach was also home to several nurseries. Pictured here is Lilydale, known for its fields of Easter lilies. The Lilydale nursery was owned by the John and Joanna Allen family and located along Girard Avenue, stretching from the railroad south to Magnolia Street. Beginning in 1913, the Allen family raised lilies for the bulbs, which were sold. Joanna also had two greenhouses, where she raised bougainvillea, orchids, and other exotic plants. (Courtesy of Paul Jermyn.)

This gladiola farm was located where the high school, middle school, stadium, and a church stand today. Shown are C.W. Thomas and his daughter, Chrissie, and son, Dick. During the 1940s, gladiolas and blue, white, and yellow Dutch irises were grown here and shipped to flower markets all over the country. Other gladiola-growers included Nettie Glass, Katherine Inglis Hendrickson, and John and Blanche Sinclair. (Courtesy of the Mary Ellen Alexander Collection.)

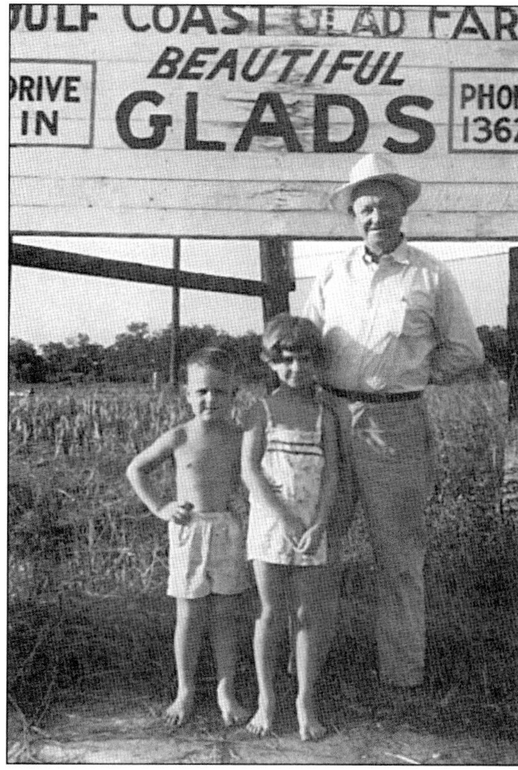

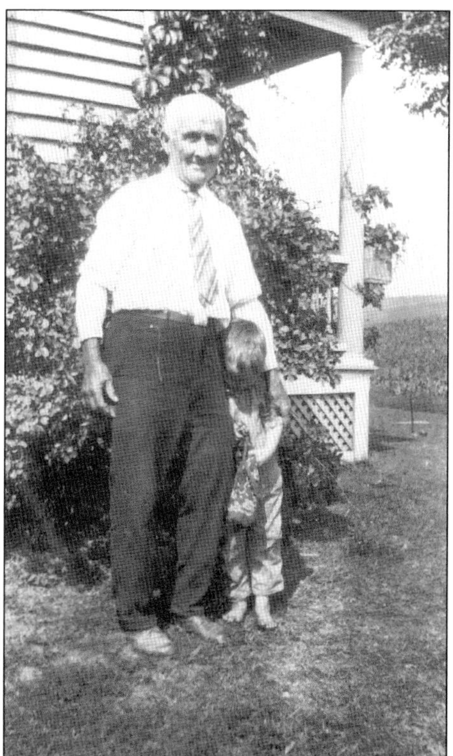

In 1929, Albert "Gar" Skellie, pictured here with William Skellie, age three, boarded a train from New York to Long Beach along with his Holstein cows so he could feed and water them along the route. The Skellies' Holstein dairy on Espy Avenue was the first of its kind in Long Beach. (Courtesy of Mable Skellie.)

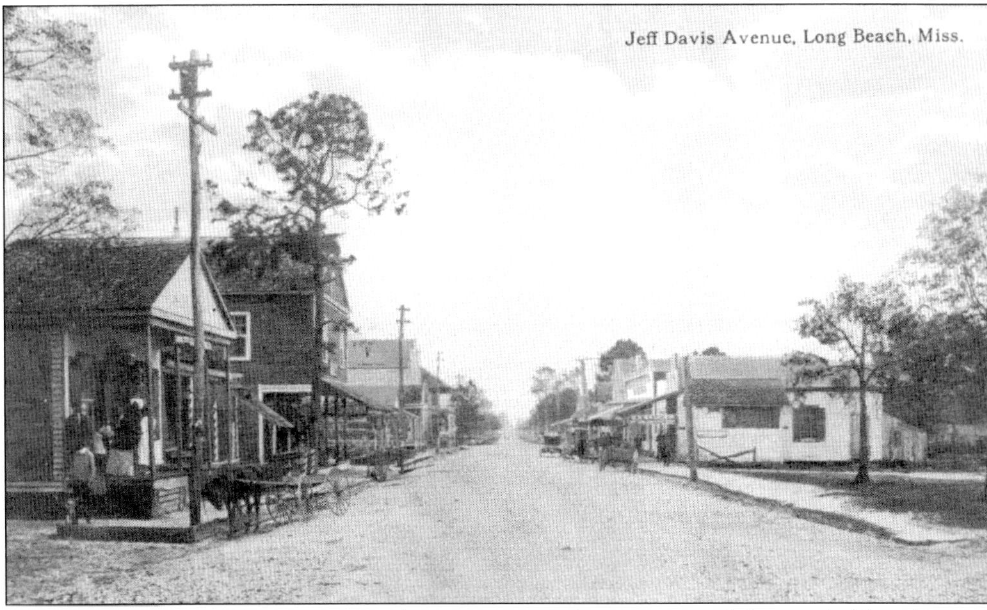

Downtown Long Beach was a quiet place in 1910. Only one automobile—probably still a rare sight in those days—can be seen. The main mode of transportation at that time would have been a horse and cart. The view in this photograph looks south along Jeff Davis Avenue. (Courtesy of Paul Jermyn.)

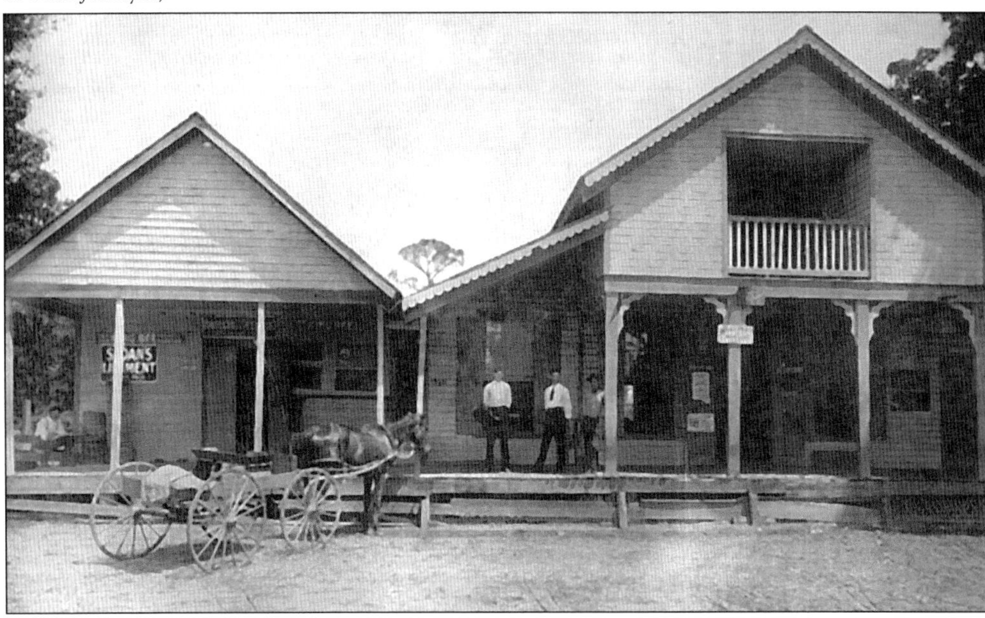

W.J. Quarles' General Store operated from 1890 to 1925. It was located at the head of Jeff Davis Avenue on Railroad Street (now the location of Exclusive Cleaners). The post office was also located in the store until 1904. The store carried groceries, dry goods, notions, seeds, fertilizer, and farm implements. The Masonic Lodge and the Order of the Eastern Star both met in a room upstairs during the 1890s. In this photograph, I.D. Toomer is seated on the left near the feed room. Clerks Oscar Quarles (left) and Owen Thomas Jr. are standing in the front. The store was later operated by J.J. Bailey. (Courtesy of the Mary Ellen Alexander Collection.)

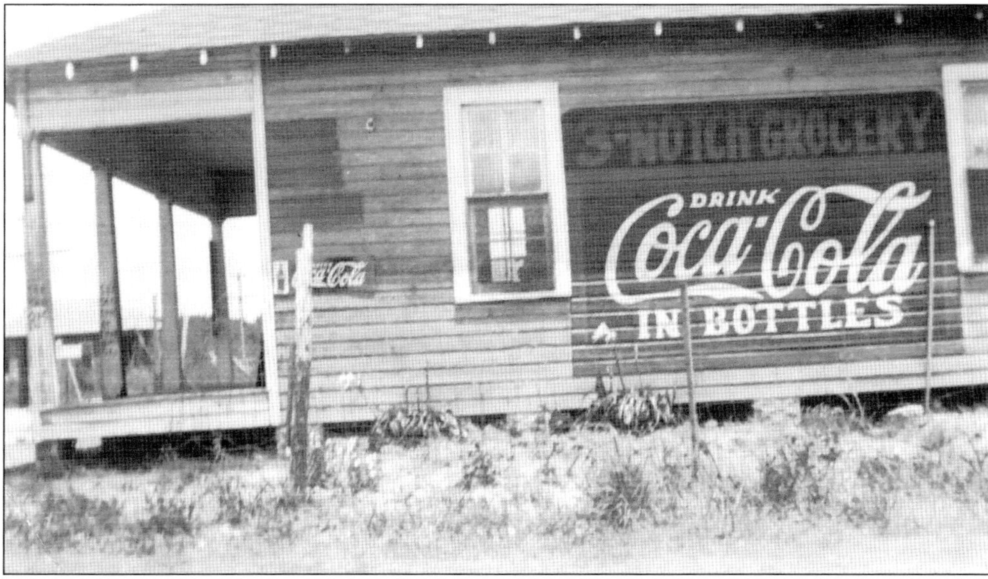

The 3-Notch Grocery was located at the corner of present-day Seal Avenue and LaRosa Road in an area known as Five Points. The grocery was owned by the Skellie family, who later opened another grocery store on Jeff Davis Avenue. (Courtesy of Mable Skellie.)

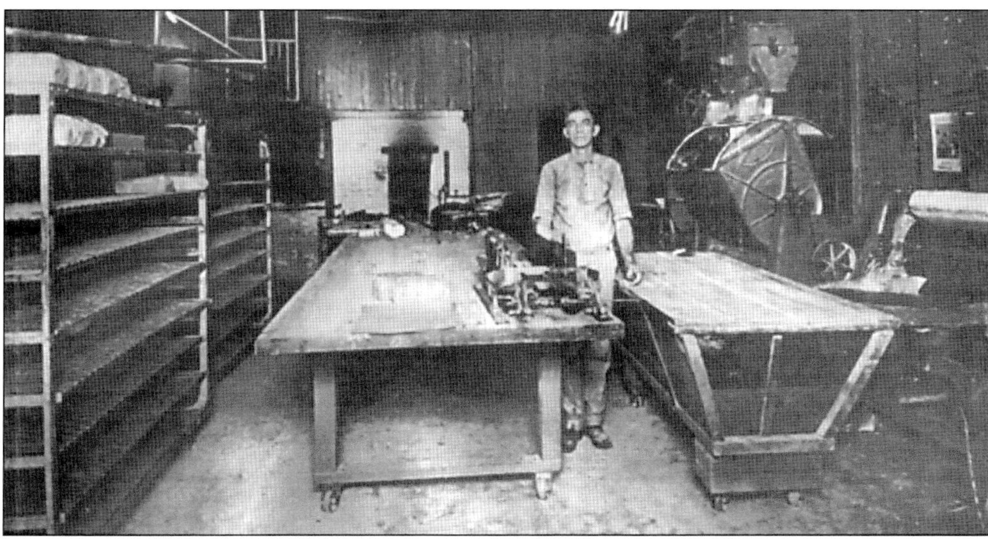

Hardtner's Bakery was owned and operated by Ernest Hardtner Sr. It was located on Jeff Davis Avenue across from the current public library (the site of the former senior citizens' center). The bakery closed during World War II after 23 years because the rationing of sugar and other ingredients made it impossible to operate the business. Many longtime citizens remember the smell of baking bread wafting through the neighborhood from Hardtner's. (Courtesy of the Mary Ellen Alexander Collection.)

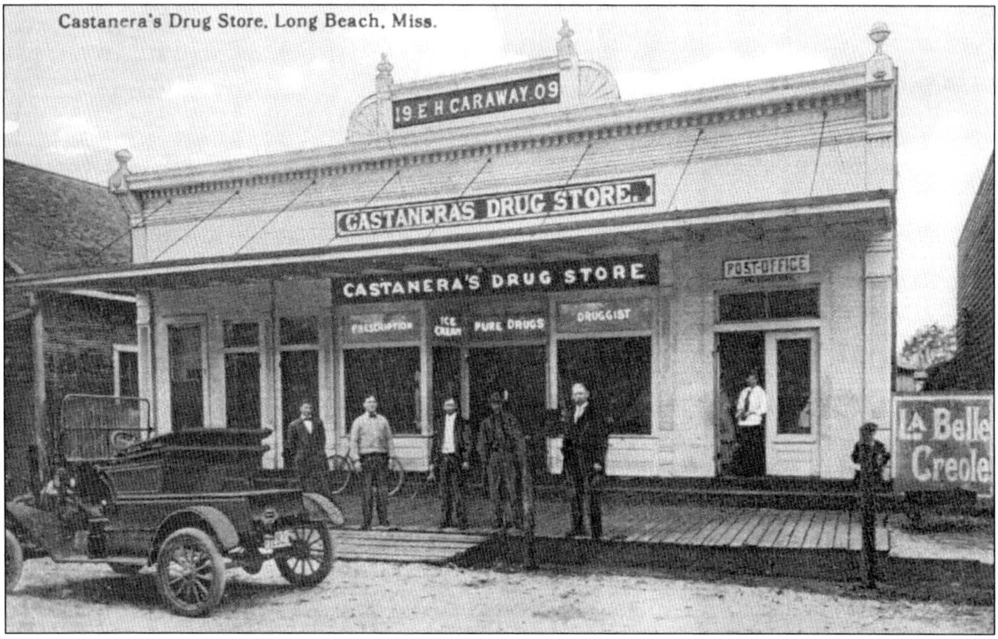

In 1909, local physician E.H. Caraway built Castanera's Drug Store on Jeff Davis Avenue. The store was operated by C.H. Castanera. Dr. Caraway's office was located in the building until 1938. This photograph was taken in 1922, when the post office was also located in the building. When people dropped by the post office to gather their mail, they usually walked over to enjoy a treat from the drugstore's soda fountain. The store was operated under the name Long Beach Drug Co. in the 1940s through the early 1950s, when William Triplett bought the business. Other owners operated a drugstore until the 1960s. The site is now occupied by the Sonic Drive-In. (Courtesy of Paul Jermyn.)

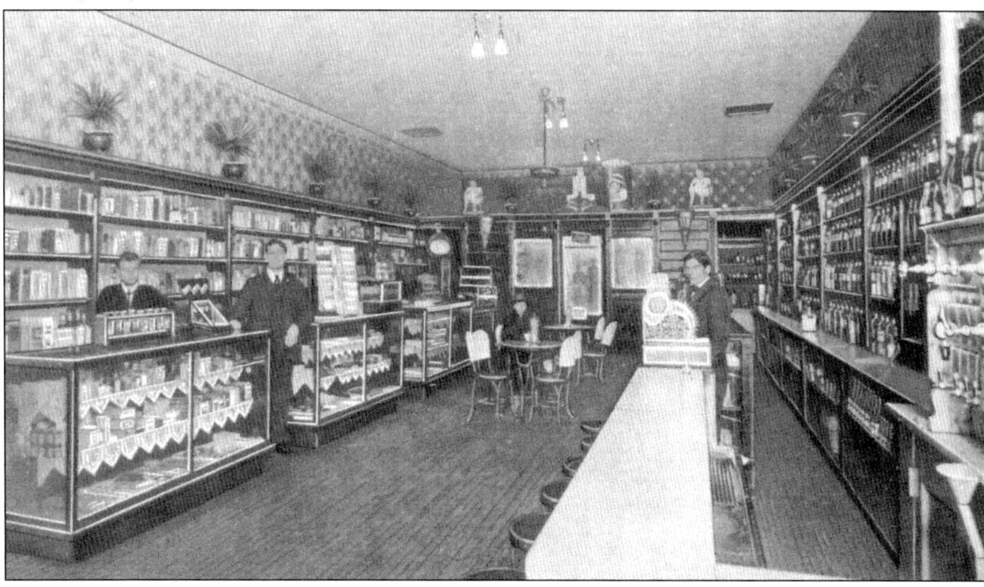

This is the interior of Castanera's Drug Store in 1919. Castanera advertised that it carried a "full line of pure drugs and all patented medicines." The soda fountain is shown on the right. (Courtesy of the Mary Ellen Alexander Collection.)

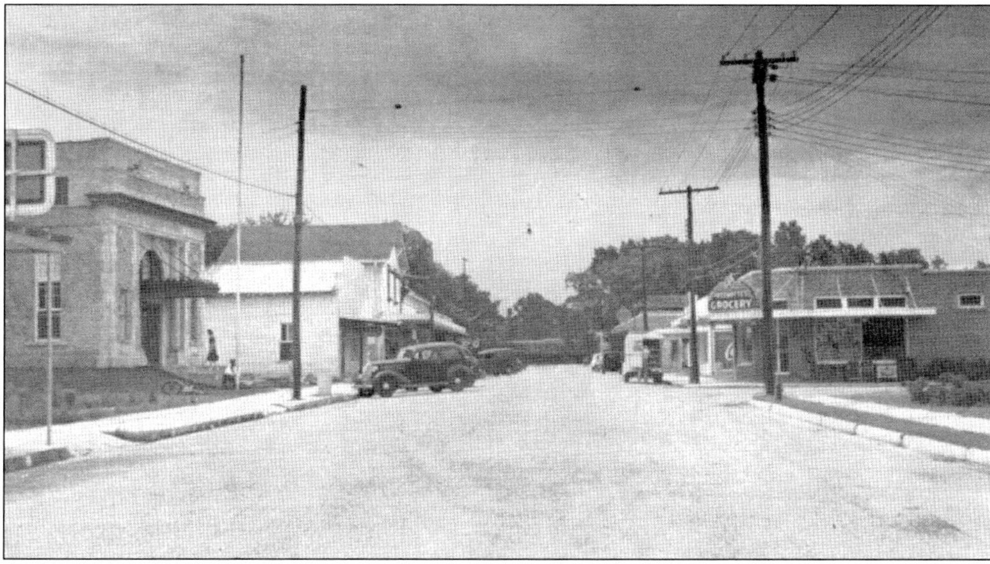

This is a 1943 postcard view looking north on Jeff Davis Avenue. At this time, the post office was located on the first floor of the bank building shown on the left, and the Masonic Lodge was on the second floor. There were several businesses located along Jeff Davis Avenue at the time, including Patenotte's Grocery on the right, along with a garage, hardware store, and a meat market. (Courtesy of the Mary Ellen Alexander Collection.)

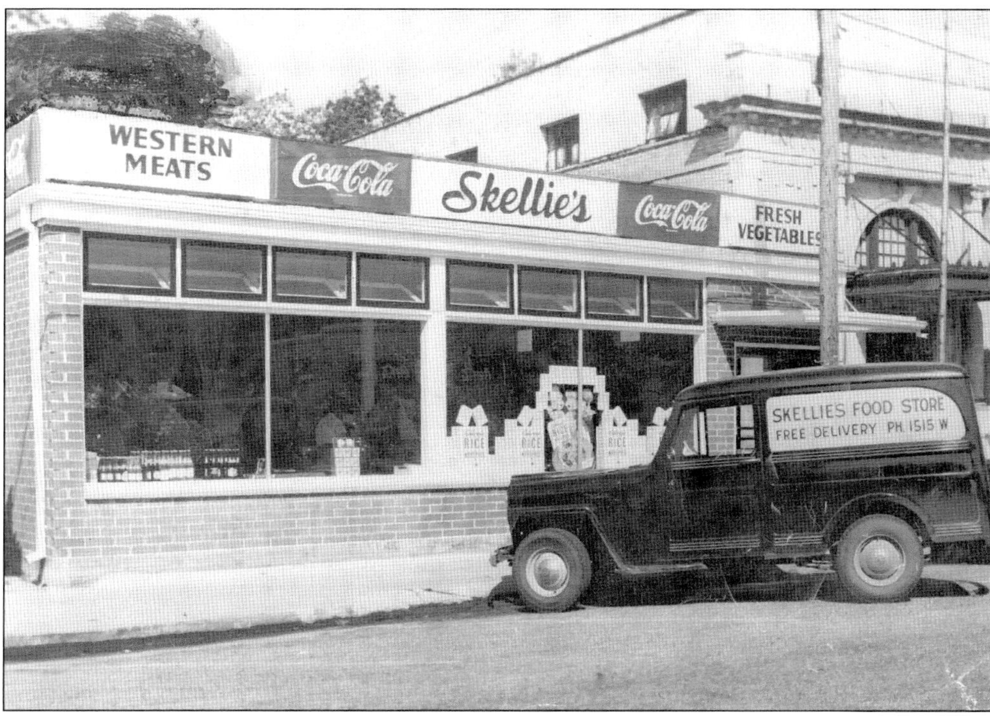

Skellie's Grocery was on Jeff Davis Avenue and offered fresh produce and meats. Exactly what was meant by "western meats" is not clear, but it probably meant meats that were not raised on local farms. The store also offered free delivery, as seen from its truck parked out front in this 1949 photograph. (Courtesy of Mable Skellie.)

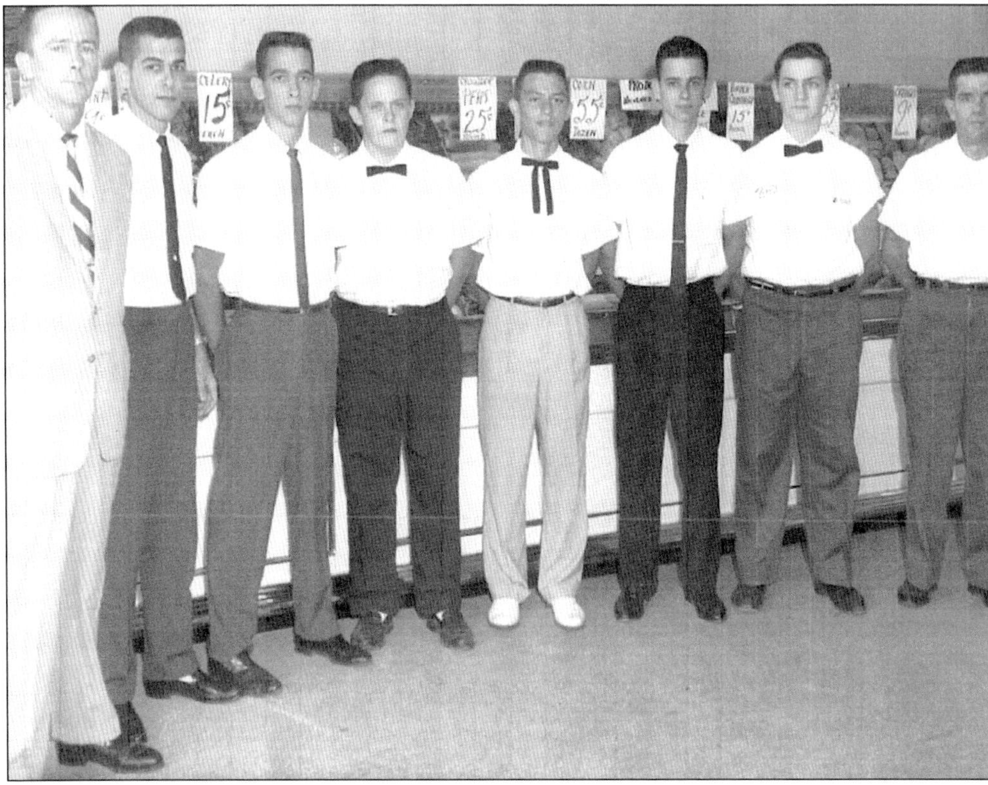

Here are the employees of Skellie's Grocery ready to go to work. This photograph was taken in the late 1950s, probably for advertising purposes. Notice the low prices on the signs in the background. Pictured here, from left to right, are William Skellie, Billy Hansen, Danny Hansen, Billy Skellie, Jasper Carrubba, Stanley Hansen, Lester Kunz, and Freddie Ball. (Courtesy of Mable Skellie.)

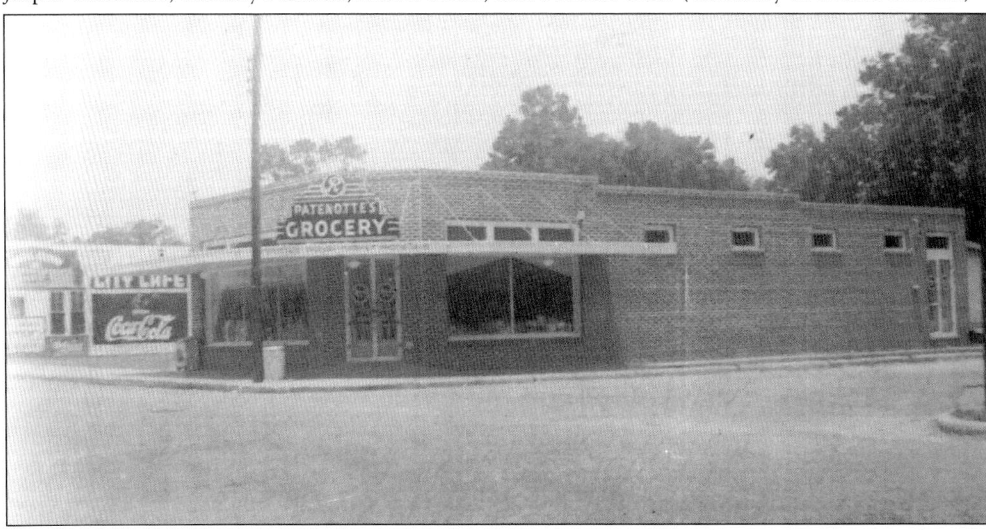

Patenotte's Grocery was owned and operated by Robert Patenotte during the 1930s and 1940s. The store was located on the northeast corner of East Second Street at Jeff Davis Avenue. Patenotte's was later sold and became Wilkerson's Grocery. (Courtesy of the Mary Ellen Alexander Collection.)

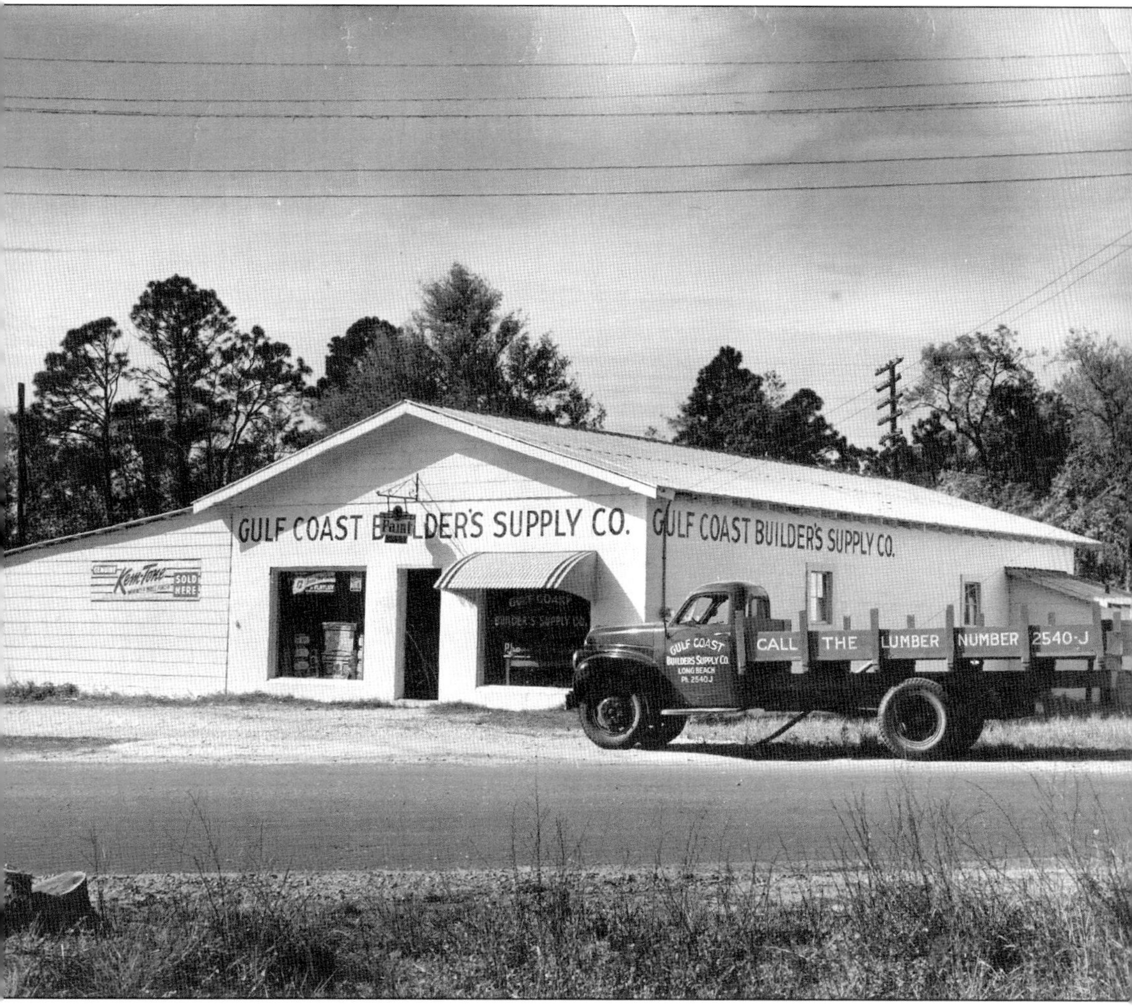

This photograph of Gulf Coast Builder's Supply was used as an advertisement in 1948. It was owned and operated by George W. Shows and offered "Prompt Delivery Service." There are various opinions as to where this business was originally located. (Courtesy of Mississippi Gulf Coast Community College Dixie Press Collection.)

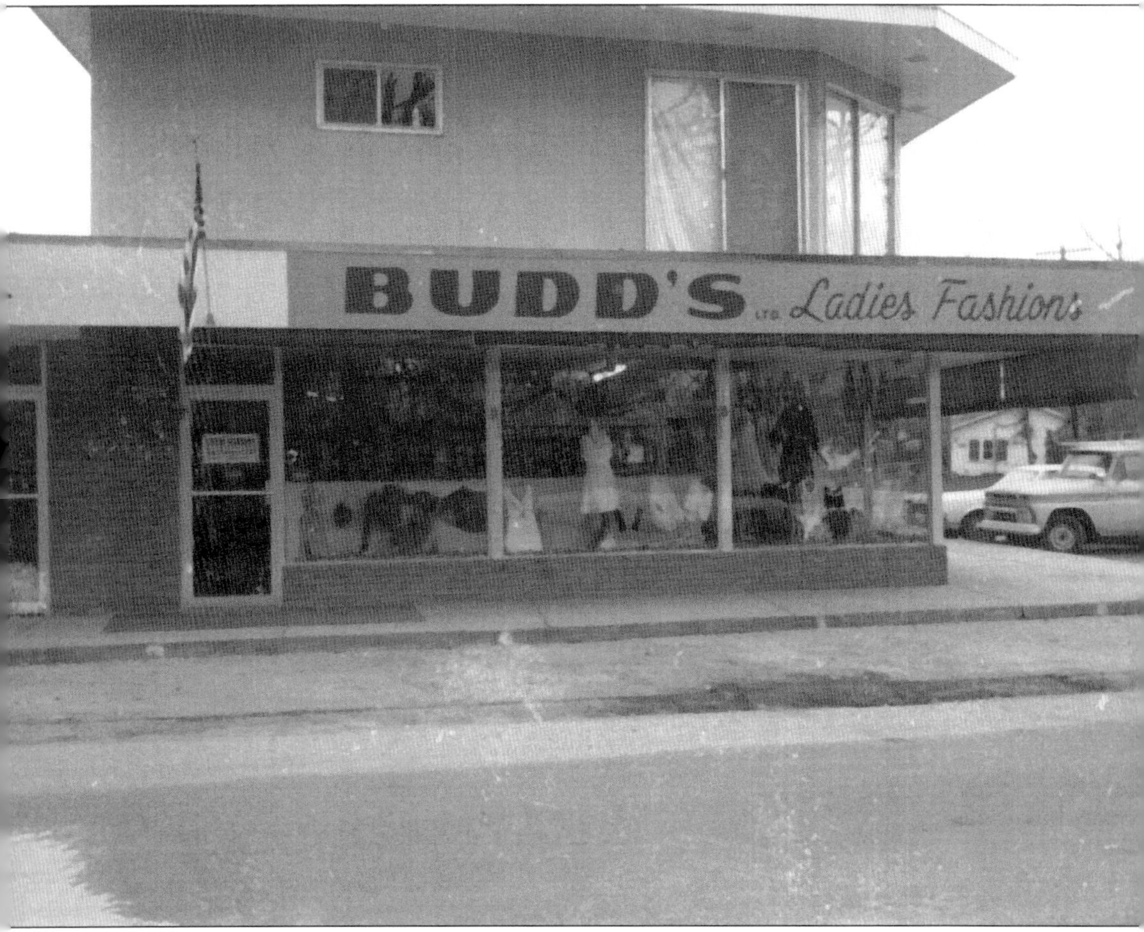

Budd's Ladies' Fashion was located on the corner of Jeff Davis Avenue and Fifth Street. The store was owned by Gladys Budd, and there was an apartment above the business. The store sold all types of ladies fashions, from casual to formal, and also offered tuxedo rentals for men. Shoppers came from as far away as New Orleans to buy clothes at Budd's. The shop was most popular in the 1970s. (Courtesy of the Mary Ellen Alexander Collection.)

The Guild-Kraft handicraft shop was located on East Beach Boulevard, although the advertising postcards for the shop list the address as Beach Park Place. The Guild-Kraft shop sold needlework and craft materials for rugs, knitting, and other art projects and was advertised as "the only one of its kind on the Mississippi Gulf Coast." One could also buy handmade baskets. The store was owned by W.T. and Mary Guild. (Courtesy of Paul Jermyn.)

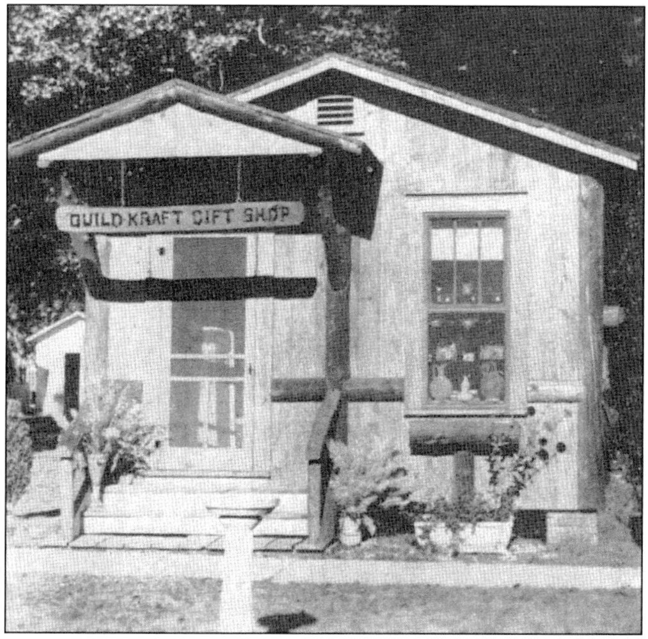

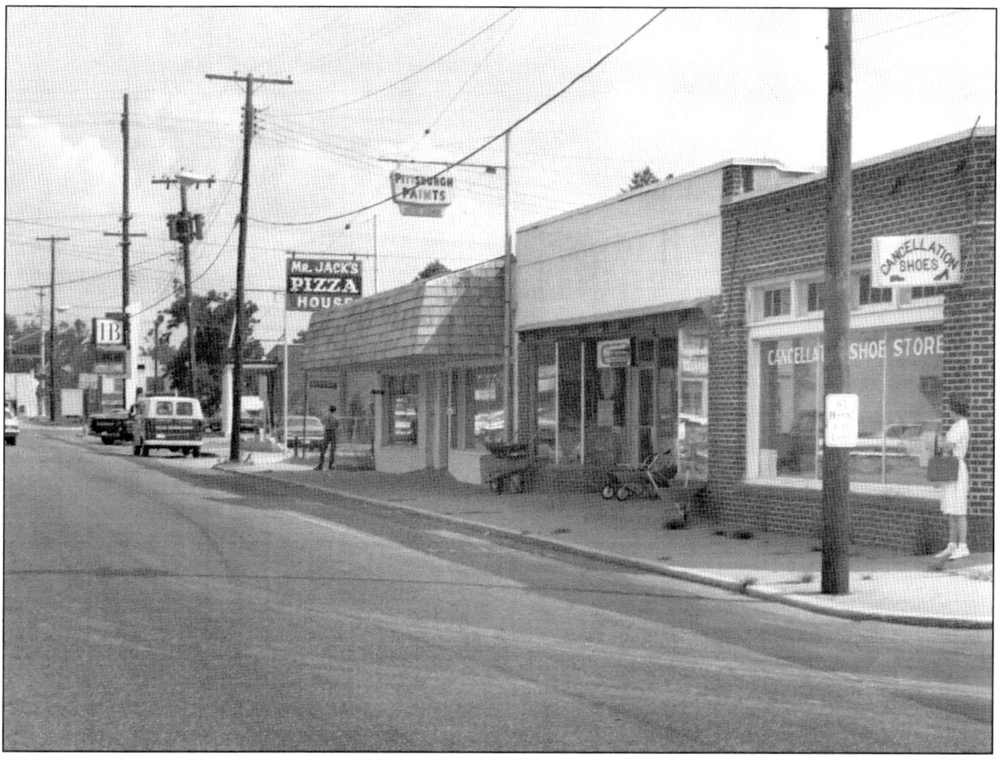

This is a view looking north on Jeff Davis Avenue with the railroad crossing at the left. Hancock Bank is just across on the right. None of the buildings shown along the left side exist today, although at one time or another, they were home to Patenotte's Grocery, the public library, Mr. Jack's Pizza, the Long Beach Chamber of Commerce, a hardware store, and several other stores. (Courtesy of the Mary Ellen Alexander Collection.)

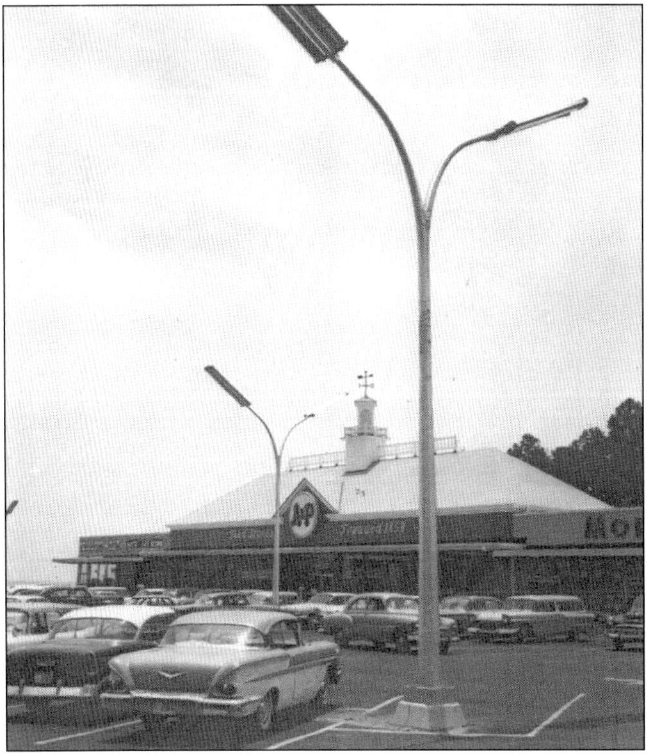

The A&P grocery is pictured here in 1962. This store was the first on the coast to be constructed in the new style of the time. It was located on the corner of Jeff Davis Avenue and Highway 90 and faced Jeff Davis Avenue. When it was destroyed by Hurricane Camille in 1969, photographs of the store (with its distinctive roof) were shown in newspapers all over the world. The shopping center was rebuilt, facing Highway 90 instead of Jeff Davis Avenue. That shopping center was destroyed by Hurricane Katrina in 2005. (Courtesy of Mississippi Gulf Coast Community College C.C. "Tex" Hamill Down South Magazine Collection.)

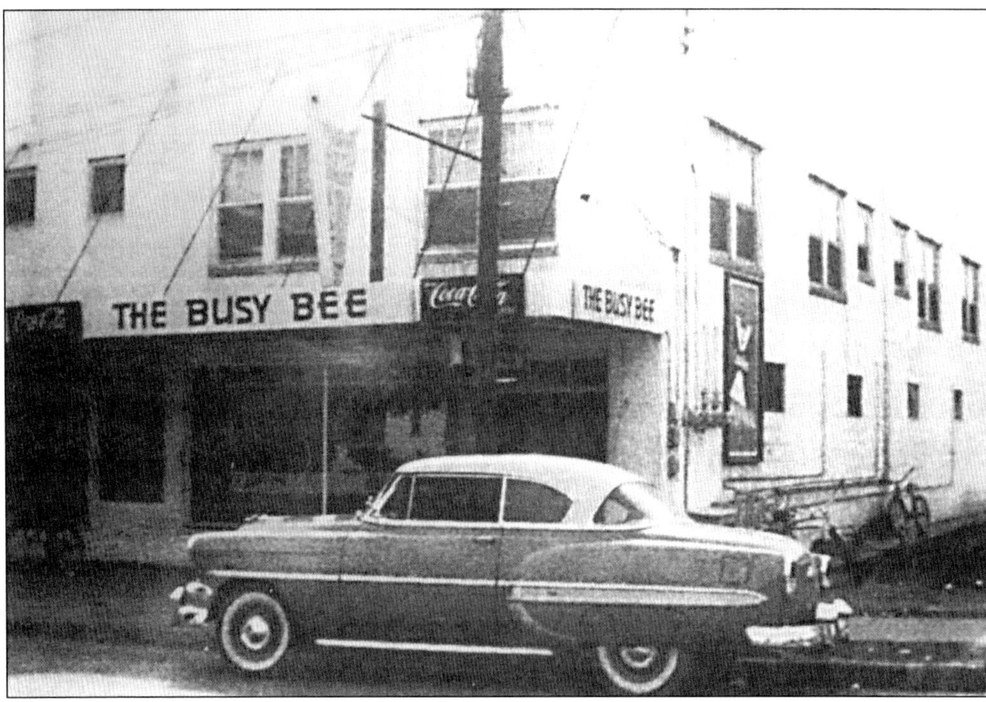

The Busy Bee was located in the LOBE Theatre Building across from the current town green. The Bee served "real hamburgers cooked fresh on a grill." It was owned by Jim and Bea Shuhardt. (Courtesy of Eddie Ware.)

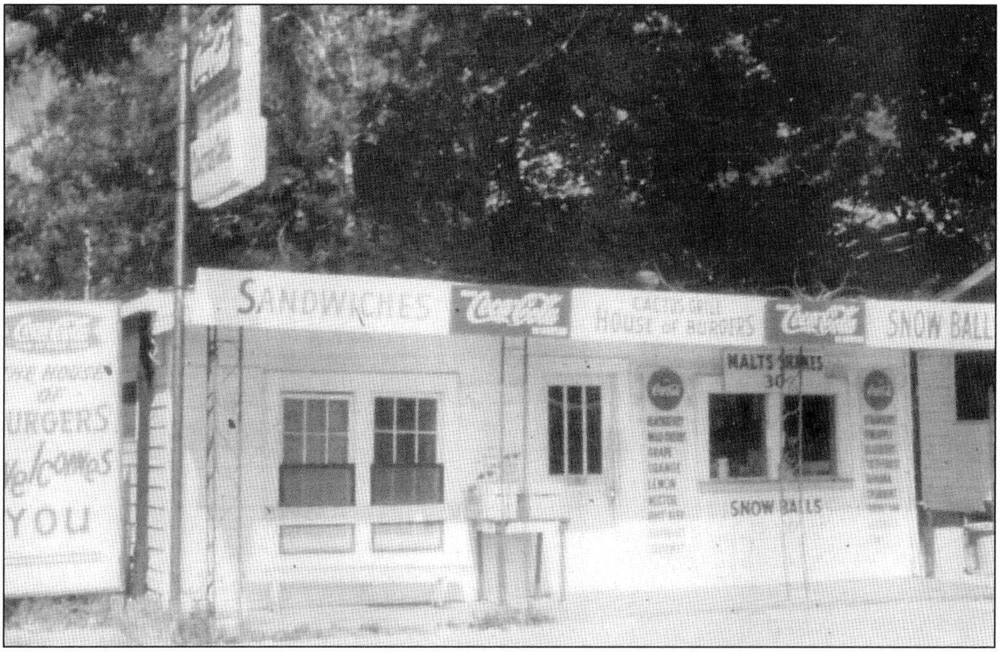

The original Cactus Grill was located on the east side of Jeff Davis Avenue, between Wilkerson's (formerly Patenotte's) Grocery and the public library. After it closed in that location, new owners built a new Cactus Grill on the corner of Pineville and Railroad Streets. At the Cactus Grill, a person could get a hamburger for 25¢ or a roast beef po'boy sandwich for 50¢. The restaurant became Amelia's in 1979 but was demolished in 1988 to make way for a shopping center. (Courtesy of Long Beach Historical Society Archives.)

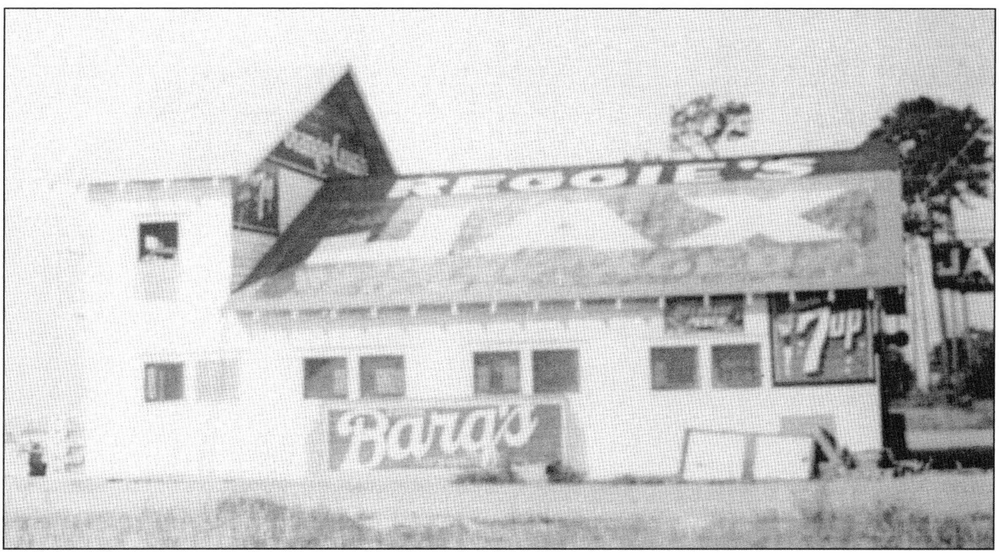

In the late 1930s and early 1940s, Reggie's Place was located at the foot of Cleveland Avenue near the water. It was the only nightspot in town, and the owner was Reginault McCaughan, son of Harper McCaughan. Reggie's was known for its tasty hamburgers and popular because of its location near the busy municipal pier. (Courtesy of the Mary Ellen Alexander Collection.)

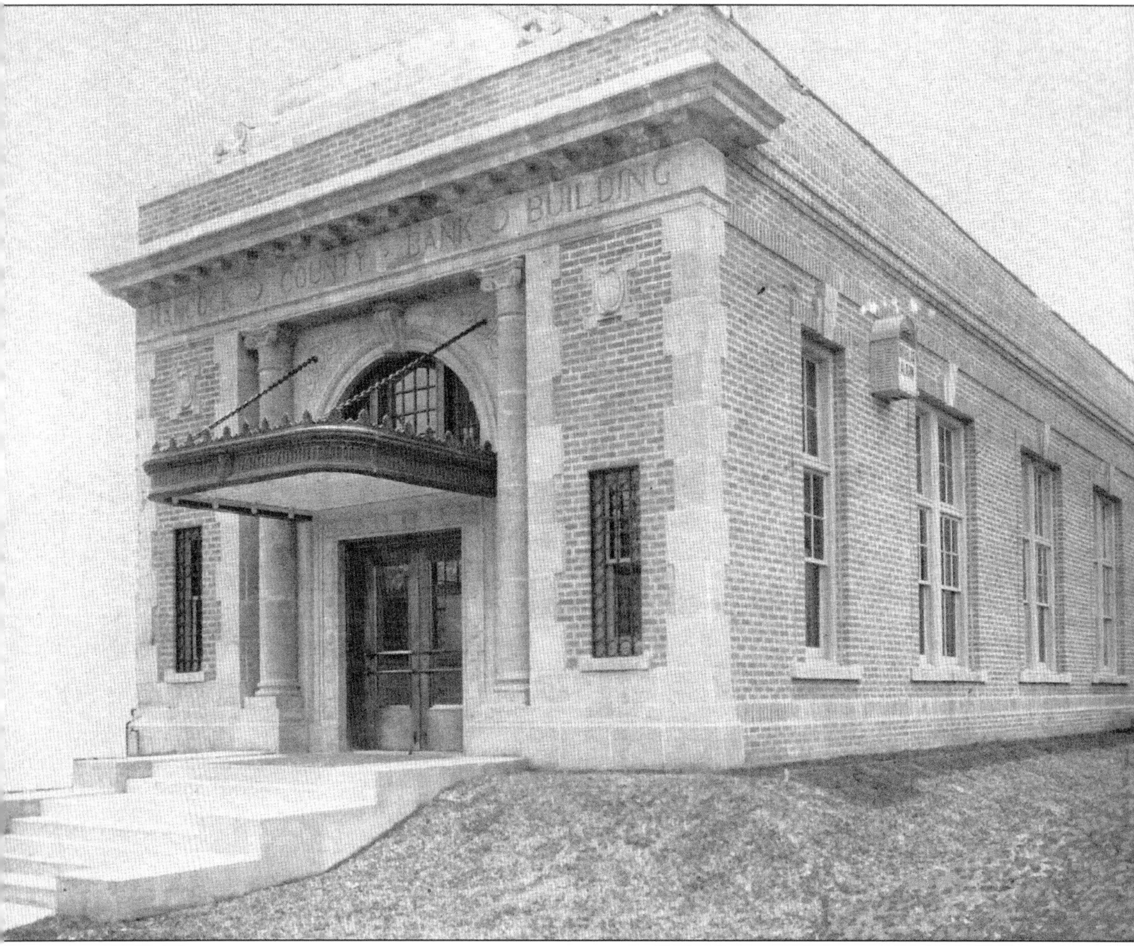

The Hancock County Bank building was constructed in 1927 as a bank to serve the local farmers. The bank moved to Gulfport in 1933, but a branch office reopened in Long Beach in 1955. The Southern Star (Masonic) Lodge No. 500 purchased the building in 1940, and a second floor was built the following year. From 1942 to 1960, the post office was located on the first floor, and the Masons met upstairs. The building has since had several tenants, and it is currently a coffee shop. (Courtesy of Mississippi Gulf Coast Community College Dixie Press Collection.)

At the time this photograph was taken in 1962, Hancock Bank had been established on the coast for 63 years. This small brick structure was eventually replaced by another, larger building. (Courtesy of Mississippi Gulf Coast Community College C.C. "Tex" Hamill Down South Magazine Collection.)

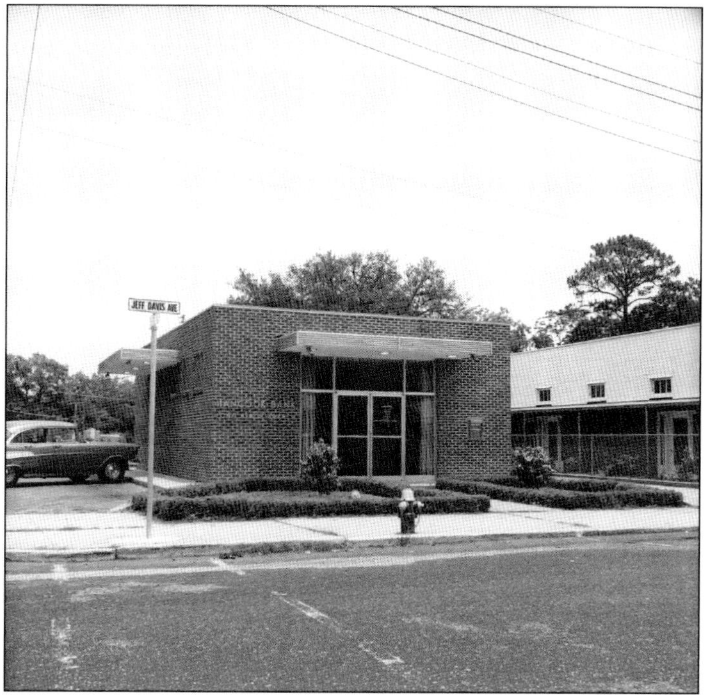

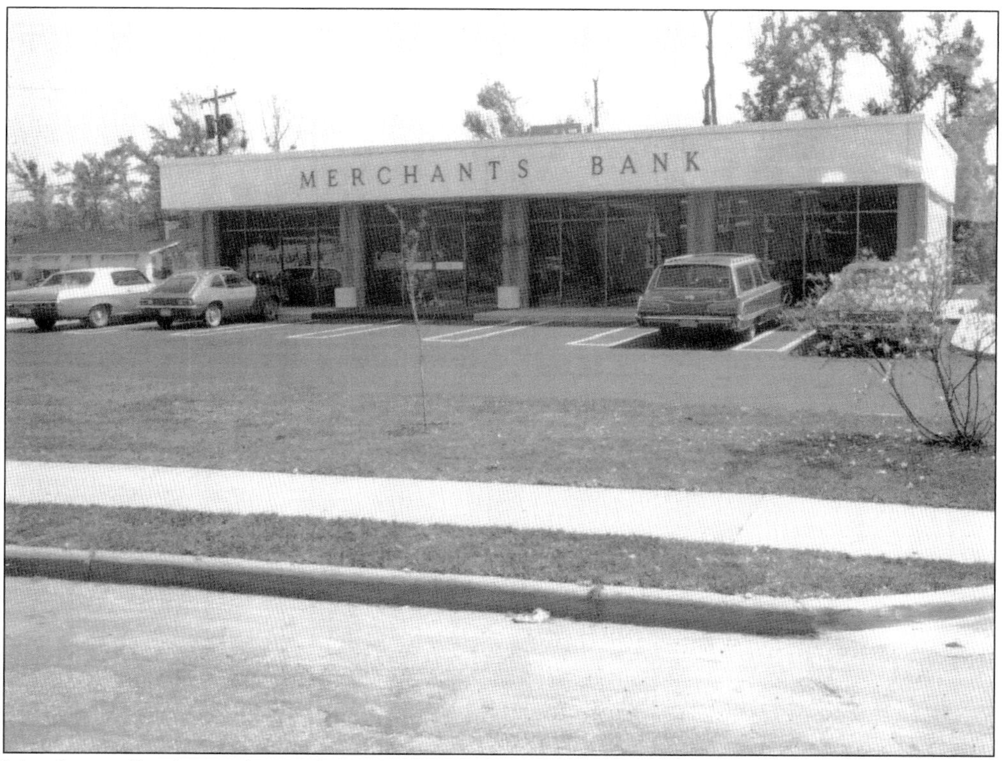

Merchants Bank was located on the corner of Jeff Davis Avenue and Fifth Street. It was destroyed by Hurricane Katrina in 2005 and not rebuilt. (Courtesy of the Mary Ellen Alexander Collection.)

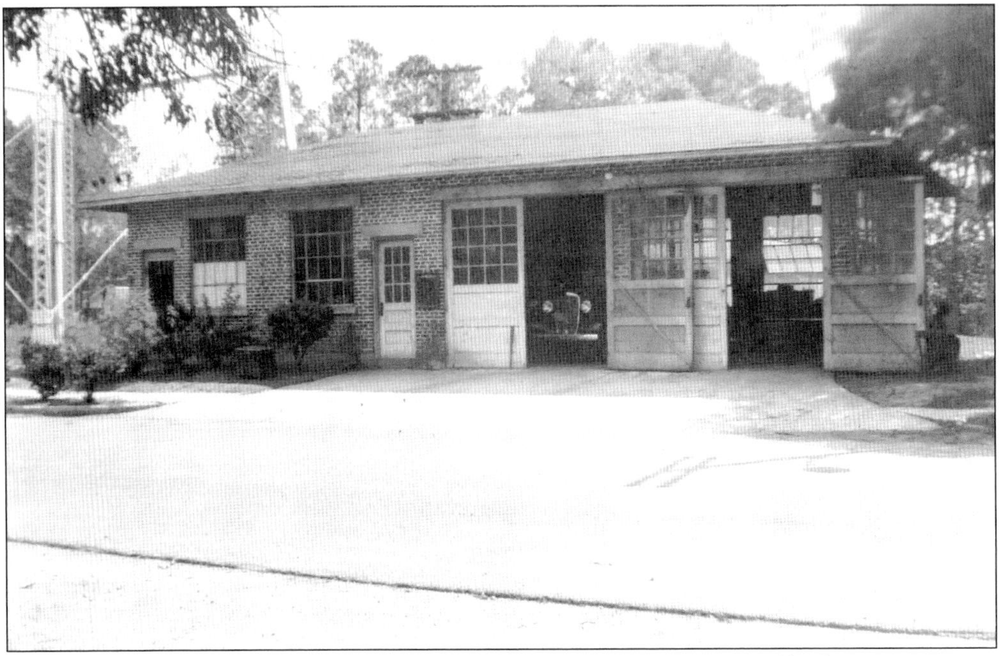

When this building was constructed in 1926, its main function was to offer fire protection to the town after a 1923 fire destroyed most of downtown. However, it would end up serving several purposes. It was the city hall (1926–1958), a fire station (1926–1980), the waterworks department (1926–1974), police station (1926–1980), and voting precinct for many years. When it was an election day or the city board needed to hold a meeting, the fire truck would be moved out to the curb. This photograph is from 1938. Although the building is long gone, it was originally located behind the current city hall. (Courtesy of the Mary Ellen Alexander Collection.)

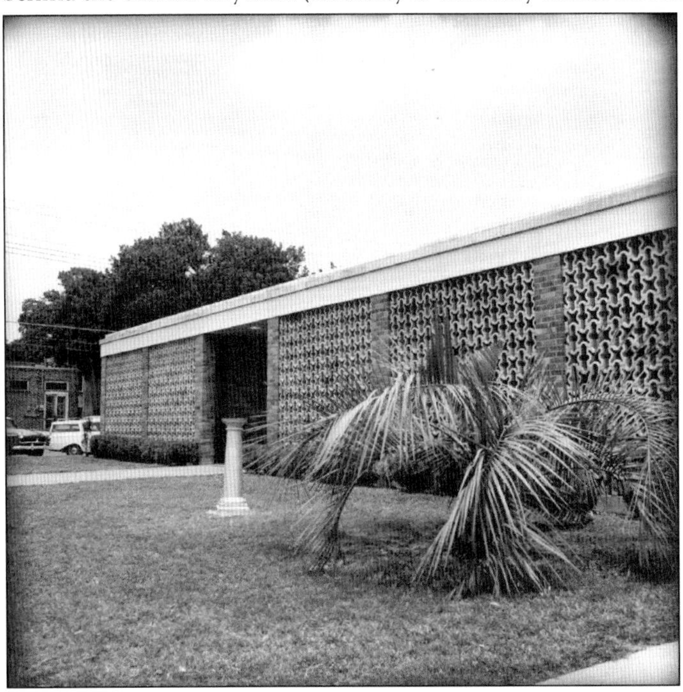

A new city hall was constructed in 1958 and housed a mayor and board of aldermen. The aldermanic style of government is still in place today. Hurricane Katrina damaged the building in 2005, and a new, beautiful two-story city hall is on the site today. (Courtesy of Mississippi Gulf Coast Community College C.C. "Tex" Hamill Down South Magazine Collection.)

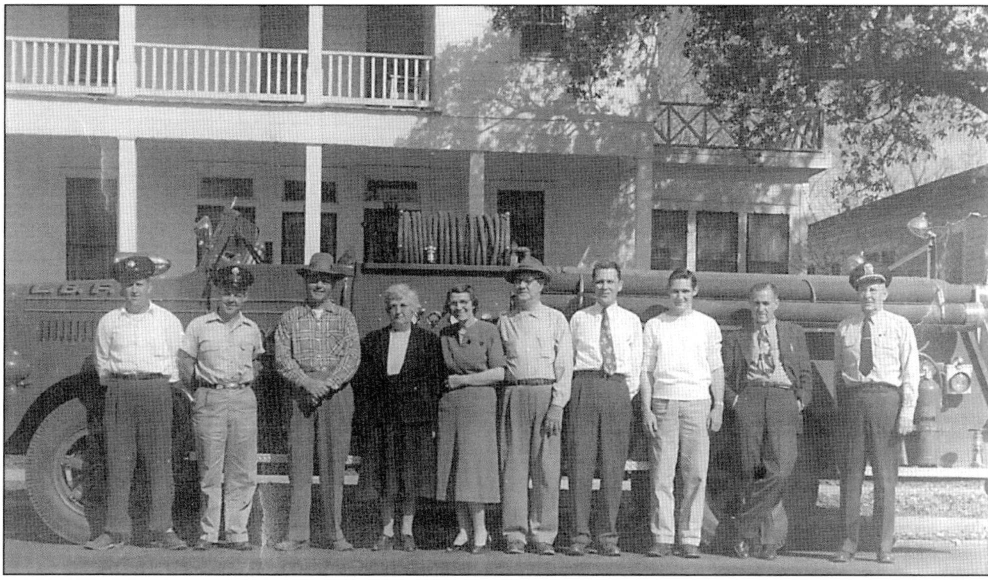

Long Beach obtained its first fire truck in 1954. Mayor H. Roy Thompson, assistant fire chief William Skellie, and fire chief Odus Woodcock traveled to the manufacturing plant in Wisconsin and drove the fire truck back to Long Beach. This photograph was taken in front of the home of the city's first mayor, J.N. Whitten. The home was moved to its present location on East Second Street so that the new Hancock County Bank could be constructed on its original site. Pictured are, from left to right, Johnny Young, assistant fire chief; R.M. Norwood Jr., fire chief; R.M. Norwood Sr., police chief, Josephine Newton, the first female alderman; and six unidentified people. (Courtesy of Long Beach Historical Society Archives.)

Minnie Dubuisson was postmistress of Long Beach from 1922 to 1956. Her certificates of appointment were signed by three different presidents—Warren G. Harding, Calvin Coolidge, and Franklin D. Roosevelt. During her tenure as postmistress, the post office was housed in several different locations—a room in Castanera's Drug Store, the Fillingim Building, and the vacant Hancock Bank Building. (Courtesy of the Mary Ellen Alexander Collection.)

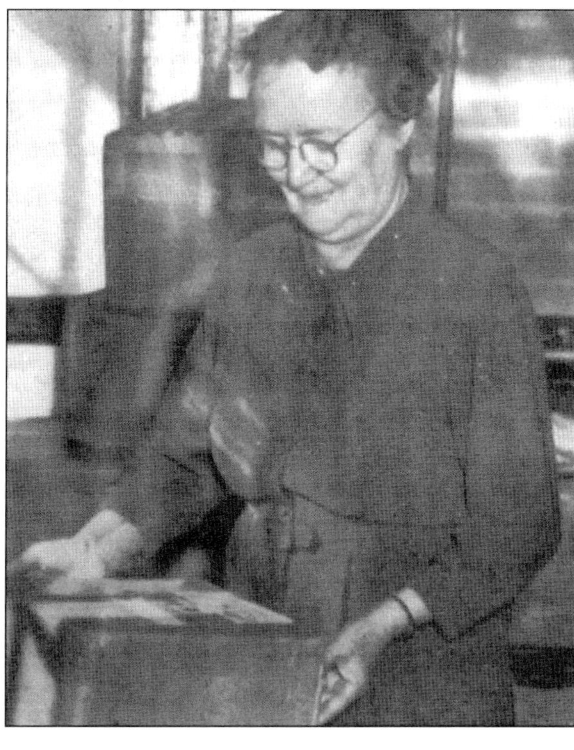

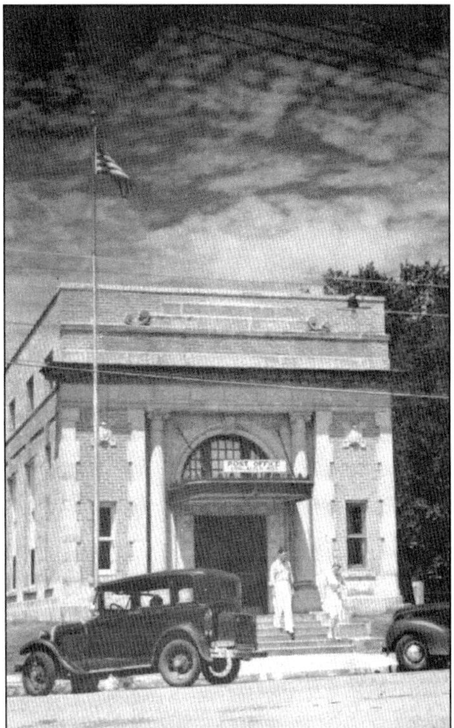

POST OFFICE, LONG BEACH, MISSISSIPPI

This postcard shows the post office, which was located in the former Hancock County Bank building from 1942 to 1960. The bank building is frequently featured on photographs of Long Beach, past and present, because it is one of the few nonresidential buildings that still stands today. The postcard is undated but would have been published after 1942, as the building was not a post office before that time. (Courtesy of the Mary Ellen Alexander Collection.)

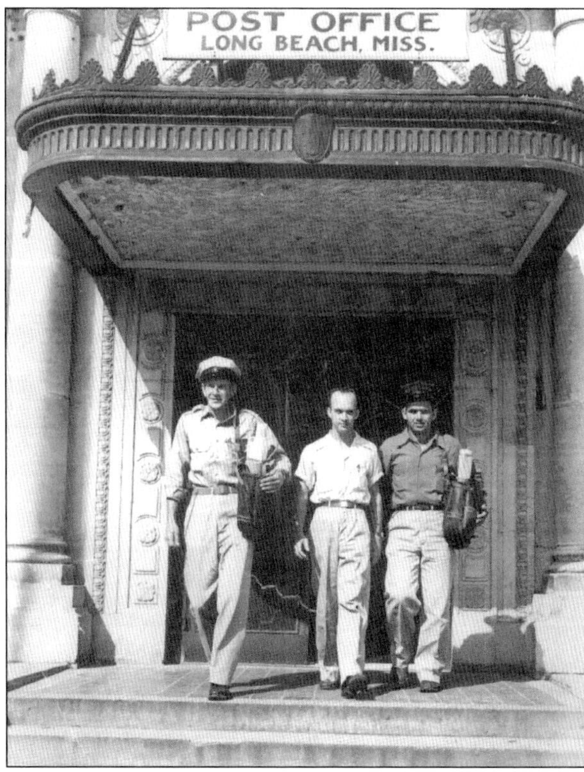

On May 1, 1947, the first mail deliveries began in Long Beach. There were two deliveries daily, and carriers walked the routes. The mailmen walking out of the post office are, from left to right, Edward Cruthirds, Jesse Sanders, and Edward Hatem. By 1949, the mail carriers began to use bicycles to deliver the mail. (Courtesy of Long Beach Historical Society Archives.)

The post office moved to this Jeff Davis Avenue location in 1960. In 1983, a new post office was opened on Burke Avenue, where it remains today. A local printing business then moved into this building. The structure was destroyed by Hurricane Katrina, and there is currently a restaurant on the site. (Courtesy of Mississippi Gulf Coast Community College C.C. "Tex" Hamill Down South Magazine Collection.)

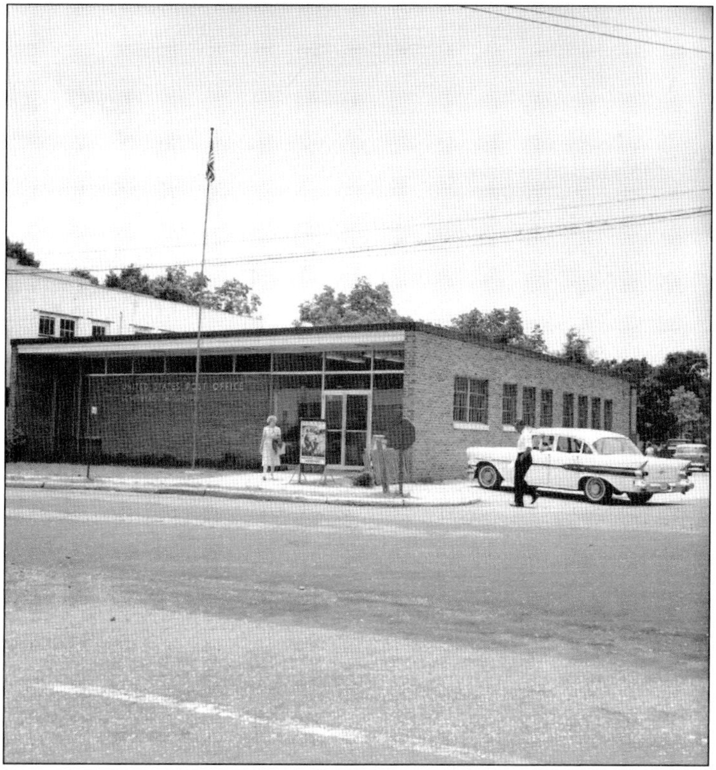

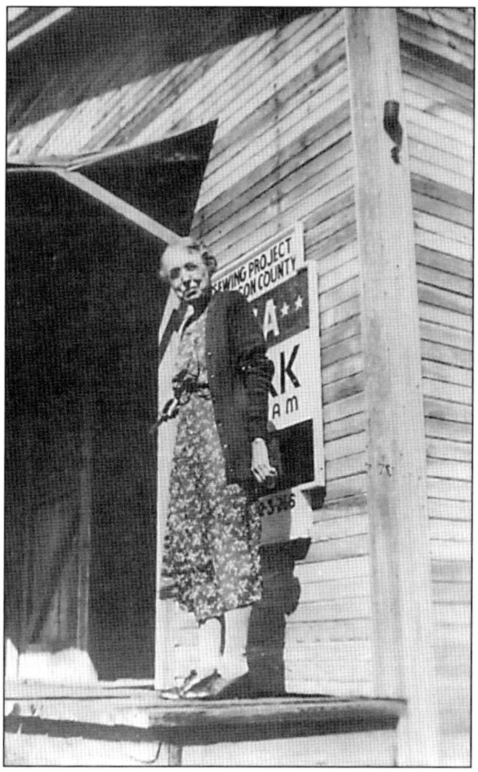

The first Long Beach Public Library was organized in 1894 (called the Garland Ferguson Library) with a collection of 250 books, but it was destroyed in the 1923 fire. Due to the Great Depression, there was no library in town until a new Works Progress Administration library was opened in 1935. It was located in a section of the vacant packing shed near the railroad tracks. Stella Buckles, pictured here on the front steps of the library, was one of the first librarians. Fruit crates served as bookshelves, and they were filled with the help of book showers. The library was later located in a store building on Jeff Davis Avenue before moving to the current site in 1966. (Courtesy of Long Beach Historical Society Archives.)

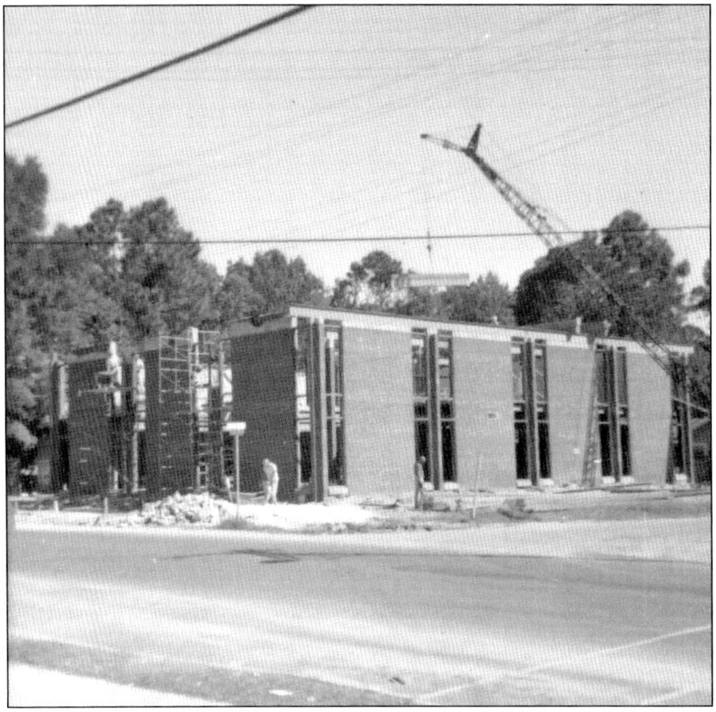

Pictured here in 1965 is the Long Beach Public Library under construction on the site of the former Fillingim home. When the library opened, it had a staff of four, five volunteer assistants, and approximately 6,500 volumes. (Courtesy of Long Beach Historical Society Archives.)

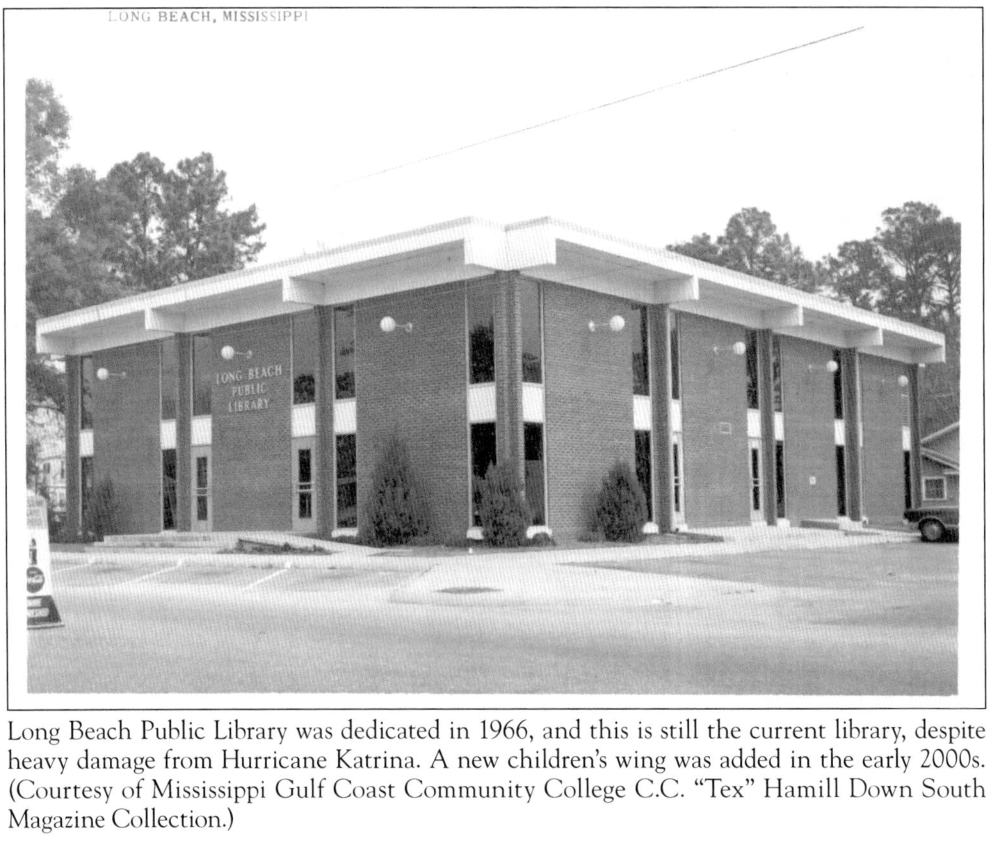

Long Beach Public Library was dedicated in 1966, and this is still the current library, despite heavy damage from Hurricane Katrina. A new children's wing was added in the early 2000s. (Courtesy of Mississippi Gulf Coast Community College C.C. "Tex" Hamill Down South Magazine Collection.)

Six

CHURCHES

The first religious organization in Long Beach consisted of missionaries from the convent of Mother Cabrini in New Orleans. The Sisters of the Sacred Heart came to Long Beach to teach catechism, and they moved into the Sacred Heart Convent, which was built on donated land. The first official organized church was the Methodist church. More churches followed the first, and today Long Beach has churches representing most major religious denominations. Churches were, and still are, a major source of social life and activity in Long Beach.

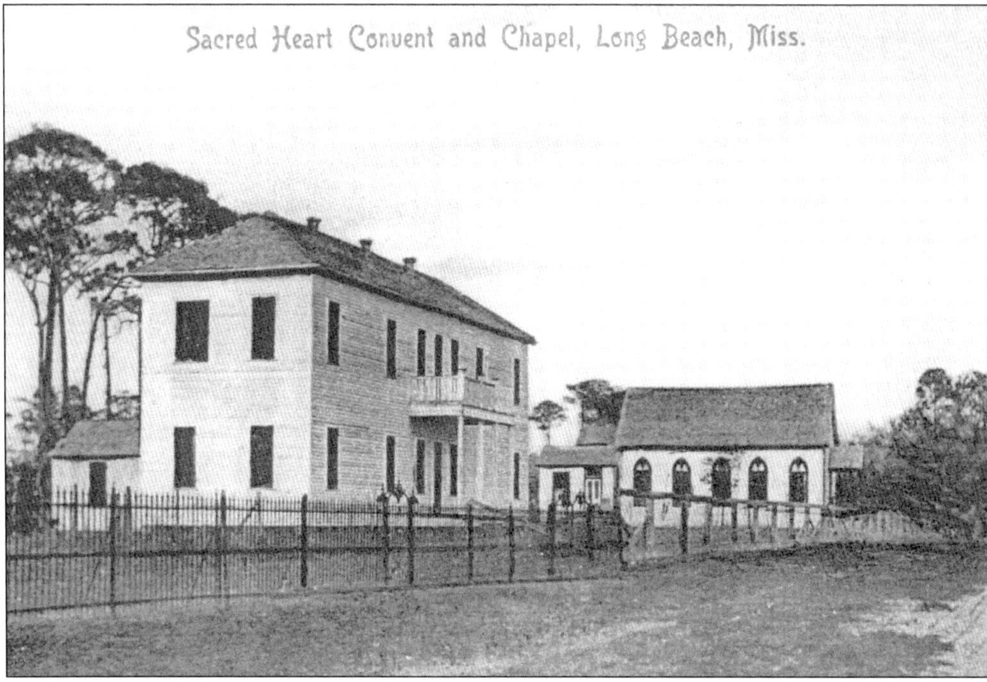

Sacred Heart Convent and Church was located on the corner of Beach Boulevard and Girard Avenue (originally Scott Avenue). The convent operated the Sacred Heart Orphanage, supervised by the Order of Cabrini from New Orleans. (Courtesy of Paul Jermyn.)

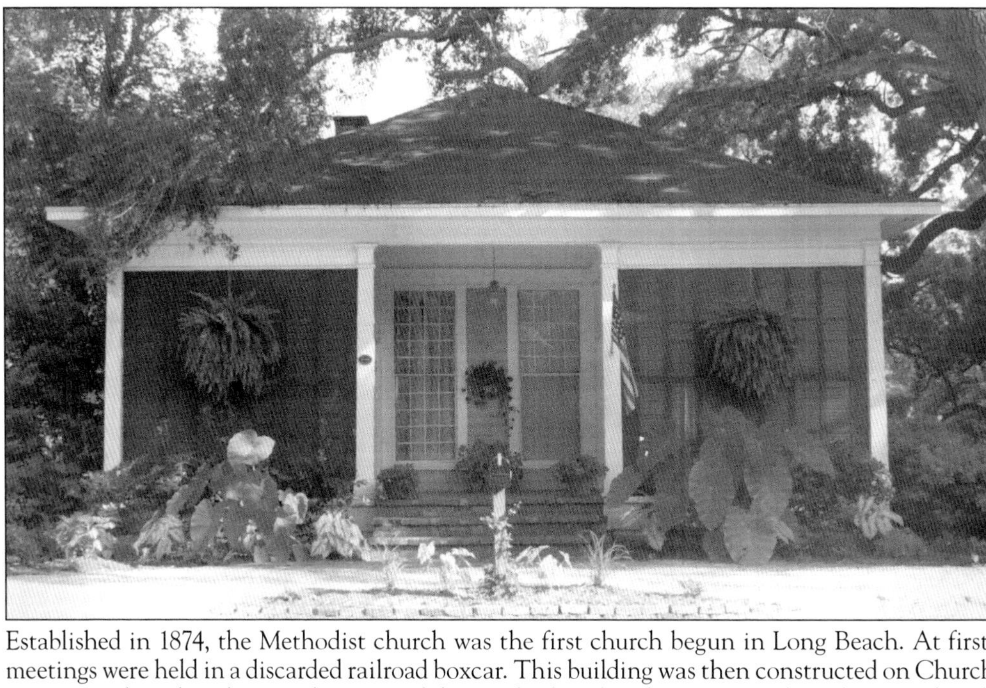

Established in 1874, the Methodist church was the first church begun in Long Beach. At first, meetings were held in a discarded railroad boxcar. This building was then constructed on Church Avenue and used as the next location of the Methodist church. In 1904, when the new church was built, this structure was moved to another location and remodeled into a private residence. (Courtesy of Long Beach Historical Society Archives.)

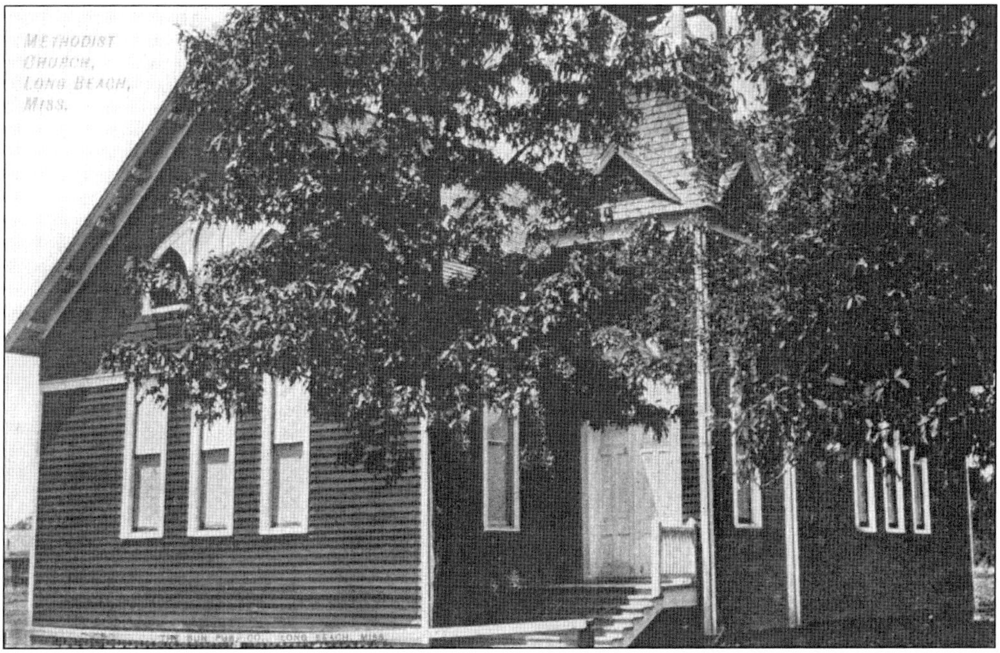

This was the Methodist church building from 1904 to 1949. The church was located on Church Street, with a parsonage just south of the main building. Fannie Donavan organized the first Sunday school. (Courtesy of Paul Jermyn.)

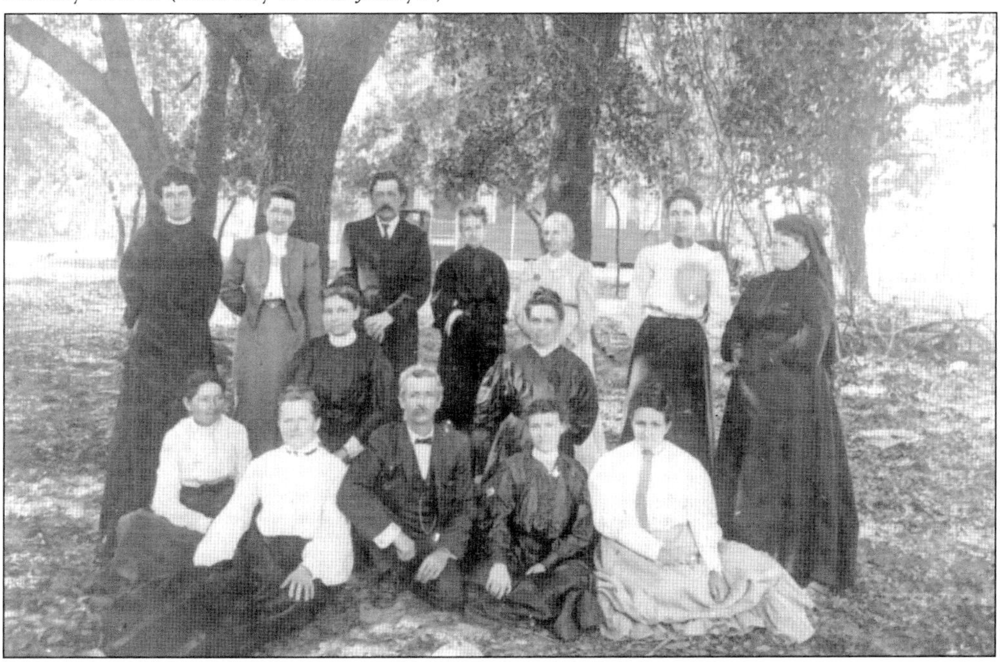

Some of the members of the Methodist church are pictured here in 1905. They are, from left to right, (first row) Matilda Gates, C.B. Gates, Mabel Galloway, and Mary Talbot; (second row) Mary Abarr, Annie Biberon, and Clara Sells; (third row) Mamie Caraway, Fannie Hicklin, Rev. J.L. Sells, Rebecca Hunnicut, Nan Abarr, Bertha Todd, and Fannie C. Donavan. (Courtesy of the Mary Ellen Alexander Collection.)

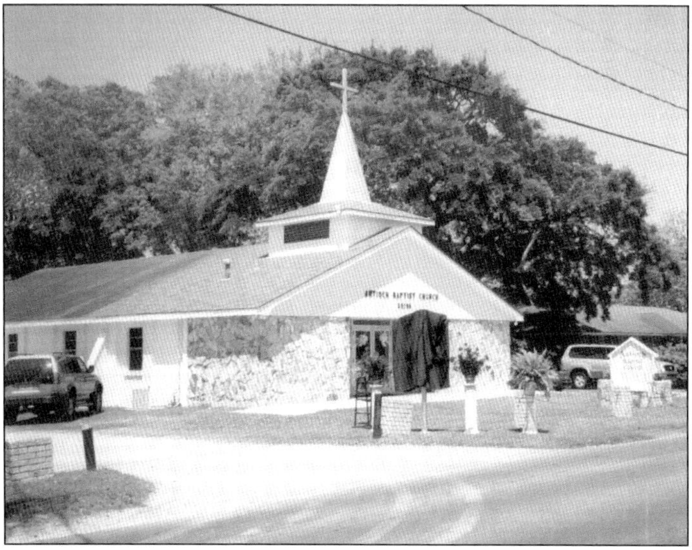

The Antioch Baptist Church was the second-oldest church in Long Beach. It was originally organized in 1880 as the Bethel Baptist Church, but the name changed sometime around 1884. The first church was built in 1881 on the site of the current church building, which was constructed in 1962. In 1905, the original property was deeded to the church by W.J. Quarles. (Courtesy of Long Beach Historical Society Archives.)

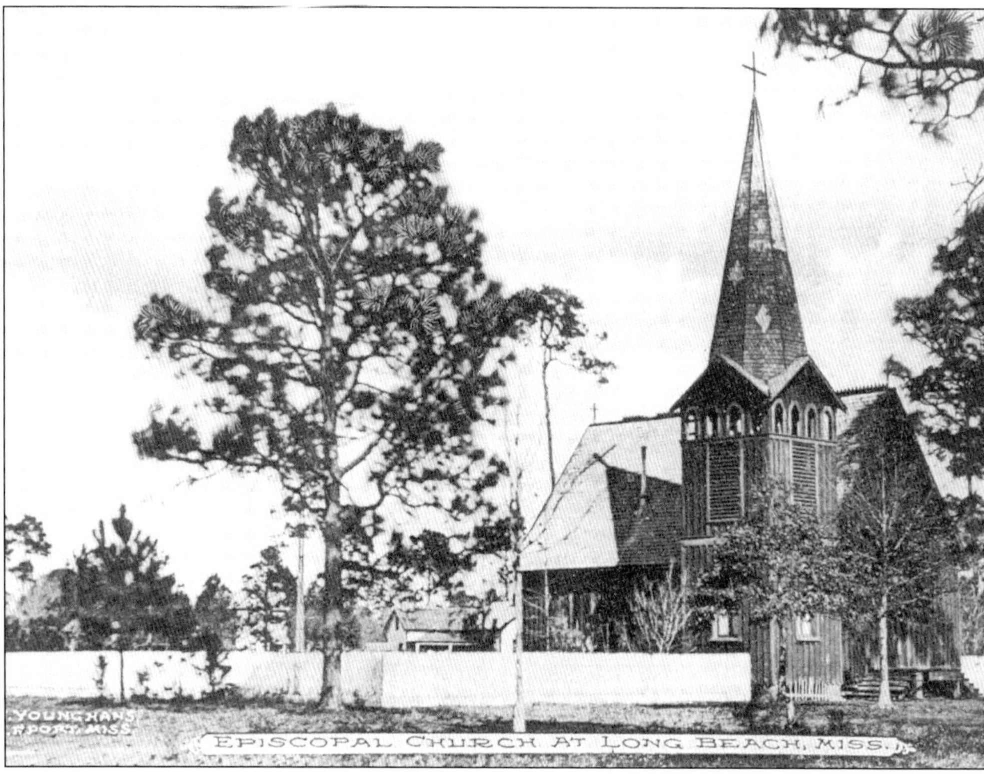

The All Saints' Episcopal Church was the first Episcopal church in Long Beach. In 1894, this building was constructed on Magnolia Street just west of Church Avenue. In 1920, the church merged with Saint Peter's by-the-Sea Episcopal Church in Gulfport. The original church building was sold to the Presbyterian church. It was torn down, and the materials were used to construct the Presbyterian church's educational building, McInnis-Wharton Hall. (Courtesy of St. Patrick's Episcopal, Long Beach.)

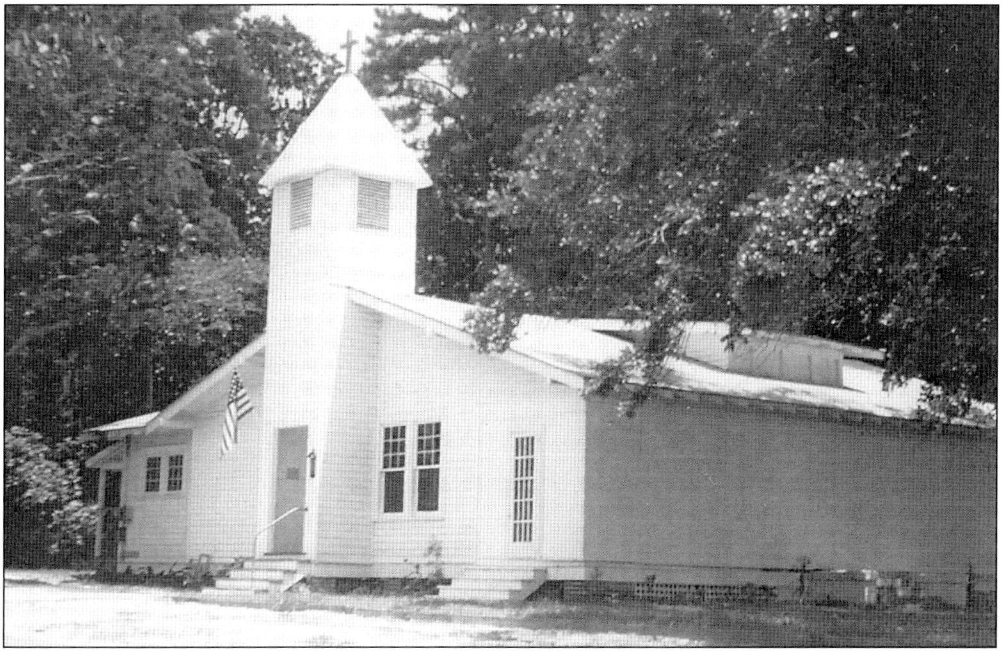

This Episcopal church photograph was taken between 1962 and 1966. In 1962, the church was reorganized and readmitted to the diocese as St. Patrick's. This church was located at 200 East Beach Boulevard at South Burke Avenue and Highway 90. This church was lost to Hurricane Camille. (Courtesy of St. Patrick's Episcopal Church, Long Beach.)

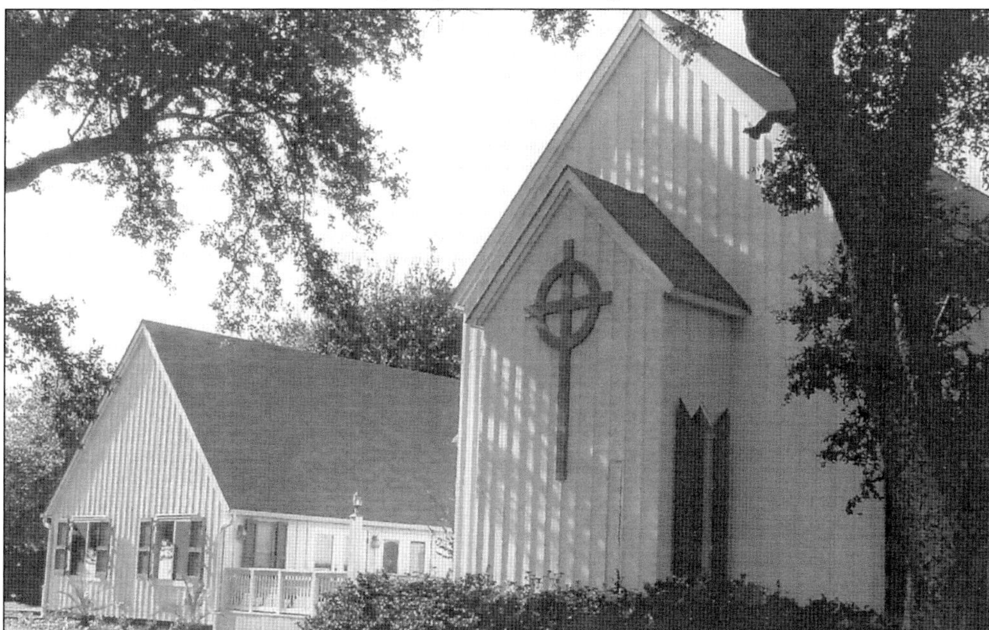

In 1989, the St. Patrick's property was sold and a new location at 452 West Beach Boulevard was chosen as the church's new home. This beautiful church was destroyed by Hurricane Katrina in 2005, and it was rebuilt north of the waterfront, on Cleveland Avenue. (Courtesy of St. Patrick's Episcopal Church, Long Beach.)

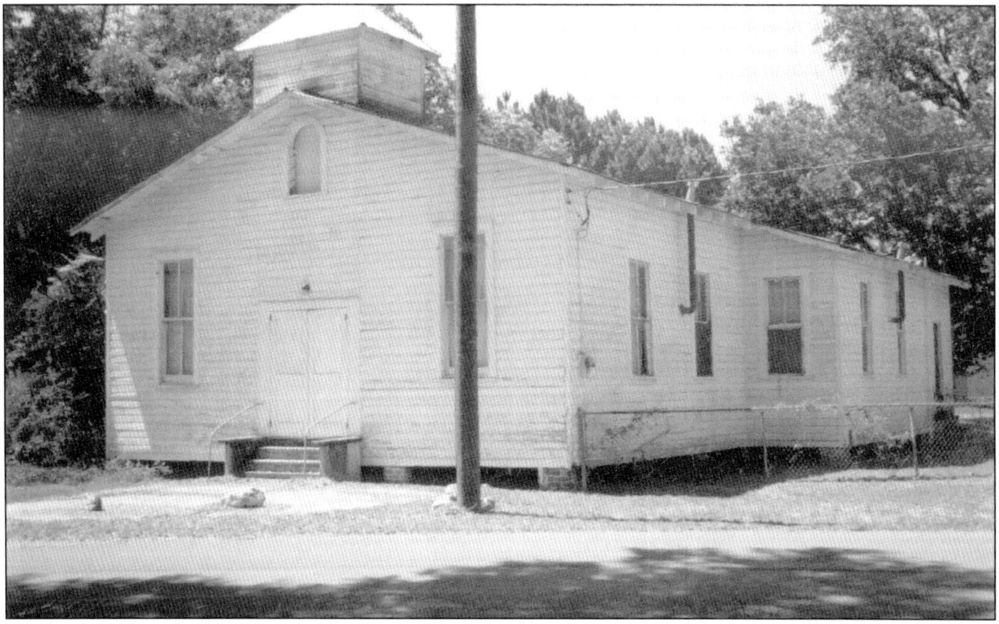

The original Mount Pilgrim Missionary Baptist Church building was constructed in 1895 on Church Lane. A school for the local children was also held in the church until a school building was constructed on the property next door. A second building was constructed after a storm damaged the first. This third church was built in 1938, with additions made in 1947. (Courtesy of the Mary Ellen Alexander Collection.)

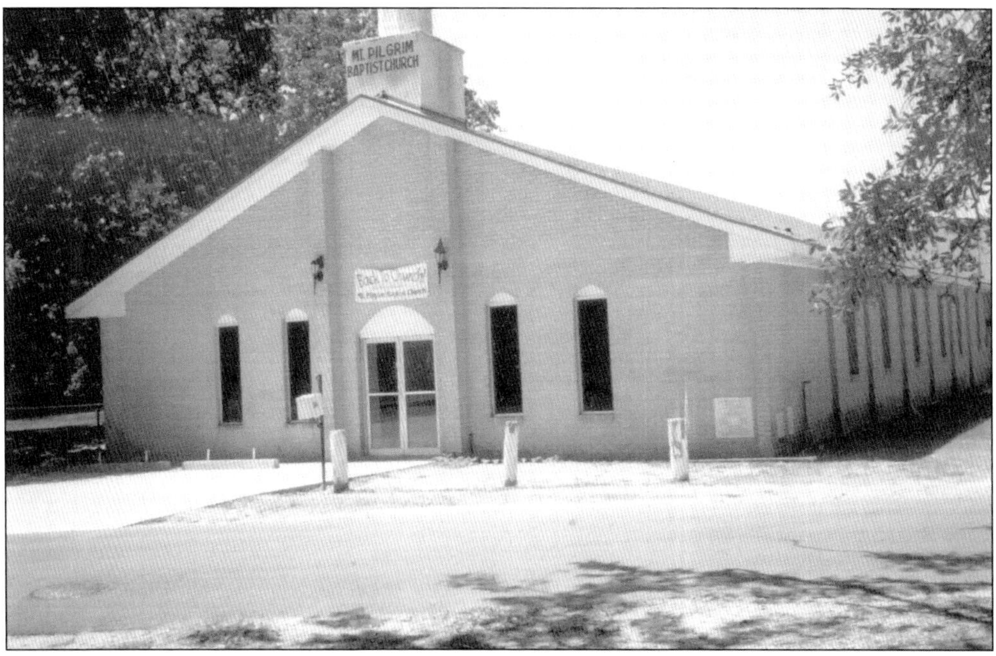

This is the current Mount Pilgrim Missionary Baptist Church building, constructed in 1966 on the site of the former school. The church has additional historical significance: plans to desegregate Long Beach public schools were made in the annex of the church in 1965. (Courtesy of the Mary Ellen Alexander Collection.)

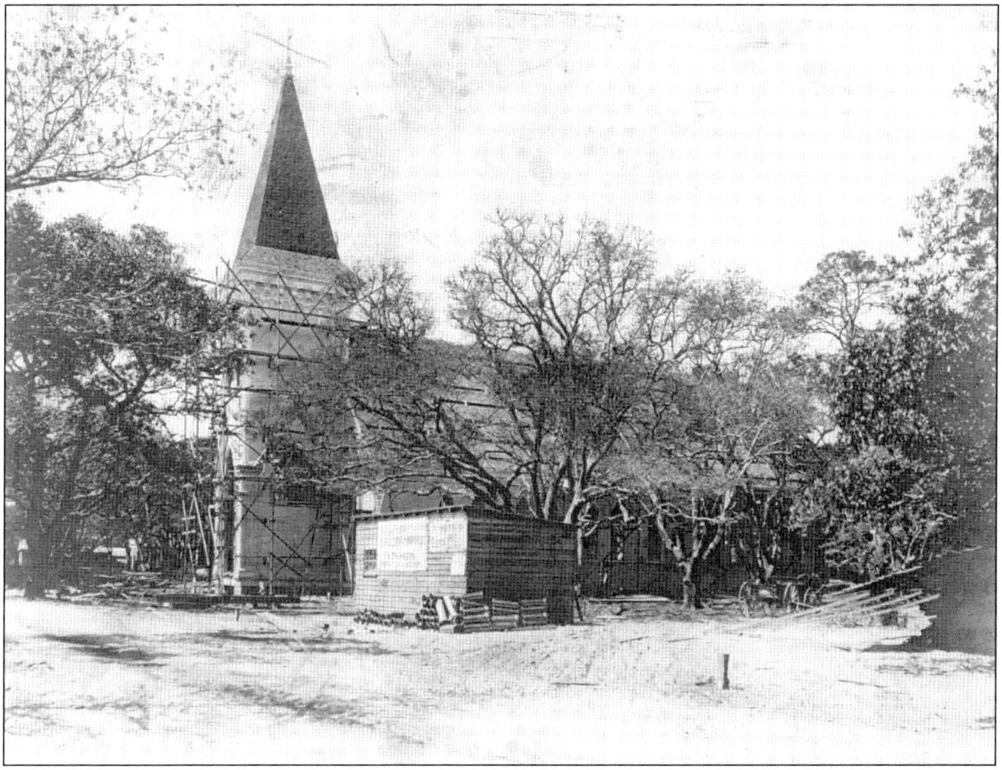

In 1905, construction of the first St. Thomas Catholic Church began. It was built of virgin pine and Louisiana cypress. Originally, mass was said by visiting priests at Foundry Hall, which was located on the site of the current city hall. (Courtesy of Eddie Ware.)

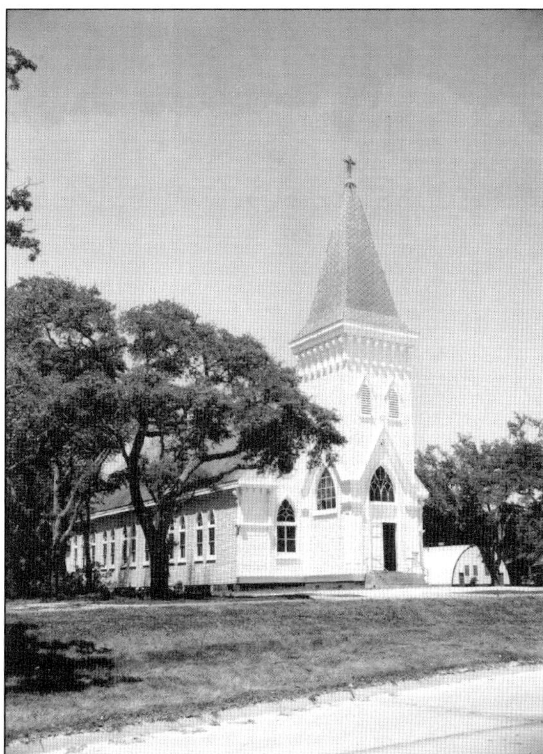

The beautiful St. Thomas Catholic Church is shown here. At onetime, as many as 40 priests said mass daily at the 13 altars. A two-story building was constructed nearby and called St. Thomas's Villa Nova. It was used as a home for the visiting priests until it burned in 1915. This church building was destroyed by Hurricane Camille. While the new church was being constructed, mass was said in the gymnasium of the nearby St. Thomas school. (Courtesy of Mississippi Gulf Coast Community College C.C. "Tex" Hamill Down South Magazine Collection.)

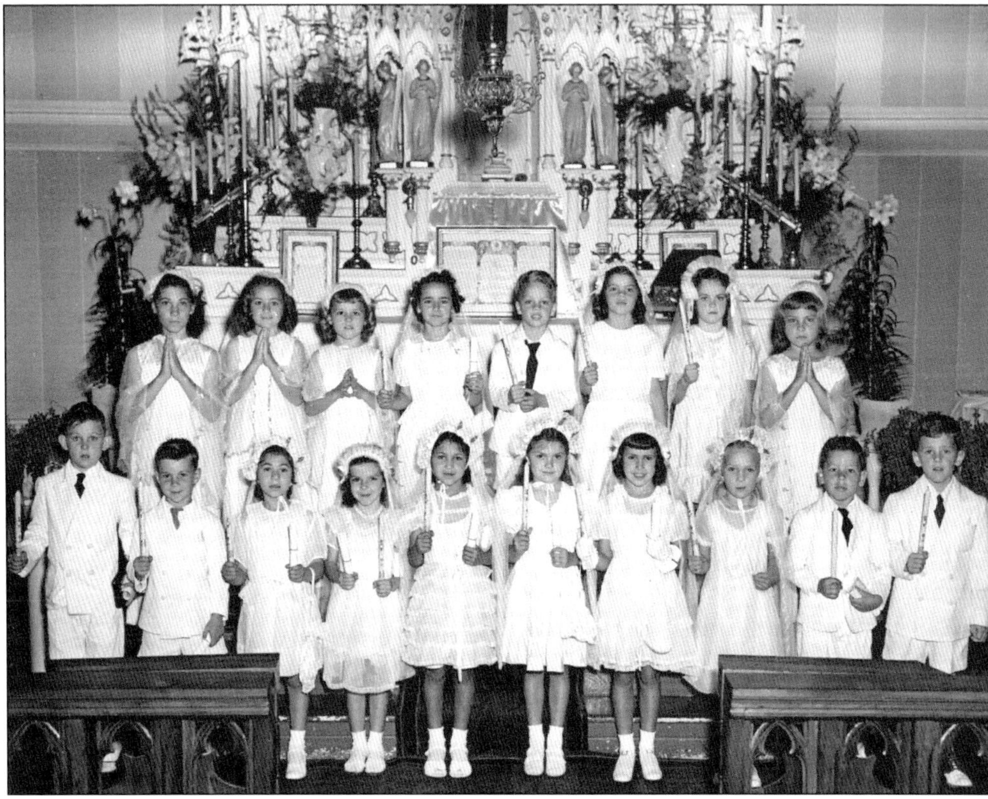

On April 24, 1949, eighteen boys and girls celebrated their first communion at St. Thomas Catholic Church. Pictured here, from left to right, are (first row) Warren Hale, Billy Ray Lopesto, Lena Lopesto, Sylvia Holley, Rose Ann Barrale, Judy Fabian, Geraldine Fennel, Anne Holmes, Wayne Ray, and Billy Hartwell; (second row) Jennette Lopesto, Mary Ellen Hatem, Barbara Ray, Rose Ann Ladnier, Robert Morrison, Peggy Blake, unidentified, and Ann Davis. (Courtesy of Mississippi Gulf Coast Community College Dixie Press Collection.)

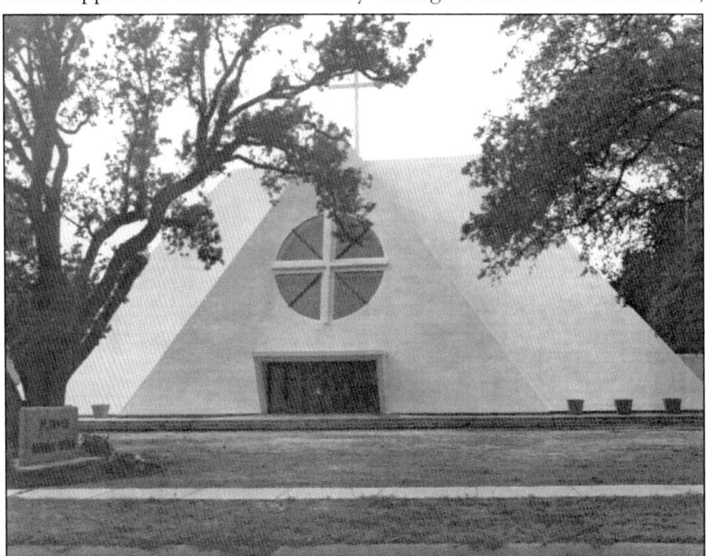

After Hurricane Camille destroyed the church, a new St. Thomas Catholic Church was constructed and dedicated in August 1972. New additions to the church were in progress when Hurricane Katrina destroyed the structure in 2005. The church has since been rebuilt on the same site. (Courtesy of Eddie Ware.)

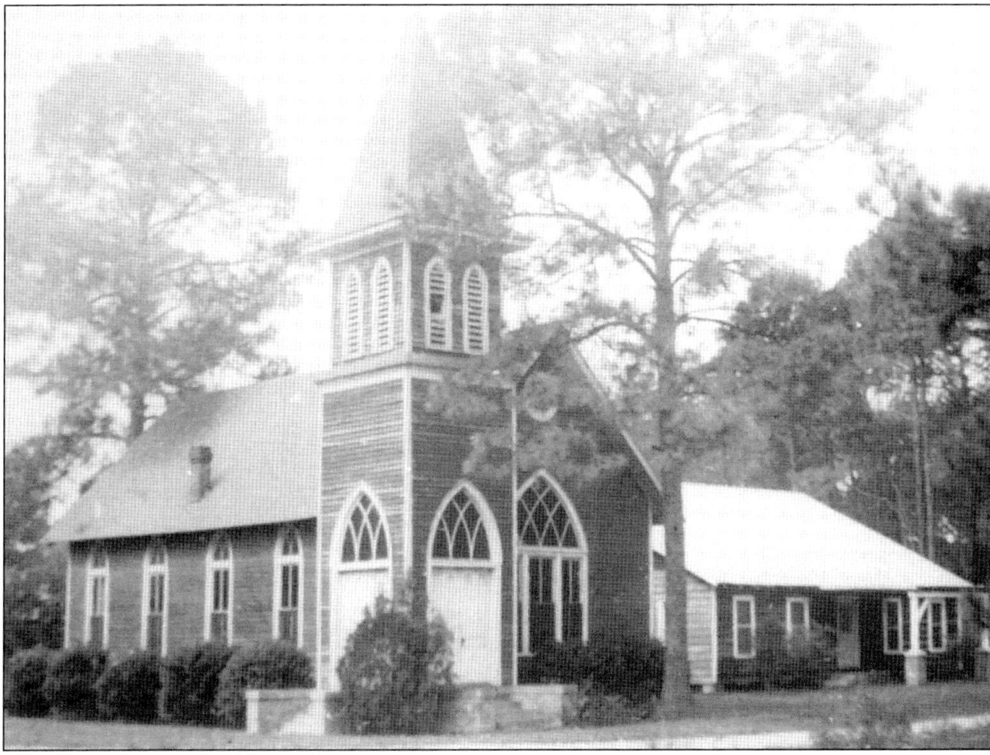

In 1909, the Presbyterian church was organized in Long Beach, and the first church building was constructed in 1912 on the corner of Burke Avenue and Third Street. The land for the church was donated by Merinda Quarles. This building served as the church from 1910 until 1964. An educational wing was added in 1936, and the church was also used for a Head Start program from 1964 to 1969. (Courtesy of the Mary Ellen Alexander Collection.)

The original Presbyterian church building was torn down after Hurricane Camille. A bell tower was added to the current building, which allowed the church bell, stored since Hurricane Camille, to once again ring out for all to hear. (Courtesy of the Mary Ellen Alexander Collection.)

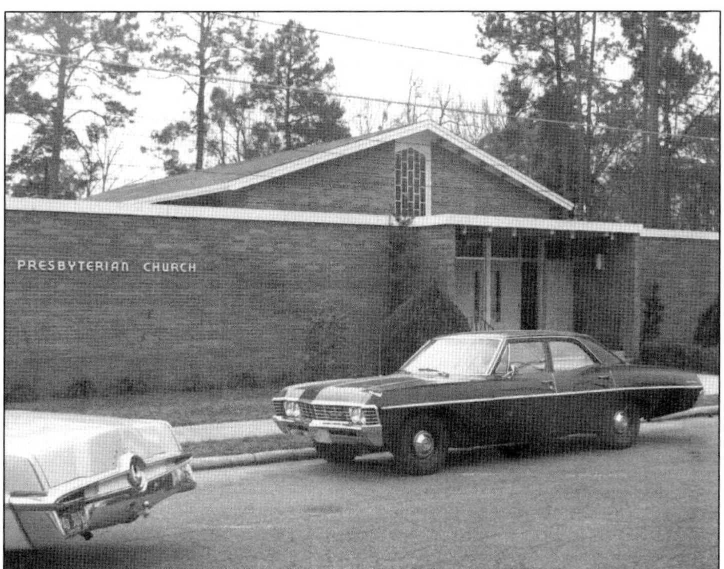

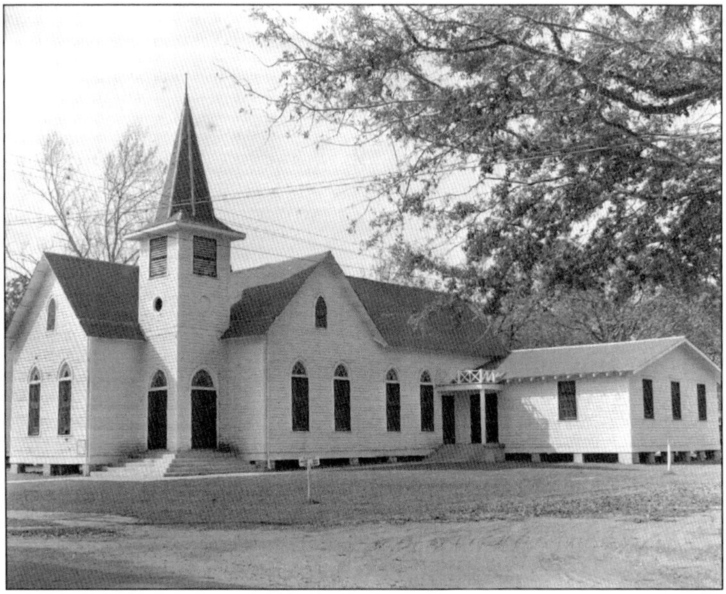

The First Baptist Church was organized in 1909. This first building was constructed in 1910, with improvements and additions until a new church building was erected on Jeff Davis Avenue. (Courtesy of Mississippi Gulf Coast Community College Dixie Press Collection.)

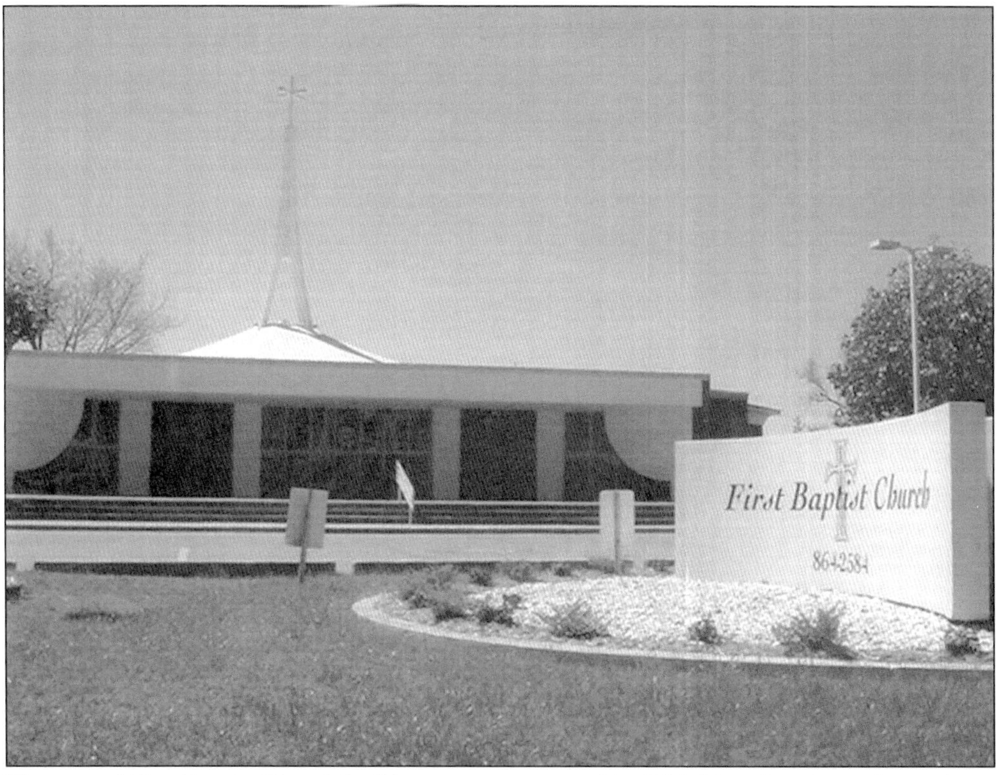

The second First Baptist Church building was constructed in 1964. This church was located two blocks off of the beach and took heavy damage from Hurricane Camille. According to a report sent to the Southern Baptist Convention in August 1969, the church building suffered more than $200,000 in damages. The water was two feet deep with a surge so powerful that pews ended up heaped towards the front of the church. The church was later destroyed by Hurricane Katrina in 2005 and rebuilt north of the waterfront on Cleveland Avenue. (Courtesy of John McCall.)

Seven

Hurricanes

The Mississippi Gulf Coast has always had its share of tropical storms and hurricanes. In the days before radio and television, sudden changes in the weather that signaled the coming of a storm were cause for fear among the inhabitants of the vulnerable coastline. Many storms had impacted the area that became known as Long Beach over the centuries, but the first that had its history recorded in photographs was the 1915 storm. Few images survive, but they show boats beached on the sand, piers destroyed, and miles of trolley tracks washed away.

Before Hurricane Katrina caused extensive destruction to the Mississippi Gulf Coast in 2005, there were two other storms that were considered historic (devastating): the hurricane of 1947 (hurricanes were not given personal names until 1953) and Hurricane Camille in 1969. Both caused injury and death to members of the community and extensive damage or outright destruction to homes, businesses, and the important tourism industry.

Many Long Beach residents will continue to live close to the beach even with the history of damaging hurricanes. Those who live along the coast are a resilient people and will never let the seasonal threat of hurricanes dampen their love of the beautiful Mississippi Gulf Coast.

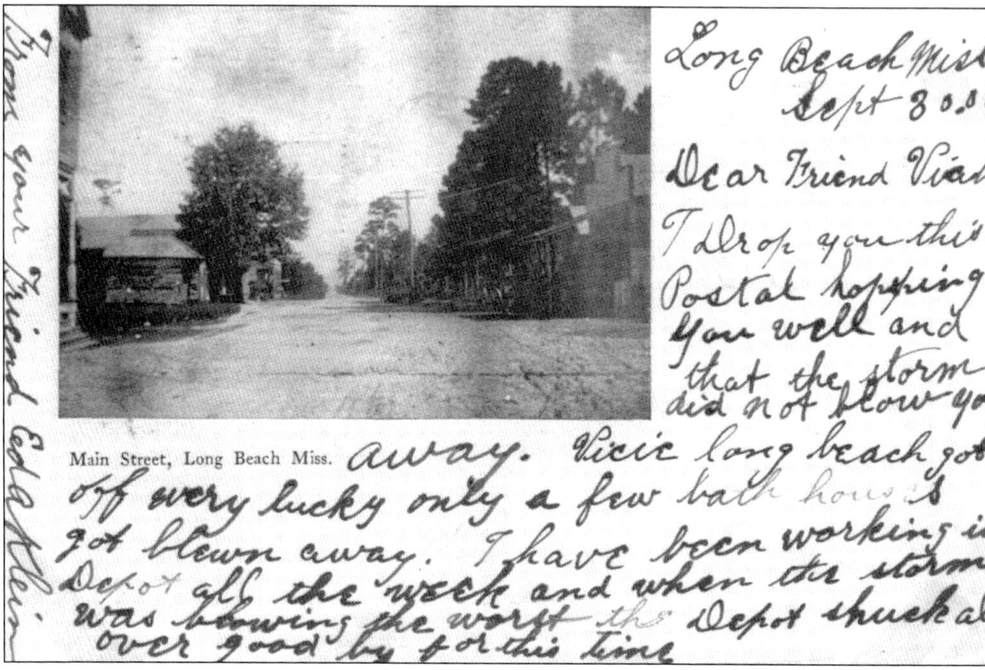

Ed A. Klein sent this postcard from Long Beach to a friend in Algiers, Louisiana, in 1906. He describes the storm that had passed through, and reports that "Long Beach got off very lucky only a few bath houses got blown away." Records show that there was a hurricane that struck the Mississippi Gulf Coast in 1906 with winds up to 90 miles per hour. (Courtesy of Paul Jermyn.)

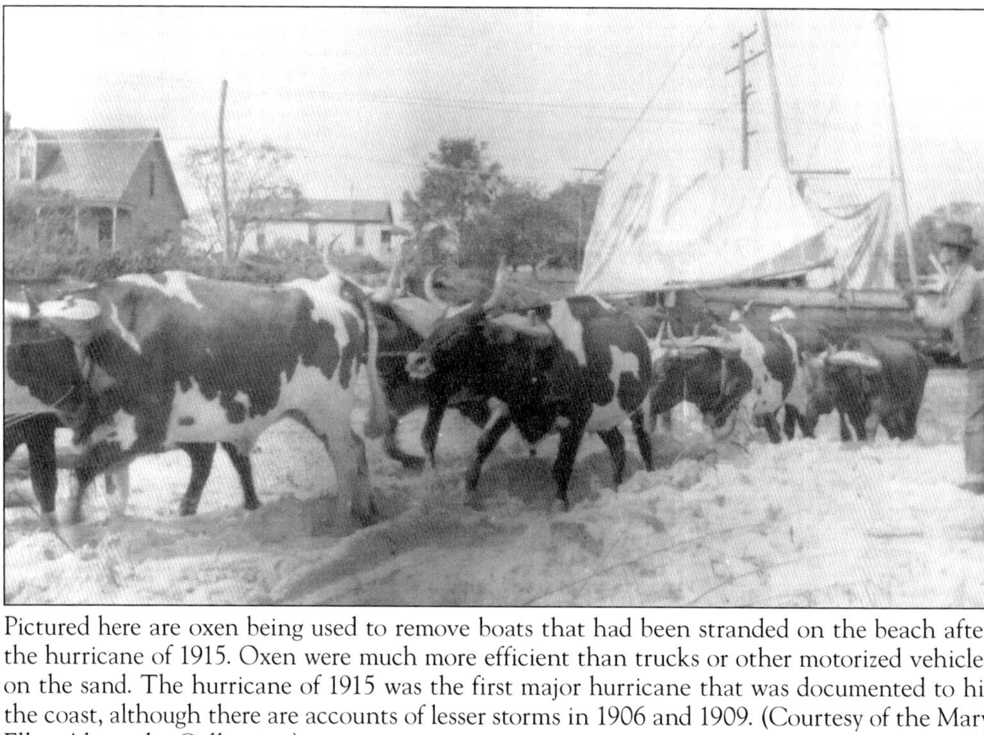

Pictured here are oxen being used to remove boats that had been stranded on the beach after the hurricane of 1915. Oxen were much more efficient than trucks or other motorized vehicles on the sand. The hurricane of 1915 was the first major hurricane that was documented to hit the coast, although there are accounts of lesser storms in 1906 and 1909. (Courtesy of the Mary Ellen Alexander Collection.)

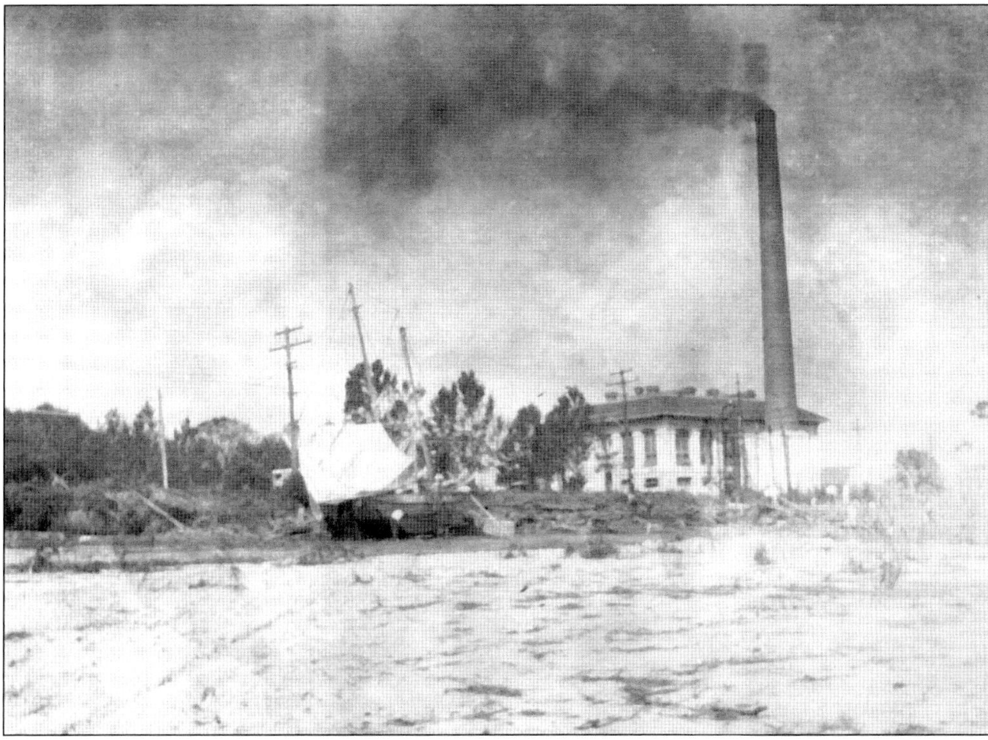

The powerful hurricane of 1915 left debris scattered along the beach. The view in this photograph looks towards the powerhouse in nearby Gulfport and shows a boat stranded far from the waterline. (Courtesy of the Mary Ellen Alexander Collection.)

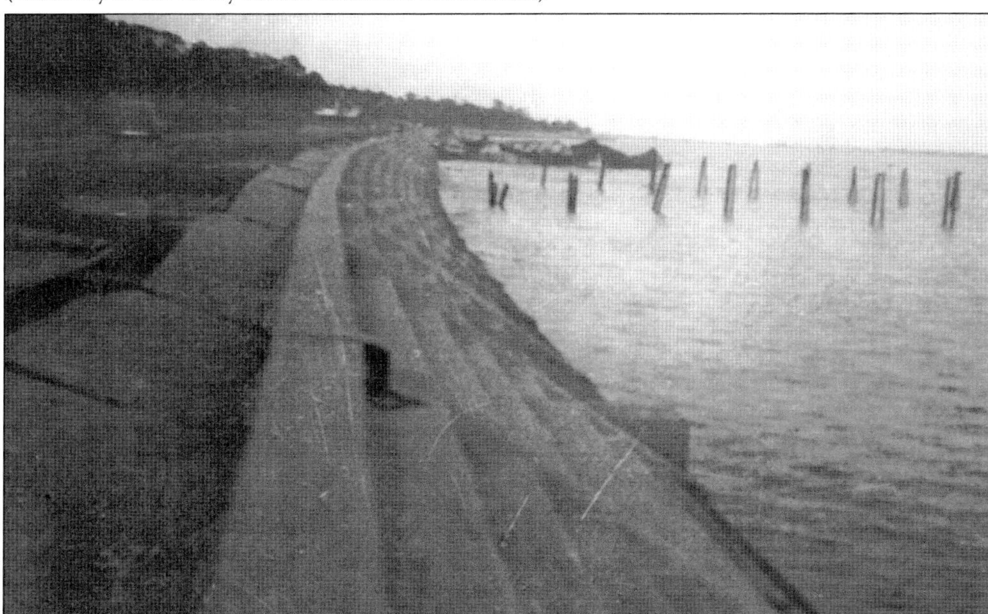

The hurricane of 1947 damaged the seawall all along the length of the coast. The buckled concrete sidewalk in this photograph is a testament to the power of the winds and water. Luckily, most of the seawall itself was not destroyed. (Courtesy of Shaw Design Group Archives.)

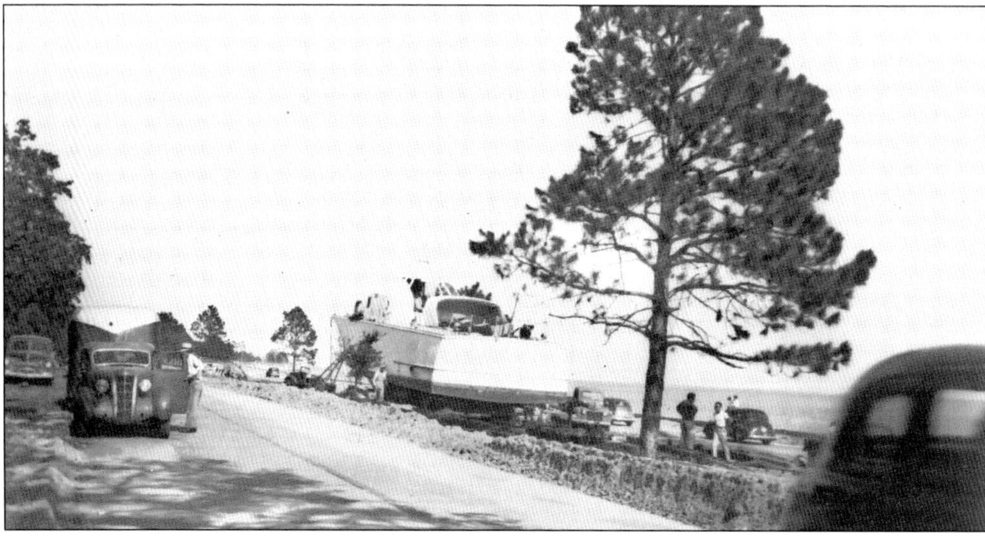

Any boats that were not secured against the storm were tossed around like toys. The hurricane of 1947 deposited this boat on Beach Boulevard. The photograph was taken just east of Gulf Park College for Women. (Courtesy of Shaw Design Group Archives.)

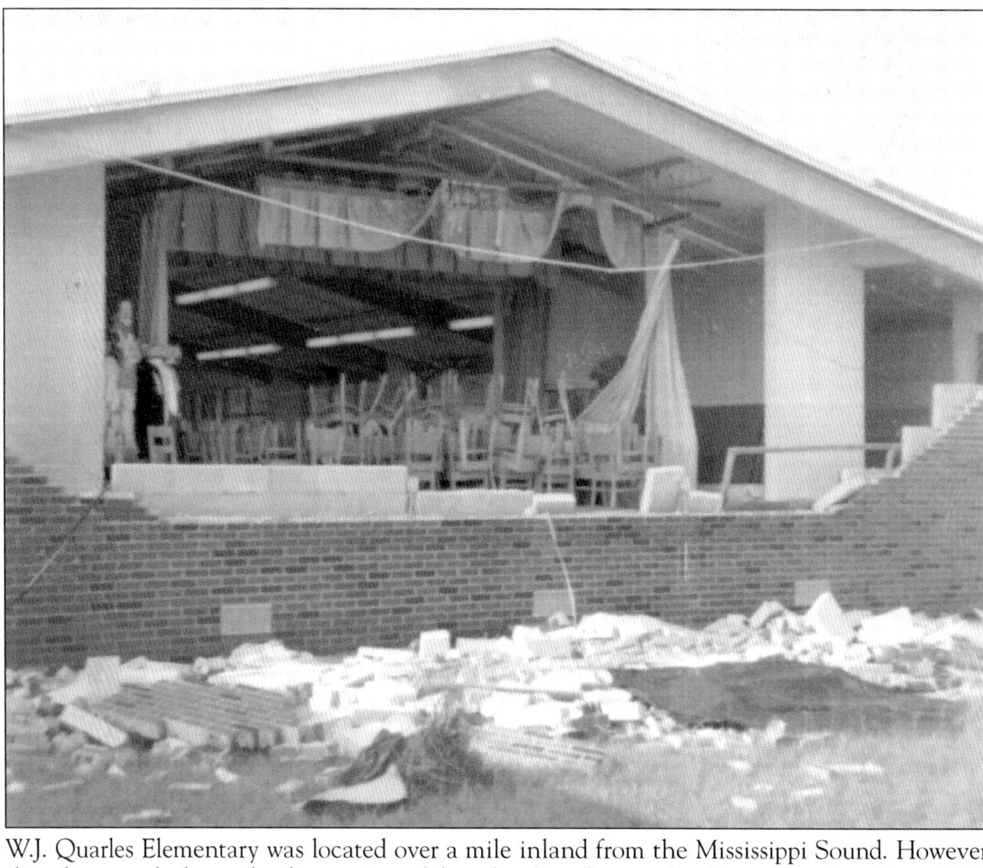

W.J. Quarles Elementary was located over a mile inland from the Mississippi Sound. However, this photograph shows the destruction of the school's cafeteria after Hurricane Camille in 1969. (Courtesy of Mable Skellie.)

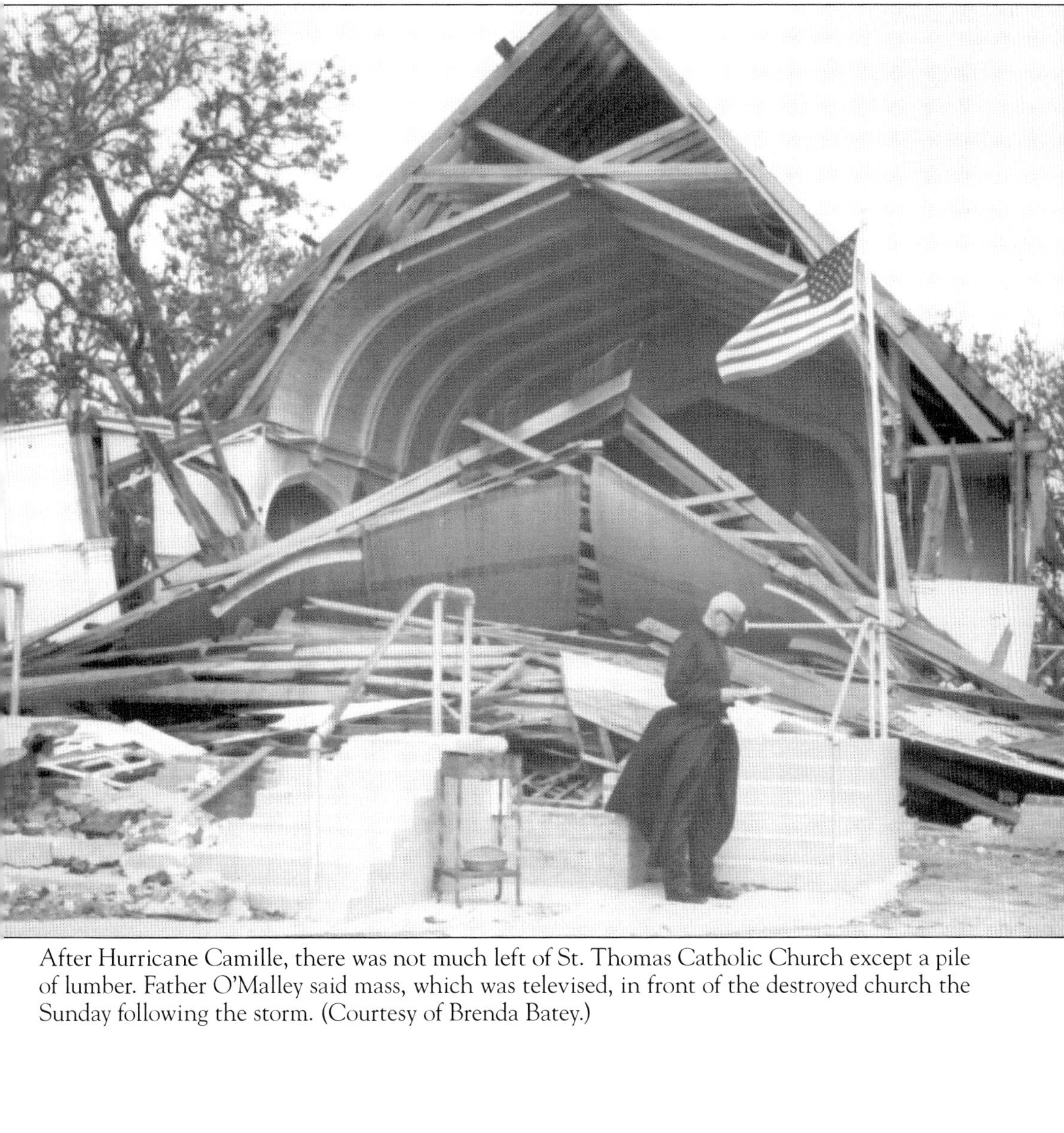

After Hurricane Camille, there was not much left of St. Thomas Catholic Church except a pile of lumber. Father O'Malley said mass, which was televised, in front of the destroyed church the Sunday following the storm. (Courtesy of Brenda Batey.)

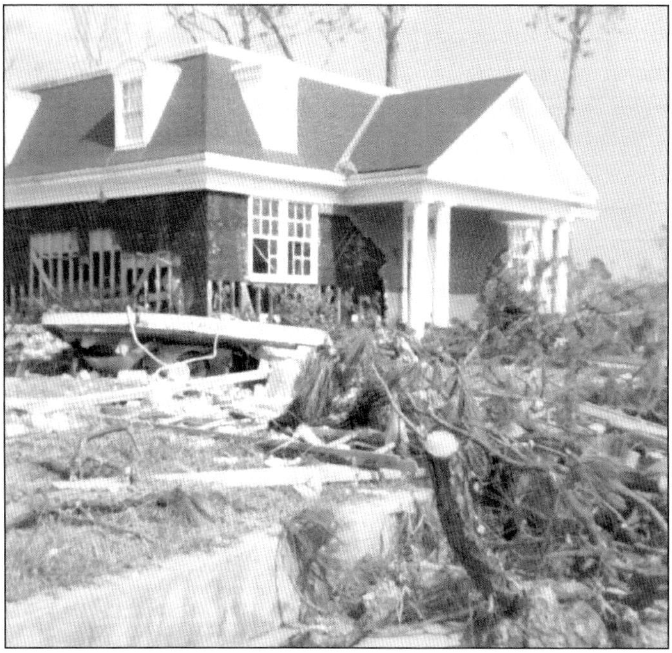

Riemann Funeral Home was almost washed away after Hurricane Camille. The funeral home was located just a block or two from the beachfront. (Courtesy of Mable Skellie.)

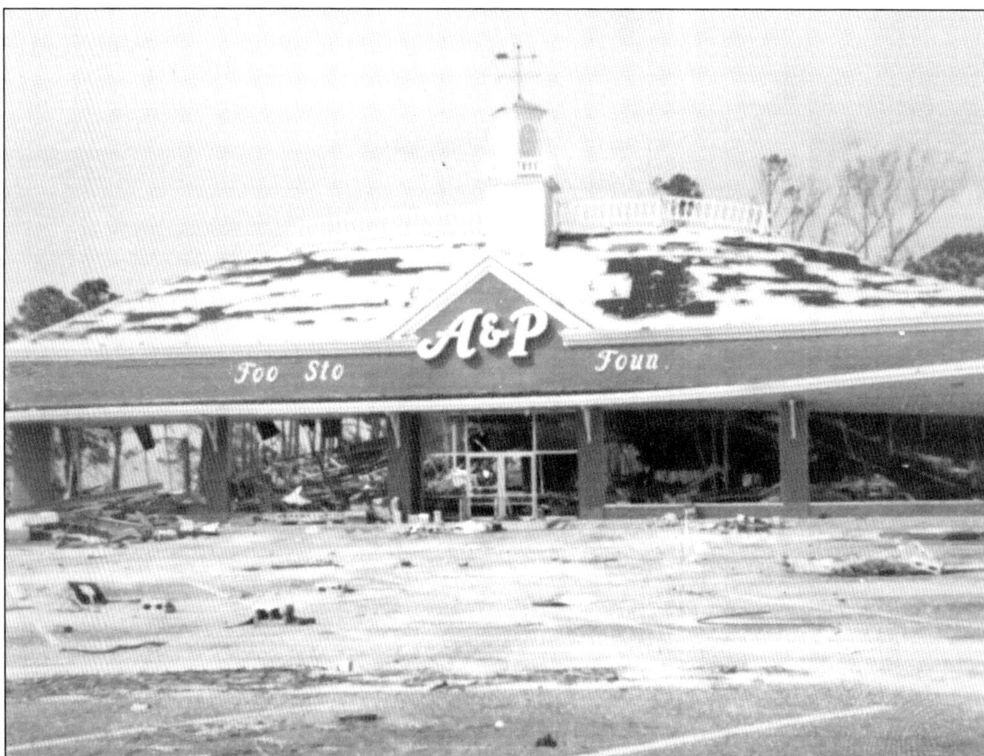

All that was left of the A&P grocery and the rest of the shopping center after Hurricane Camille was an empty shell and its distinctive rooftop. The shopping center also contained a drugstore, hardware store, and beauty shop, along with several other businesses. The center had been constructed in 1962. (Courtesy of Mabel Skellie.)

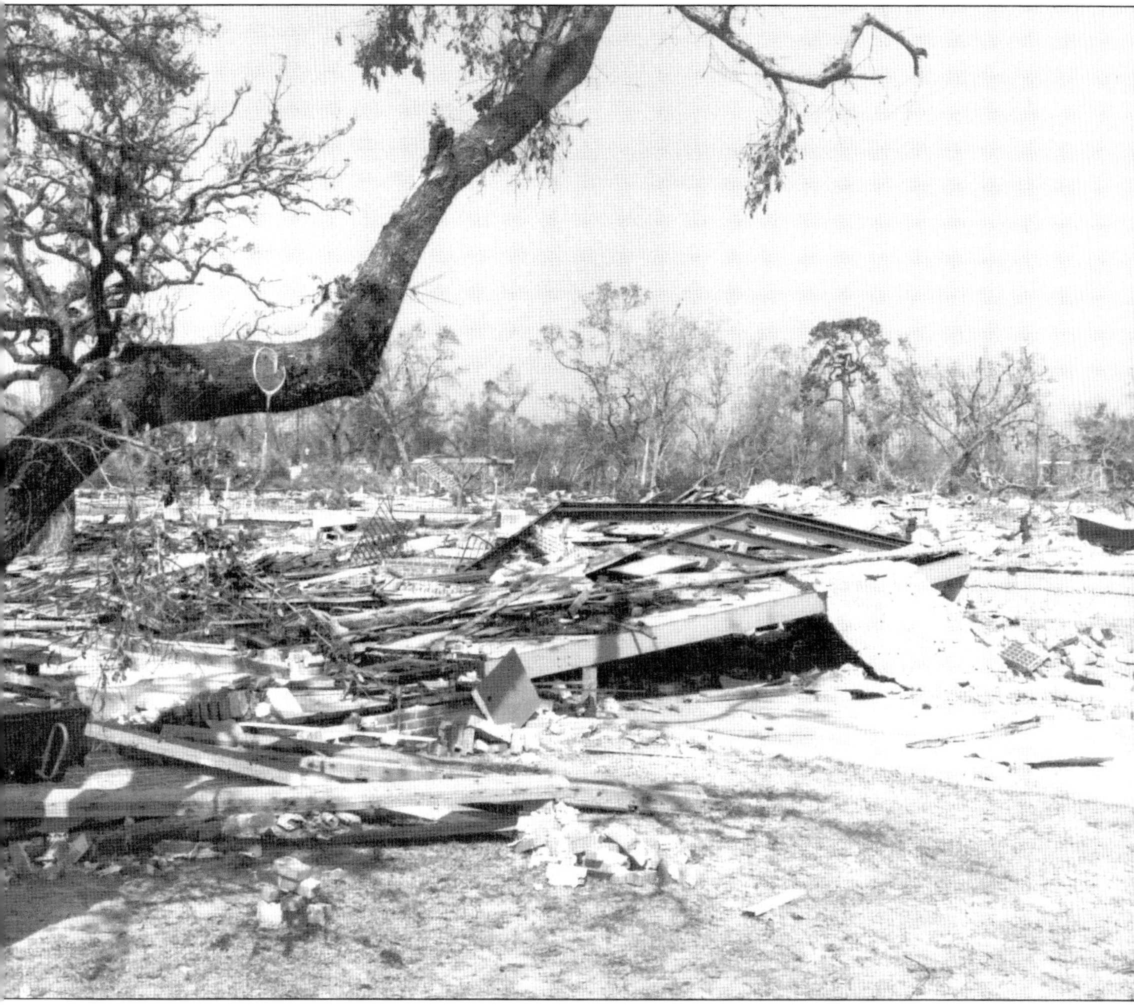

This unidentified home was one of hundreds of houses that were destroyed by Hurricane Camille. When a destructive hurricane strikes, there are hundreds of photographs that are almost identical to this one, showing how all landmarks are washed away. (Courtesy of Brenda Batey.)

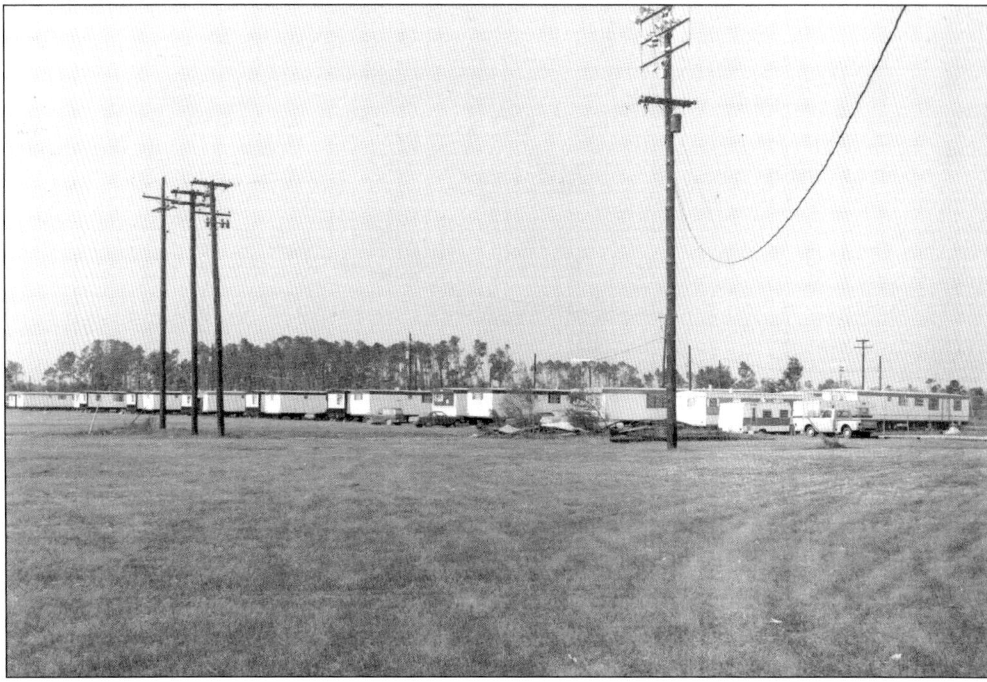

Trailers were hastily set up for emergency workers' use after Hurricane Camille. Trailers were also brought in as temporary housing for those left homeless by the storm. (Courtesy of Brenda Batey.)

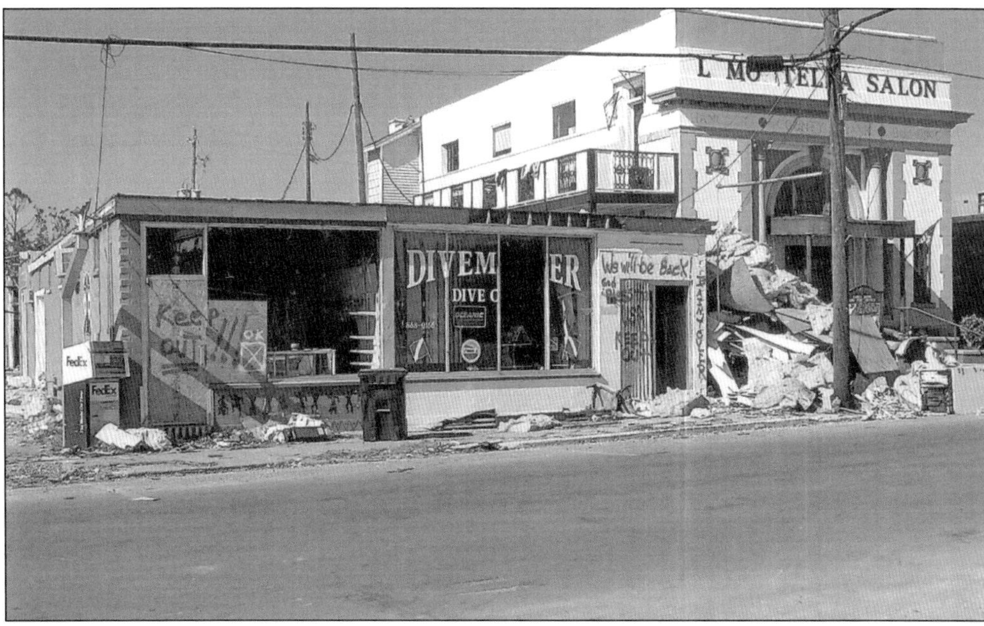

The building that had been the original Hancock Bank Building on Jeff Davis Avenue was one of the few remaining structures that was even recognizable after Hurricane Katrina blasted through the Mississippi Gulf Coast on August 29, 2005. The buildings to the left have since been torn down and new shops constructed. The sturdy old bank building was repaired and is now a coffee house. (Courtesy of Donald Dana.)

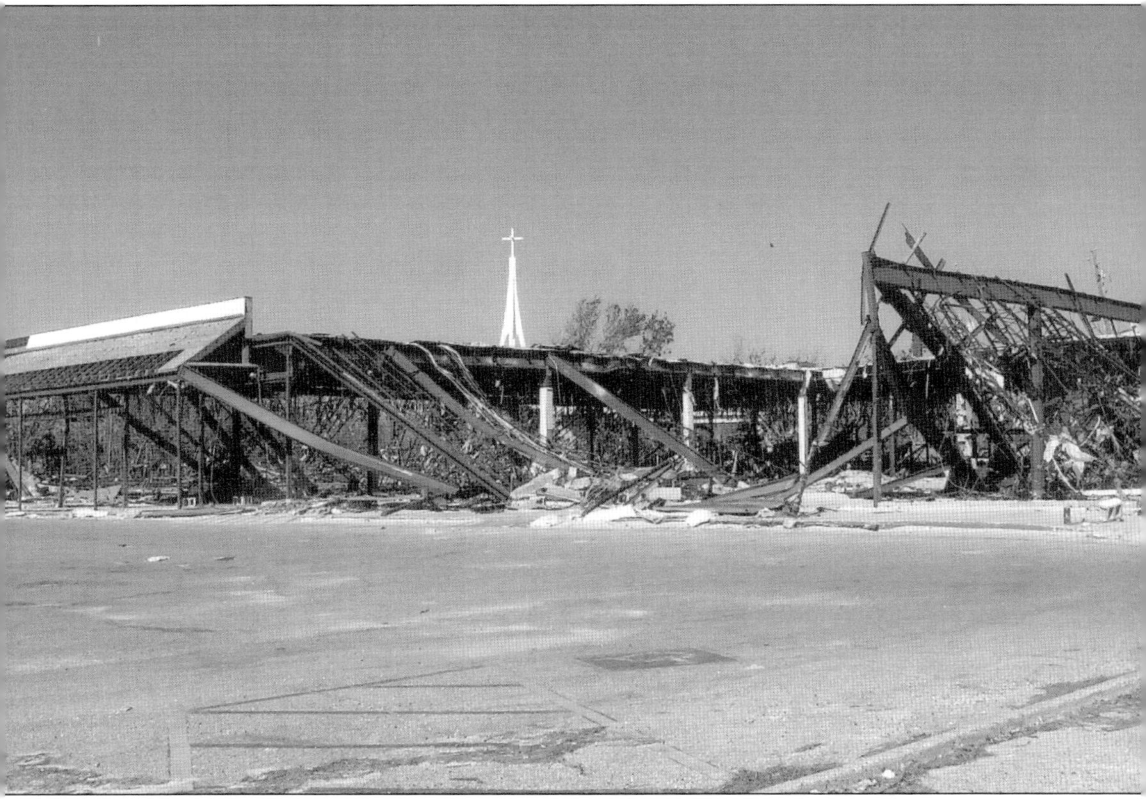

Hurricane Katrina left little of the First Baptist Church on Jeff Davis Avenue standing. The church, which had survived Hurricane Camille in 1969, was no match for the storm of 2005. Only the steeple was left, and it has since been installed at the new church on Cleveland Avenue. (Courtesy of Donald Dana.)

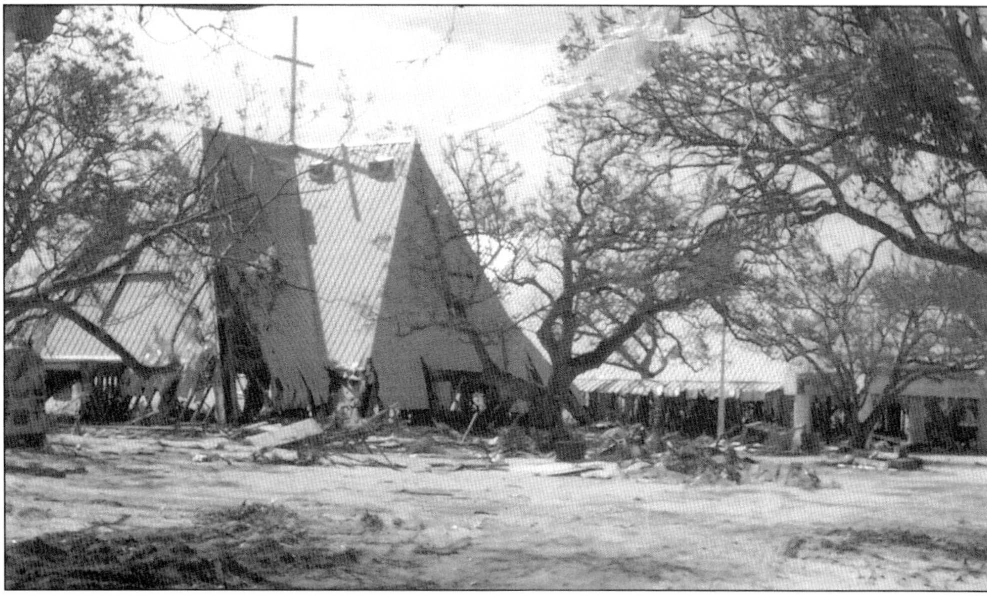

St. Thomas Catholic Church was washed through by Hurricane Katrina, and only the roof was left. A new church has been built on the site, which is just to the west of the University of Southern Mississippi's Gulf Park campus. (Courtesy of the University of Southern Mississippi Gulf Coast Library.)

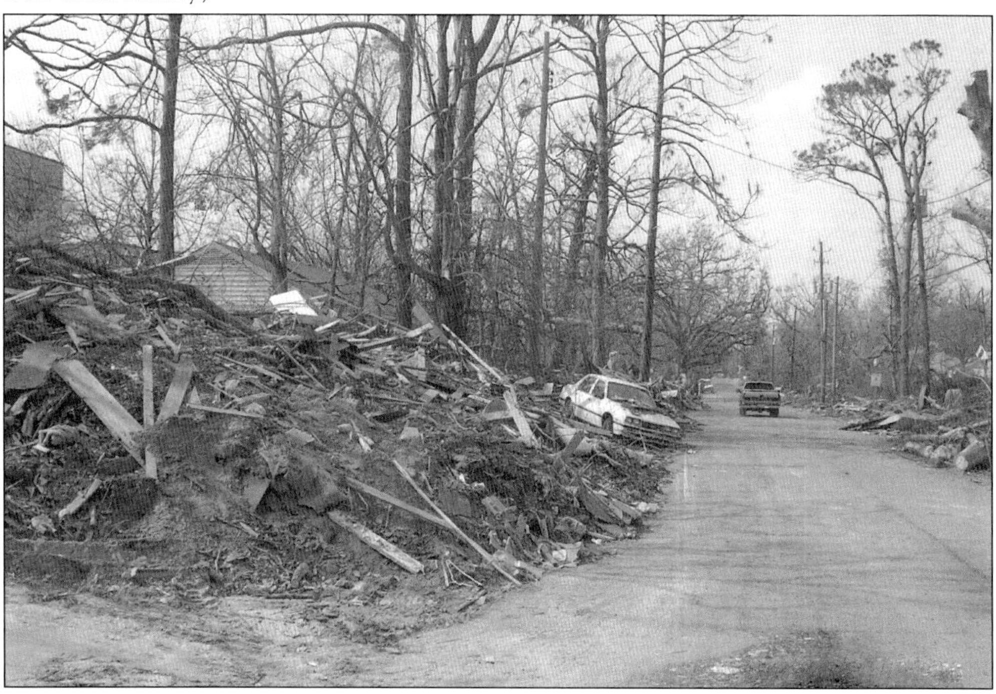

Beach Park Place runs north and south from the beach to Railroad Street. This photograph was taken almost three weeks after Hurricane Katrina and shows the mountains of debris that had been cleared from the road. There were hundreds of other streets in Long Beach that contained similar piles of debris, waiting to be picked up for disposal. (Courtesy of the University of Southern Mississippi Gulf Coast Library.)

Hardy Hall was another historic building on the university's campus that was heavily damaged by Katrina. The first floor was washed through, and the second and third floors sustained extensive damage as well. A room on the first floor of Hardy Hall had been the original home of the Gulf Park College for Women archives, and it was fortunate that the collection had been moved to the new library in 2002. (Courtesy of the University of Southern Mississippi Gulf Coast Library.)

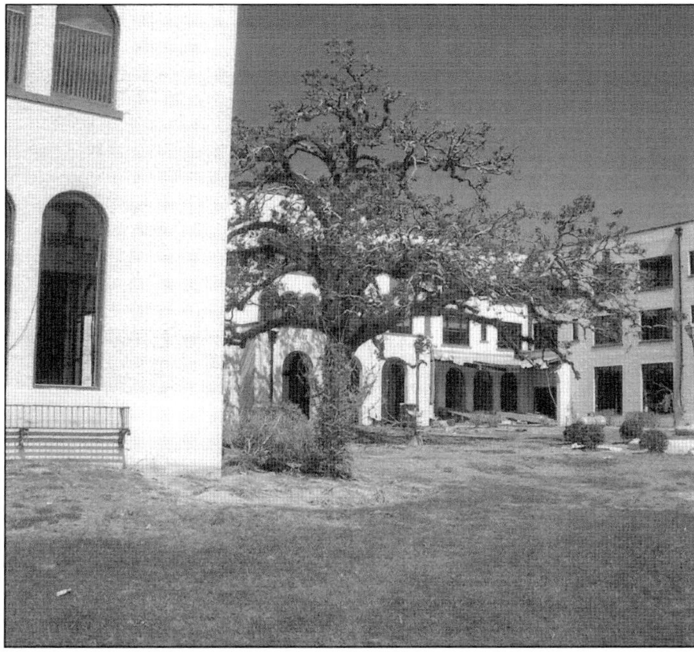

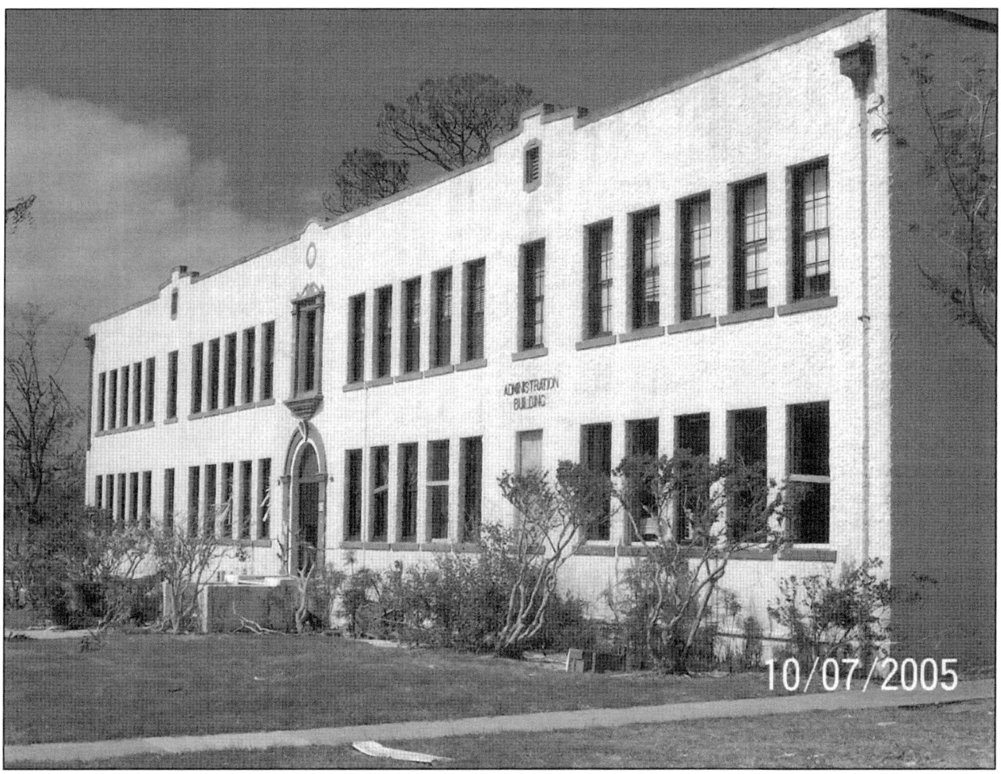

The administration building on the University of Southern Mississippi Gulf Park campus suffered extensive damage from Katrina and was later demolished. The original foundation remains as a green space and provides a footprint of the original building's outline. (Courtesy of the University of Southern Mississippi Gulf Coast Library.)

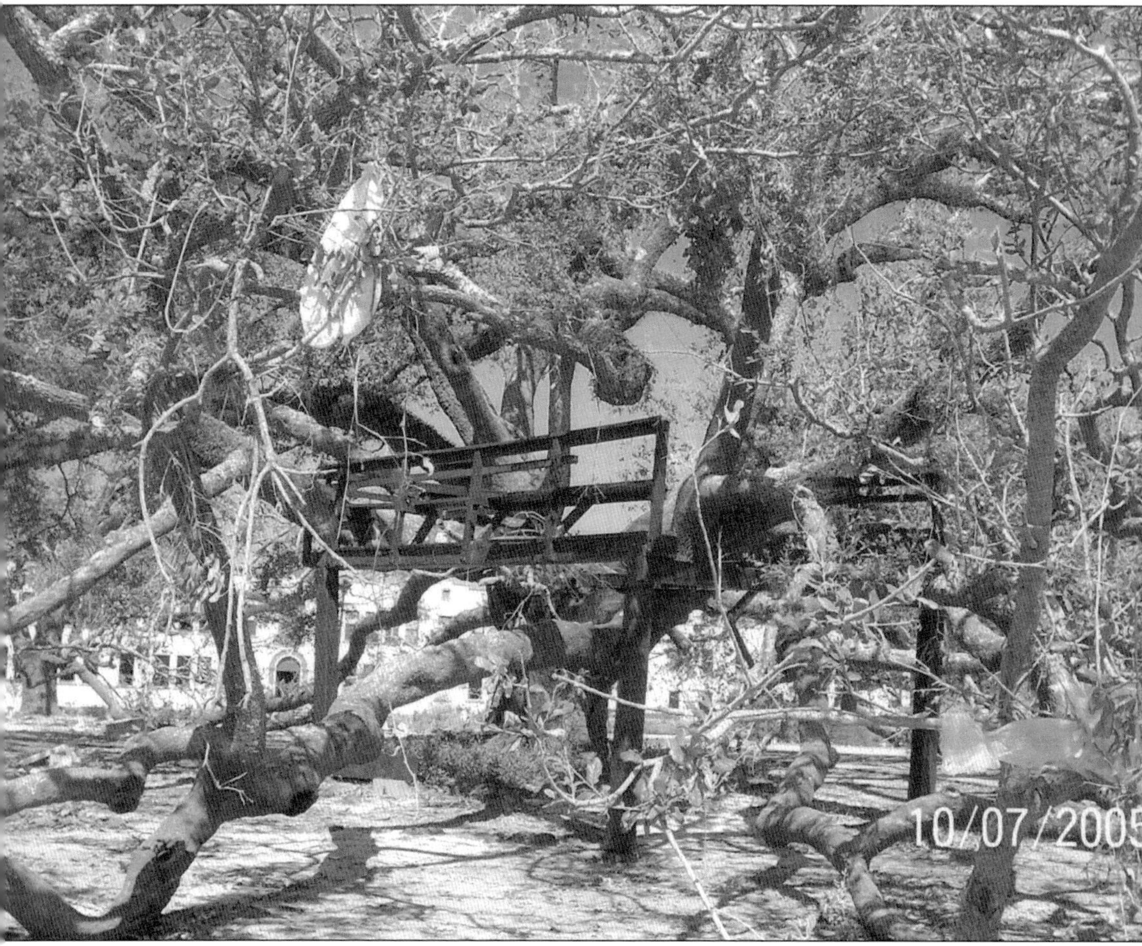

Although Hurricane Katrina did not topple the 500-year-old Friendship Oak on the University of Southern Mississippi Gulf Park campus, it did inflict damage to the tree. It has since recovered, but the historic platform that once circled the oak was not replaced. Thousands of venerable oak trees survived the storm, but their branches were bare, stripped of all leaves by the damaging winds. Some of the trees, like the Friendship Oak, sported pieces of cloth or plastic grocery bags as a kind of macabre decoration for months. (Courtesy of the University of Southern Mississippi Gulf Coast Library.)

Eight

Leisure and Everyday Life

Long Beach residents and visitors have always enjoyed the outdoor life. Fishing, catching shrimp, crabbing, and hunting were popular in the early days and are still popular today. The waters of the Mississippi Sound are protected by the barrier islands that lie a few miles offshore. The shallow waters create a very good environment for boating, skiing, and swimming. There were camps for families and day camps for the young, where they could learn archery, horseback riding, and handicrafts. Long Beach residents have also been very active in civic duties. During World War II, there were book drives, plays, and pageants to raise money for the war effort; war stamps were sold, and scrap was collected. Long Beach has also been known as a destination for tourists. At onetime, tourist camps, cottages, and motel courts dotted the beachfront. Most are long gone, mainly due to the occasional hurricanes, but tourists still visit.

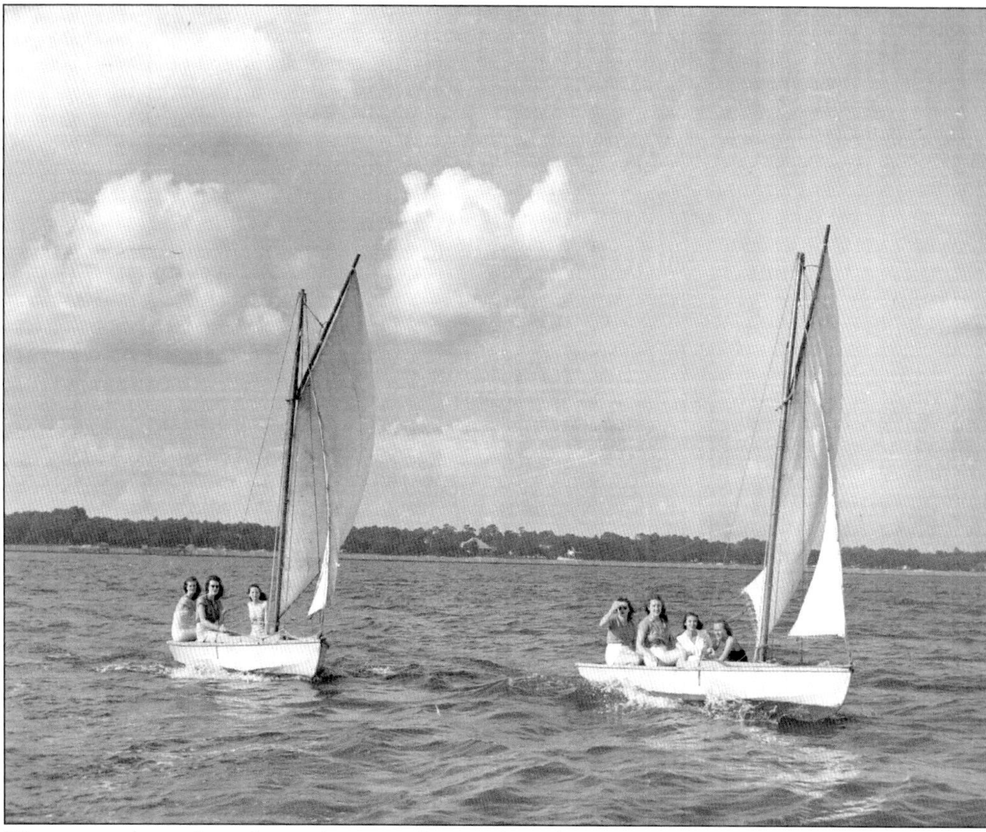
Water sports have always been a big part of living along the Mississippi Gulf Coast. Here, some young women enjoy an afternoon of sailing. (Courtesy of the Mary Ellen Alexander Collection.)

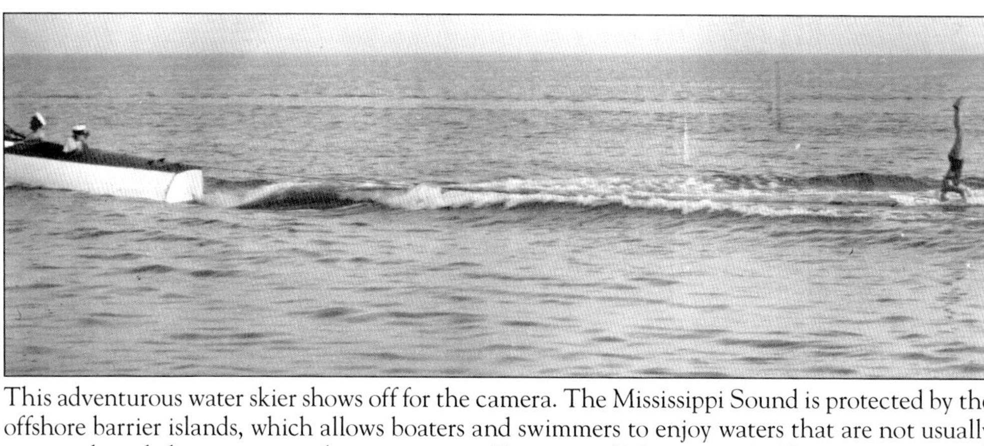
This adventurous water skier shows off for the camera. The Mississippi Sound is protected by the offshore barrier islands, which allows boaters and swimmers to enjoy waters that are not usually too rough and choppy, except during a storm. (Courtesy of Mississippi Gulf Coast Community College Dixie Press Collection.)

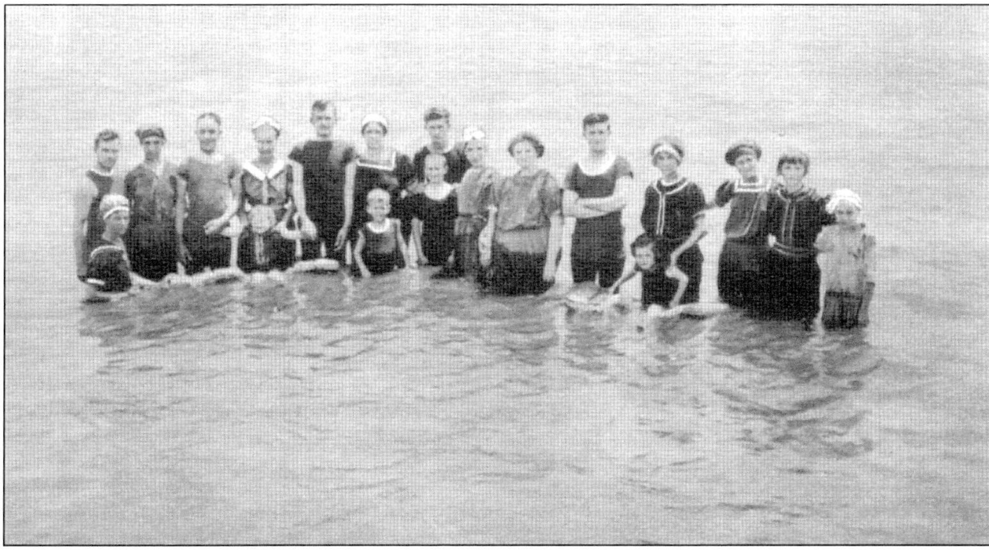

These swimmers from the 1920s are enjoying their dip in the waters of the Mississippi Sound. Except for man-made boat channels, the waters are shallow, usually allowing a bather to wade a long distance out from the shore without encountering deep waters. (Courtesy of Paul Jermyn.)

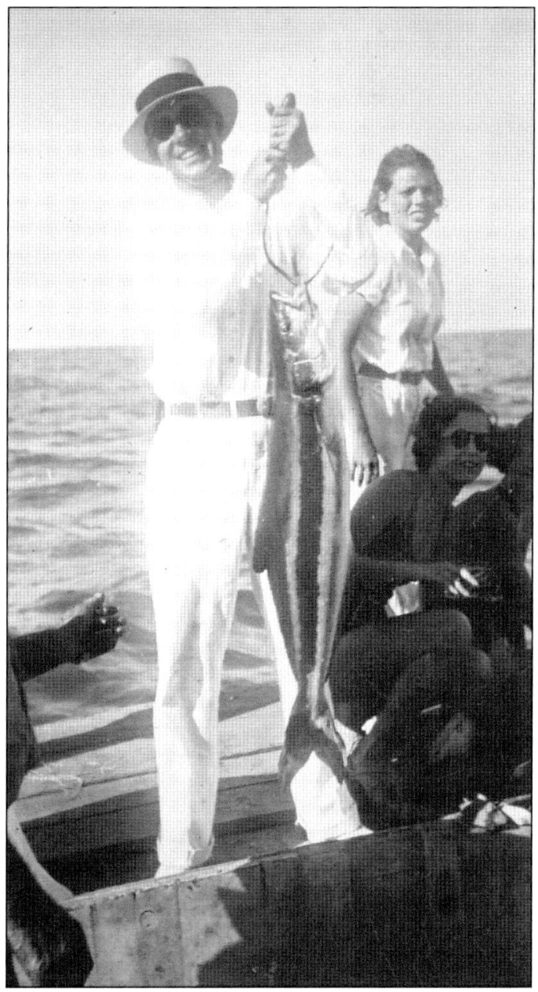

Rupert Cooke poses with 26-pound lemon fish caught near Ship Island in 1935. Reliable sources reported that Cooke, the business manager at Gulf Park College for Women, made sure that the fish was served at the college as part of the evening meal that day. (Courtesy of Mississippi Gulf Coast Community College Dixie Press Collection.)

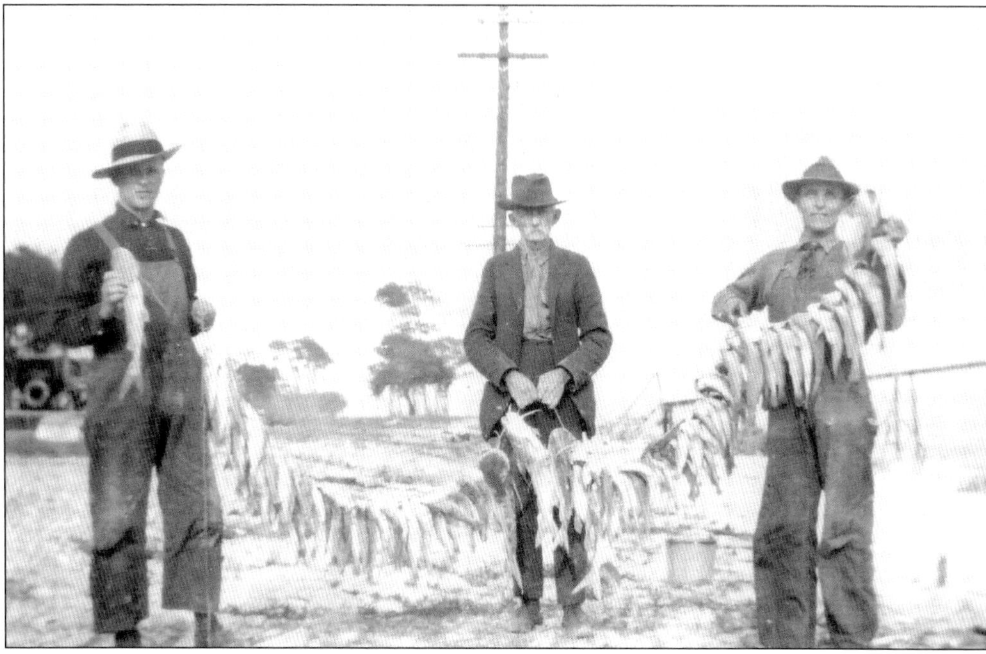

Three fishermen show off their catch in this undated photograph. Frank P. Watrous is in the center. (Courtesy of the Mary Ellen Alexander Collection.)

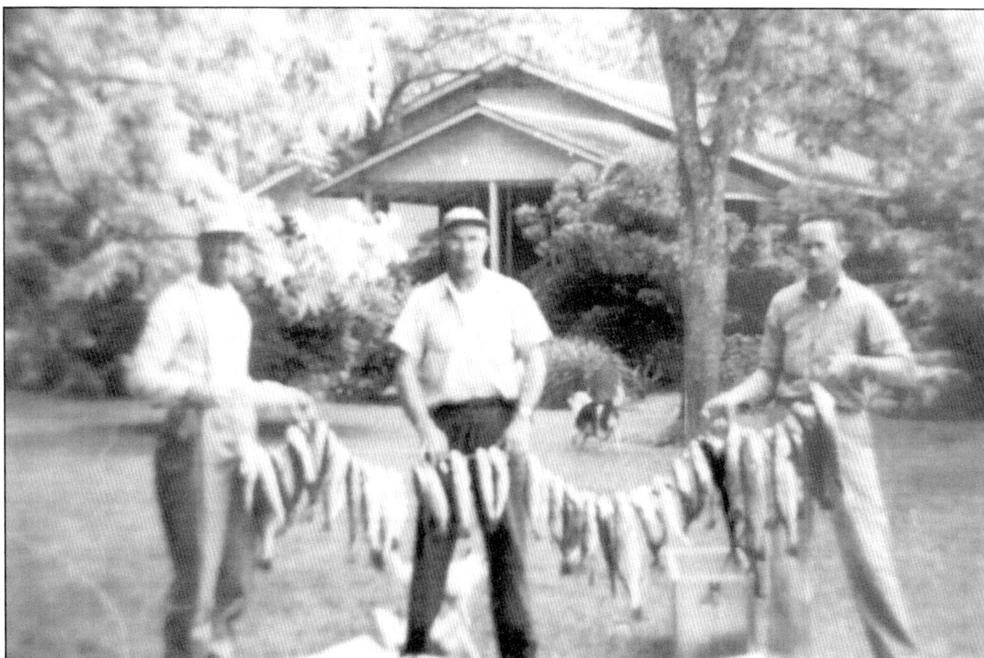

This newer photograph is almost a mirror image of the previous photograph, demonstrating that some things never change. Pete Carrubba (left), Bill Dugan (center), and William Skellie proudly hold their catch of speckled trout. (Courtesy of Mable Skellie.)

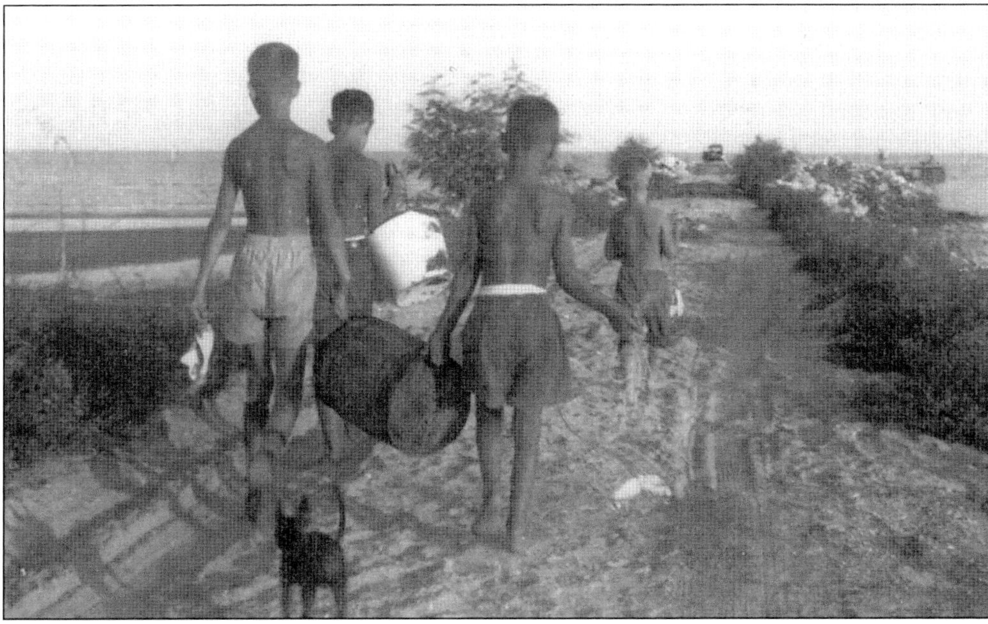

The first municipal pier was built in the 1930s, and it was located at the end of Cleveland Avenue, extending out for over 1,000 feet. This pier was destroyed by the hurricane of 1947 and was replaced by piles of riprap (pieces of roadway and sidewalk rubble), pictured here in 1953. Children were fond of crabbing and fishing on the "Rock Pile," as it was known. (Courtesy of Long Beach Historical Society Archives.)

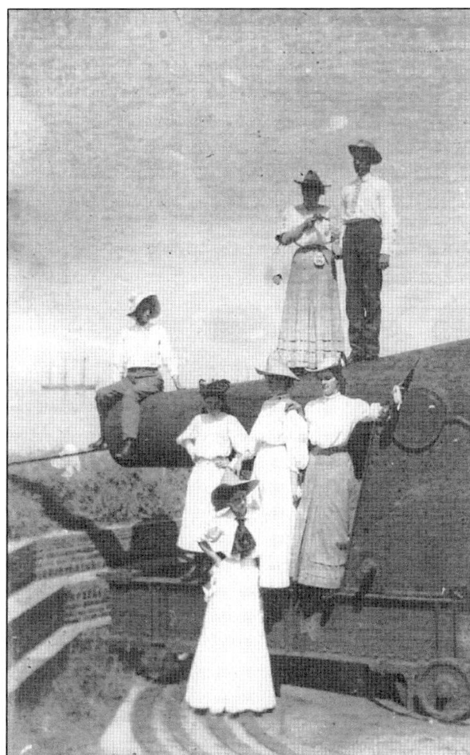

In 1904, a young, fun-loving party of Long Beach residents, including May Quarles (Watrous) and Alice Quarles (Toomer), visits the Civil War–era Fort Massachusetts at Ship Island. Many coastal residents and tourists made the 12-mile boat trip to Ship Island to enjoy the white sands and rougher surf of the barrier island. Here, some of the young men and women decide to switch hats. May Quarles had written a title under the photograph and called it *The Bonnet.* (Courtesy of the Mary Ellen Alexander Collection.)

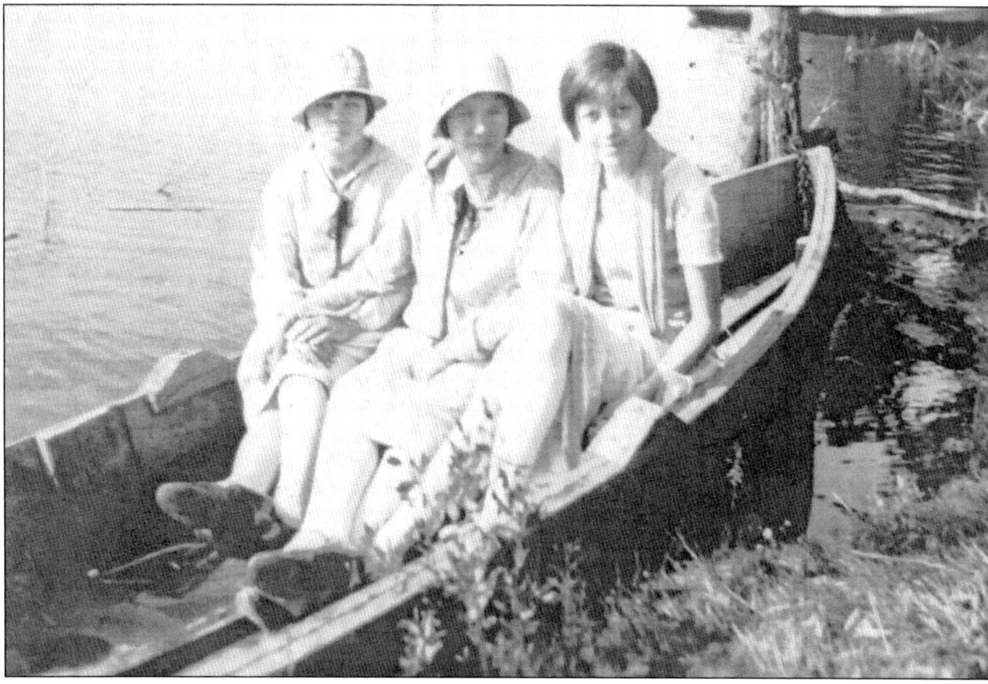

This 1917 photograph shows three friends—Annie Alexander Beech (left), Fanny Alexander Salters (center), and unidentified—getting ready to row across the Bayou Portage after leaving church to have Sunday lunch at the home of relatives. The home could only be reached by boat. (Courtesy of Otis Beech.)

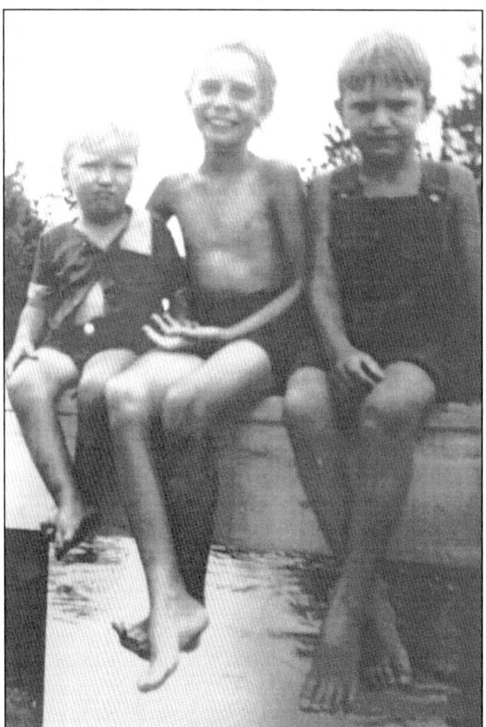

The bridge over Bayou Portage was a place for children to gather to play and swim. Otis (right), Cleo (center), and Jerry Beech are pictured here in 1938. The bridge was on South Beatline Road near Lover's Lane. (Courtesy of Otis Beech.)

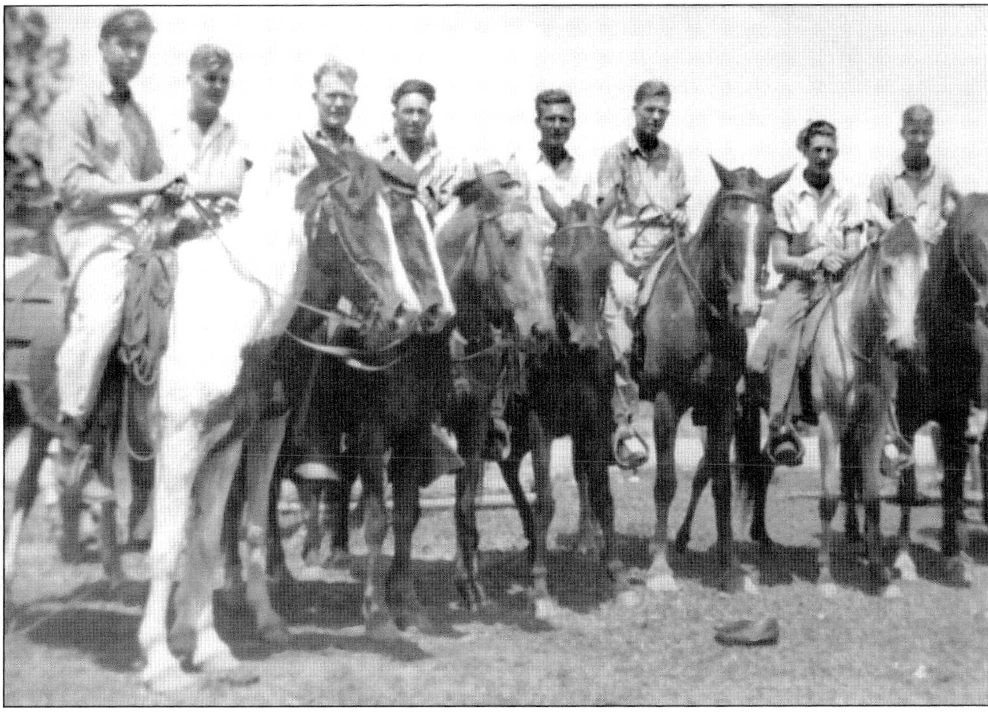

Friends, from left to right, Clyde Collins, Herman Allen, Wiley Allen, Goober Willett, Hubert Beech, Philip Allen, Junior Allen, and Buddy Allen, who lived in north Long Beach, would meet on weekends and ride horses north and west to an area near Wolf River and west of Red Creek Road. Using old bedsprings as a spit over a fire pit, they would camp and barbecue goat, wild hog, or whatever meat they could catch. They would run foxes with Philip Allen's walker foxhounds all weekend. (Courtesy of Otis Beech.)

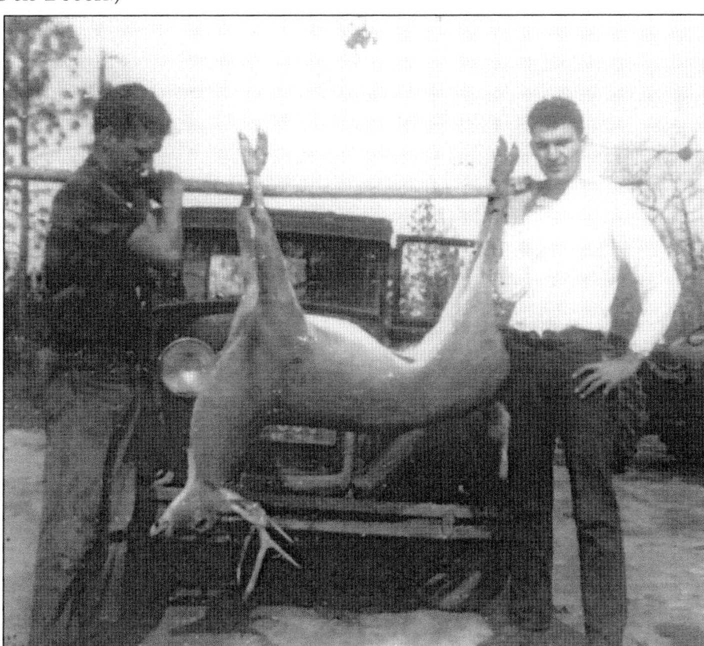

Deer hunters Gravis Alexander (left) and Otis Beech show off their prize in 1958. (Courtesy of Otis Beech.)

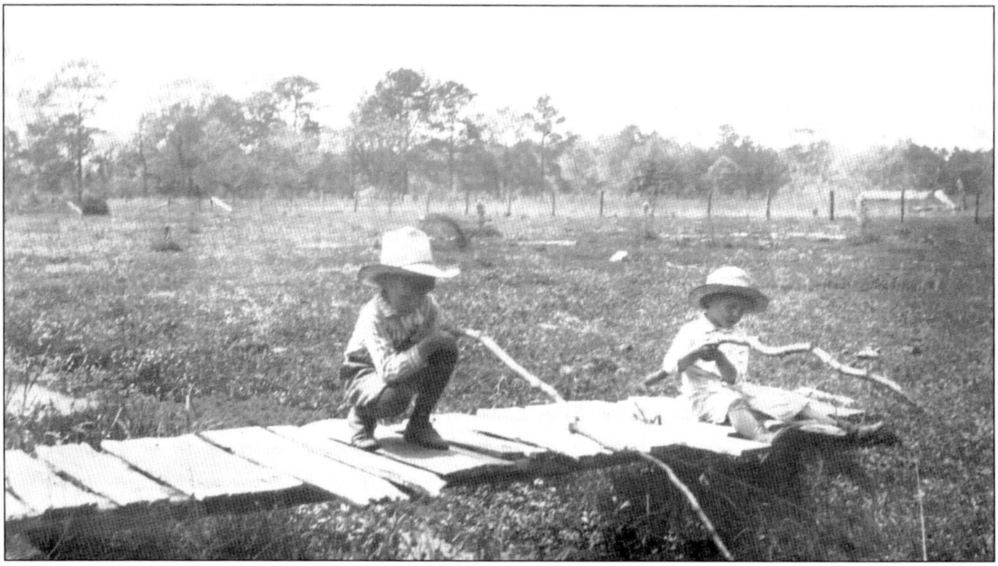

In this late 1920s photograph, these children look like they are fishing, but they are probably just having fun playing in what little water remains in this boggy area. (Courtesy of the Mary Ellen Alexander Collection.)

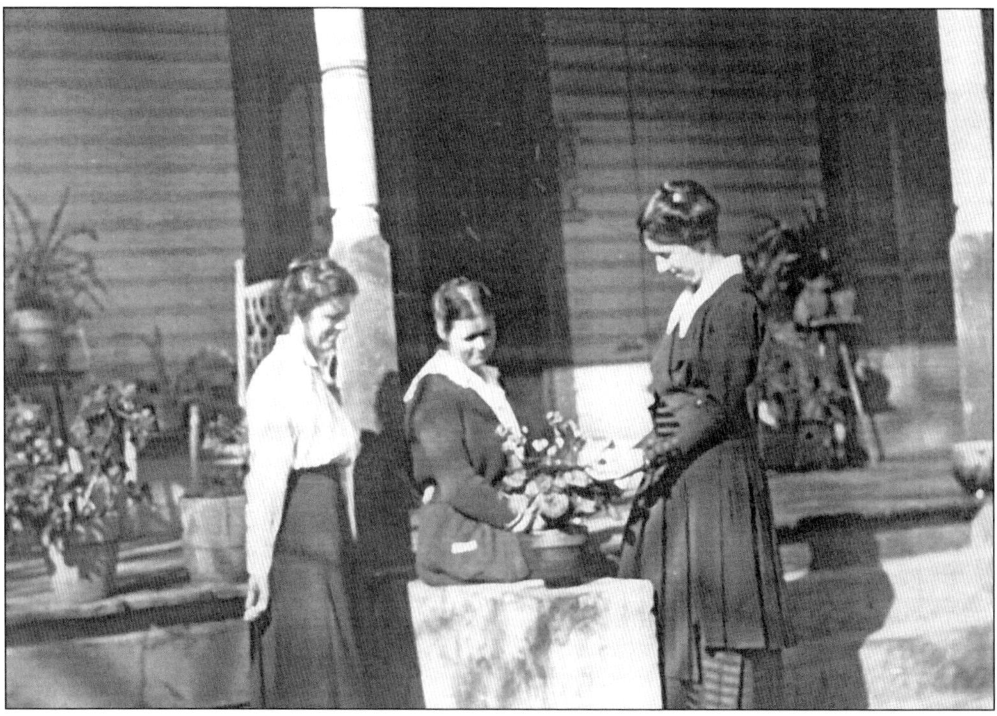

Born in 1886, May Quarles (Watrous) was the second daughter of William James Quarles and Merinda Young Quarles. Here, photographed about 1904, she is on the right, enjoying pleasantries with unidentified friends. They are in front of the Quarles House, originally on Railroad Street and now a historic property relocated near the family cemetery on Old Pass Road. (Courtesy of the Mary Ellen Alexander Collection.)

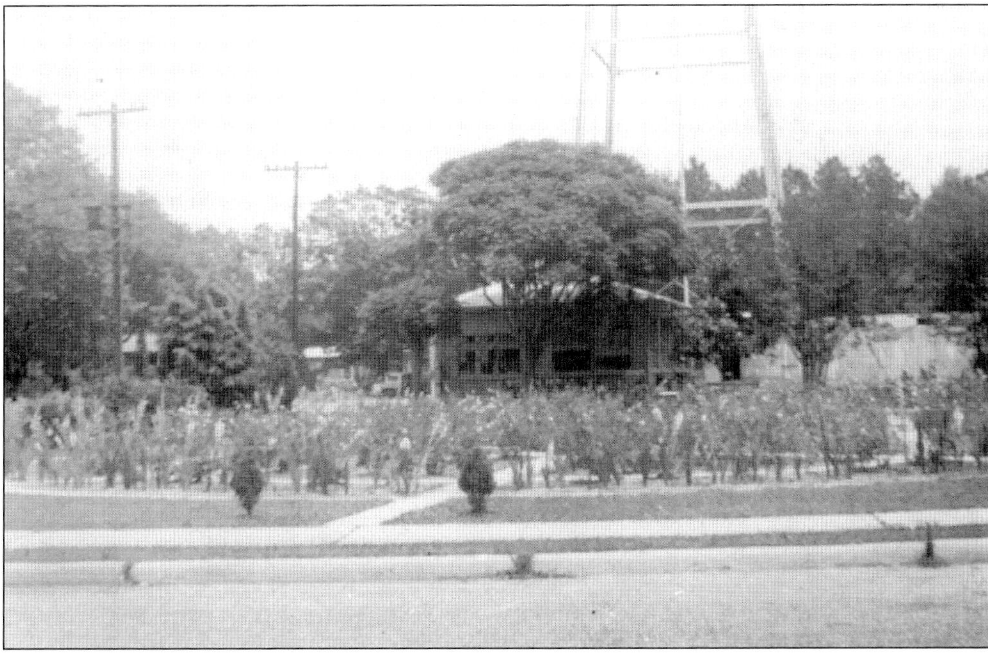

In 1931, the Long Beach Garden Club organized a rose garden on Jeff Davis Avenue after entering a rose garden contest. The city planted and cared for 650 hybrid tea roses. The Works Progress Administration paid for paved paths through the garden, and Melodia Jones donated a sundial in her mother's memory. The sundial was located in the center, with the paths radiating out. At time that the garden was created, there was only one other like it in the state, in Jackson. In 1958, city hall was built on the site of the original rose garden, and new rose bushes were planted near the original garden. (Courtesy of the Mary Ellen Alexander Collection.)

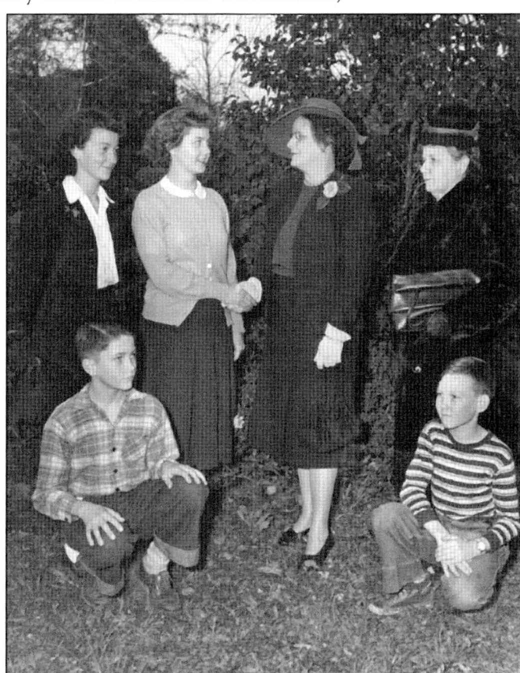

This is the Junior Long Beach Garden Club in 1949. The new officers are Betty Mae Husband, treasurer, on the left. The president of the club, Dorothy Parker (second from left) is being congratulated by Margaret Smith (third from left) and Louise Lindsey (right). Seated are Darby Gilmer, secretary, and John Ed Pearson, vice president. The Junior Garden Club won many awards and had the distinction of once winning the National Certificate of Merit. (Courtesy of Mississippi Gulf Coast Community College Dixie Press Collection.)

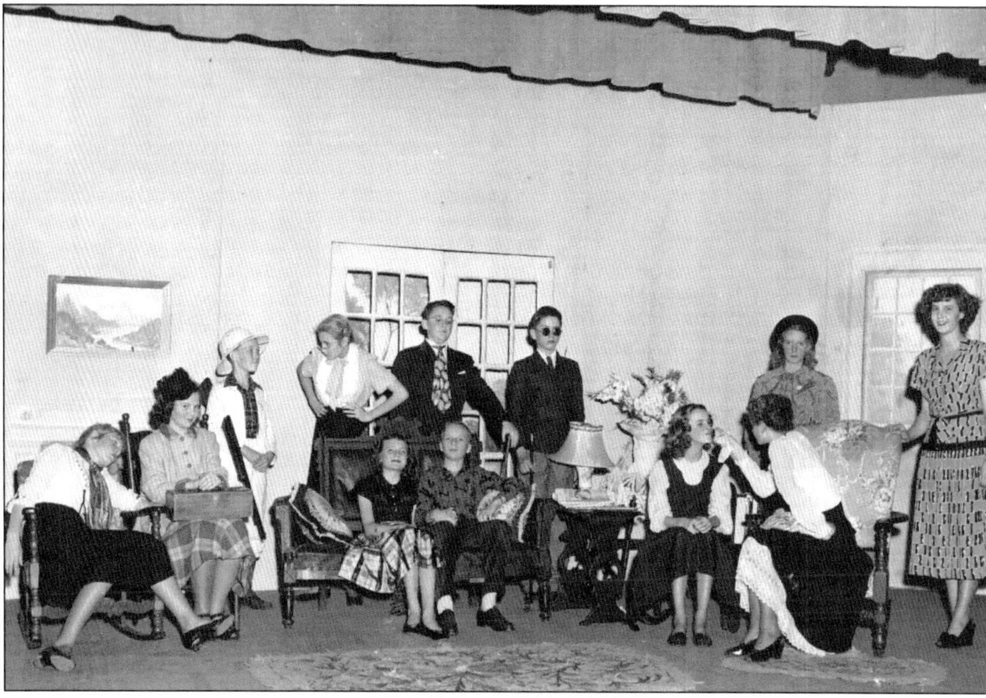

The Junior Garden Club presented the three-act comedy *Three Old Maid Aunts* at the high school auditorium in 1949. Doris Parker, president of the club, acted as master of ceremonies. The group also presented a Clown Dance, an Onion Dance, and songs between acts (including "A Lonely Petunia in the Onion Patch"). The performance was so successful that the participants were asked to perform it again and again at local schools. (Courtesy of Mississippi Gulf Coast Community College Dixie Press Collection.)

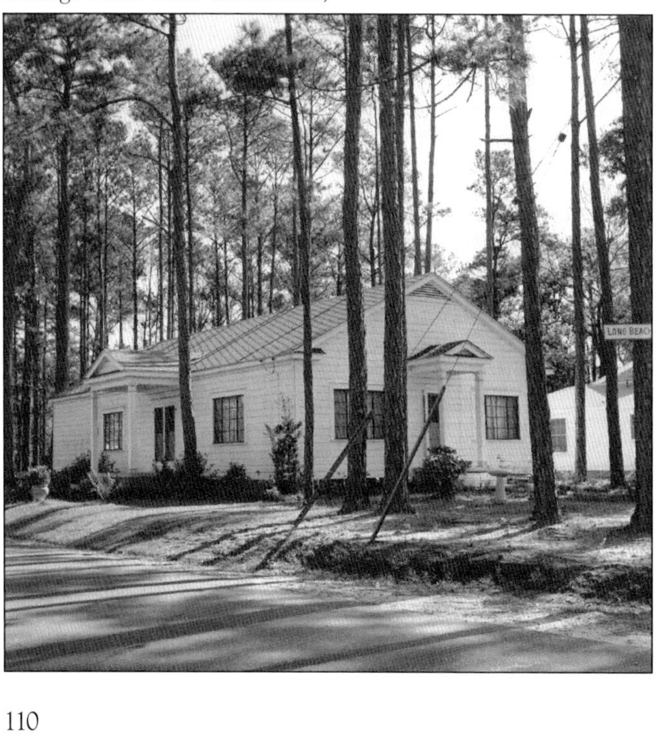

The original garden club building, pictured here in 1957, was located at Burke Avenue and Fifth Street. The Long Beach Club was the first garden club in the state to have its own clubhouse. (Courtesy of Mississippi Gulf Coast Community College C.C. "Tex" Hamill Down South Magazine Collection.)

The War Memorial Association worked diligently to create the war memorial to honor Long Beach's soldiers. Pictured here, from left to right, are (first row) Minnie Ervin, Anne Simmons, May Watrous, and Inez Woodward; (second row) Mrs. Ed Johnson, Lucy Maddux, Minnie Dubuisson, Lucy Quarles, Agnes Hendon, and Blanche Klein. (Courtesy of the Mary Ellen Alexander Collection.)

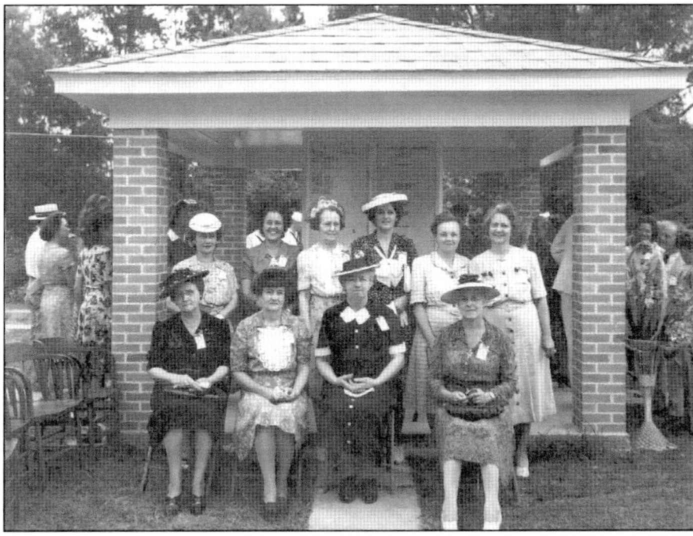

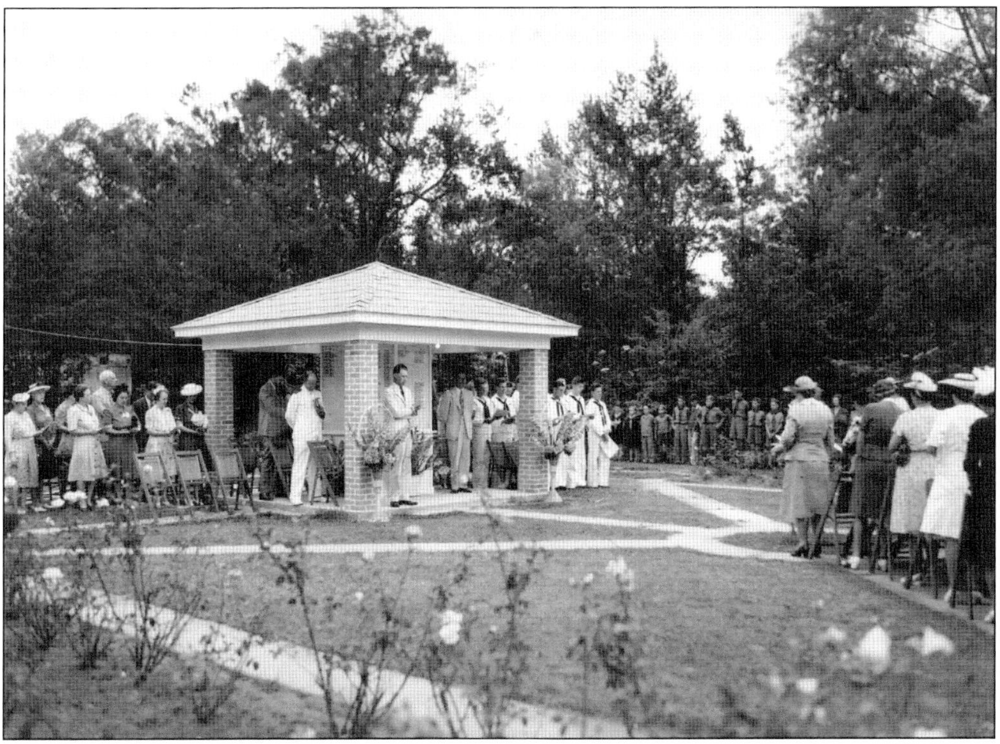

The World War II memorial was dedicated on June 3, 1945. Senior chaplain at the naval base P.C. Edgar was the guest speaker, and there was a choir composed of members of the Navy. The honor roll bore the names of 304 Long Beach men and women who served during the war. A special ceremony was held in July to honor the 10 Long Beach men who died in action (years later, a previously unknown 11th name was added). The memorial was relocated to War Memorial Park on Church Avenue in 1958 in order for the new city hall to be built on the site. The memorial was destroyed in 1969 by Hurricane Camille, and a new memorial was built next to the city hall in 1998 through the efforts of the newly formed Long Beach Historical Society. (Courtesy of Mississippi Gulf Coast Community College Dixie Press Collection.)

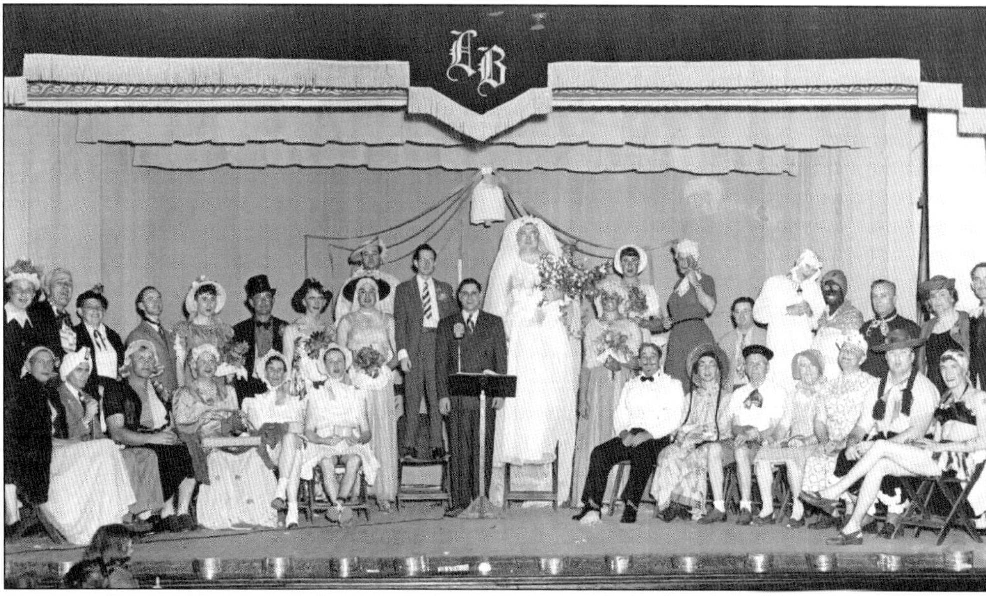
A womanless wedding was held in 1950 by the War Memorial Association to raise money for the memorial and establish a park and playground. The groom is Sam Maxwell (he was later mayor), the bride is Peyton Burkhalter, the best man is Frank Alexander, the maid of honor is Kenneth Woodward Jr., and the preacher is Jimmy Fillingim. (Courtesy of Mississippi Gulf Coast Community College Dixie Press Collection.)

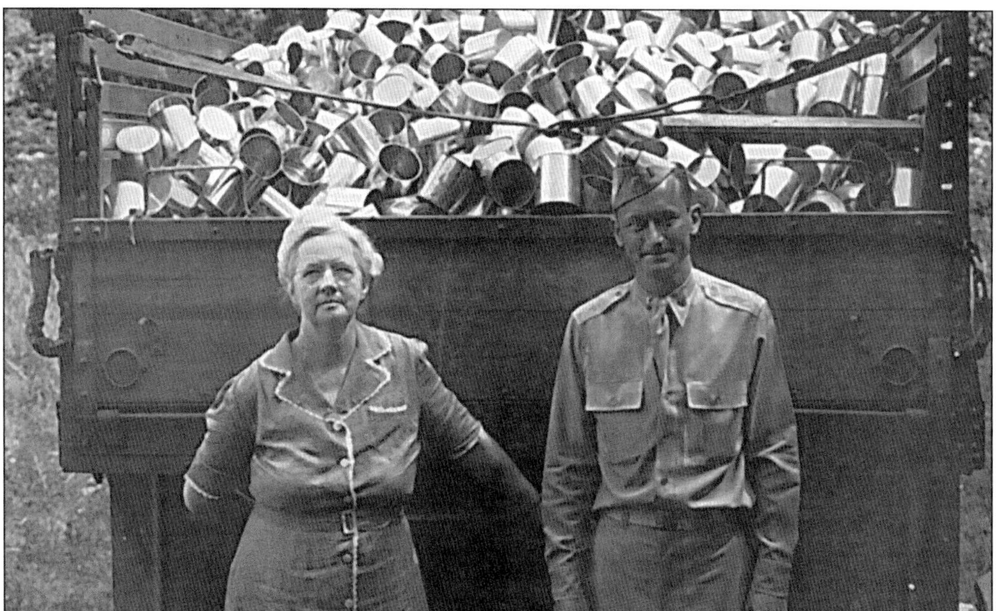
During World War II, many local citizens collected scrap for the war effort. May Quarles Watrous had been the first home demonstration agent for Harrison County and led the tin can drive for the area. She asked the workers in her gardening, canning, and school lunch programs to save their cans. This unidentified salvage officer from Gulfport Army Air Field is shown with Watrous as he picks up some of the 11,000 cans collected by her volunteers. (Courtesy of the Mary Ellen Alexander Collection.)

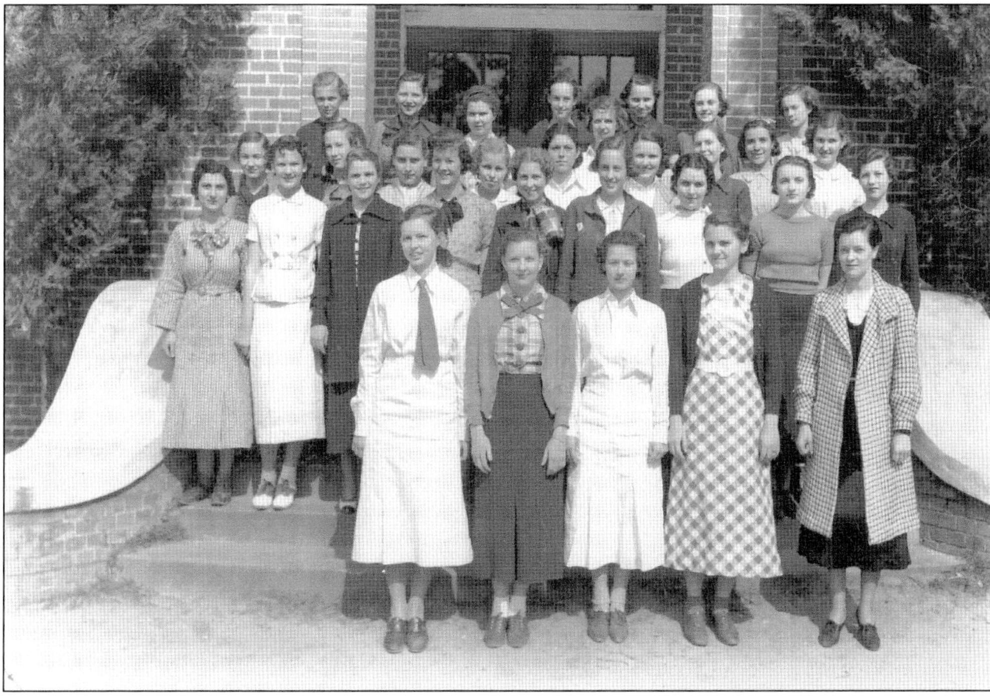

The Girls Reserves group is shown in 1936. The Reserves were formed in 1918 to foster patriotism and war work. The nationwide group was part of the YMCA, and the membership was made up of junior high and high school girls. The girls promoted health, service, knowledge, and spirit. On the front left is 15-year-old Mary Ellen Watrous. (Courtesy of the Mary Ellen Alexander Collection.)

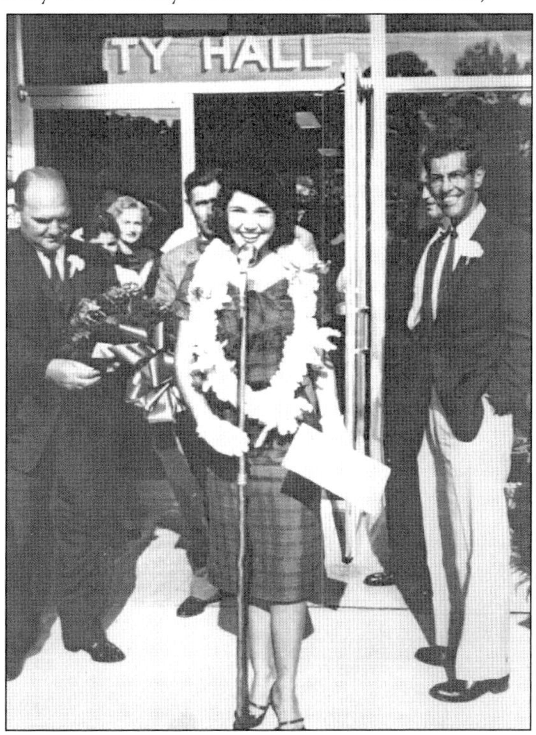

Native Mississippian Mary Ann Mobley visited Long Beach during her reign as Miss America 1959. Mayor Bob Reed is standing behind her, and Pete Carrubba, the city attorney, is at right. (Courtesy of Long Beach Historical Society Archives.)

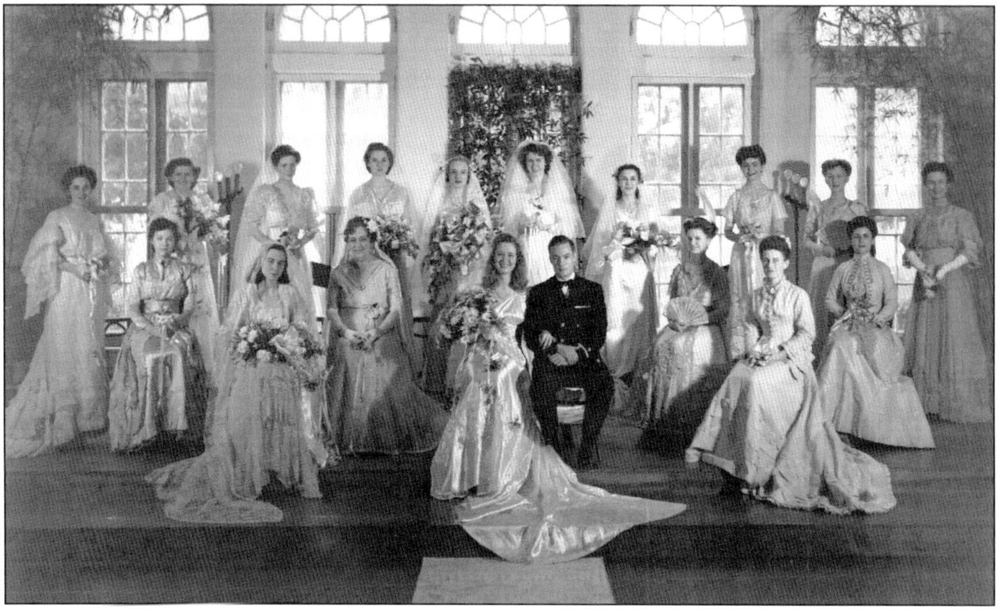

In 1945, the Garden Beach Society held a wedding gown tea at Gulf Park College for Women. Members of the society and students from Gulf Park modeled the wedding dresses, new and old. Several hundred dollars were raised and donated to the coast's Army and Navy hospitals. (Courtesy of Mississippi Gulf Coast Community College Dixie Press Collection.)

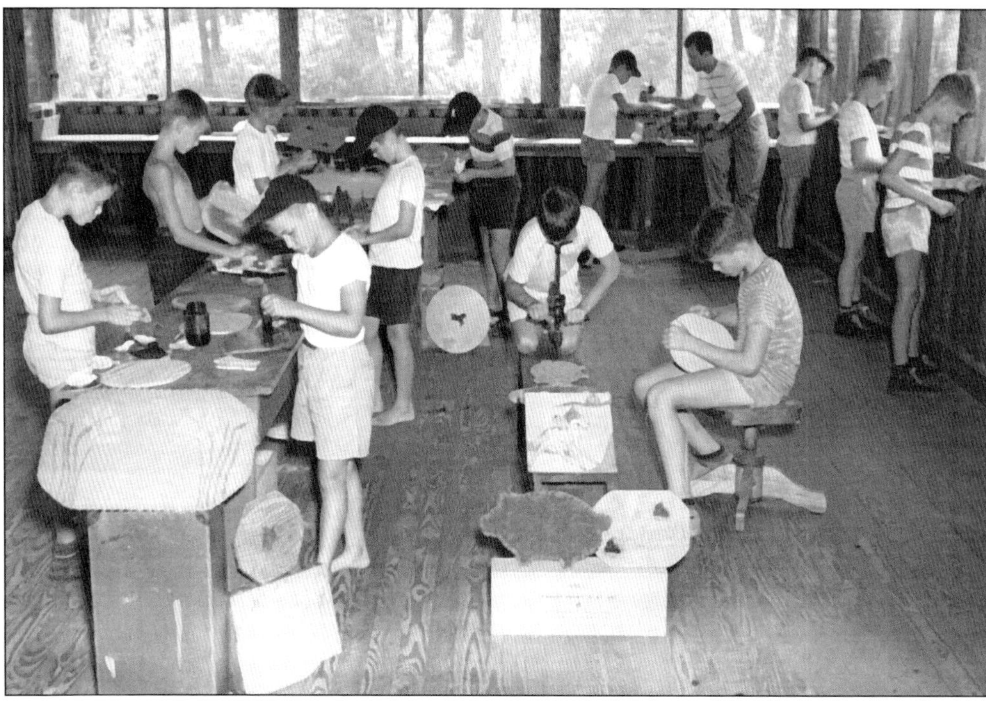

Camp Happy Day was a day camp that was held during the 1960s. The camp was located on the E.O. Hunt property. The daily fee was $5 and included activities such as the arts and crafts shown here. Children learned ceramics and other creative nature crafts. (Courtesy of Mississippi Gulf Coast Community College C.C. "Tex" Hamill Down South Magazine Collection.)

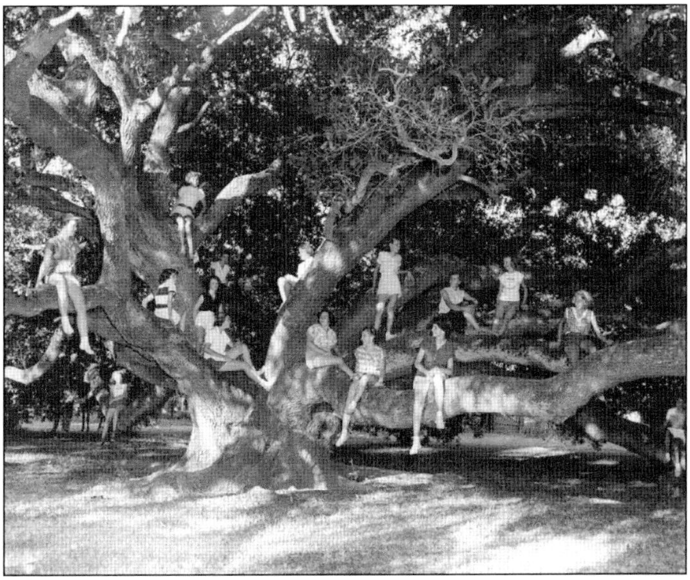

The E.O. Hunt oak tree spread 135 feet across at the time. The tree was registered as Happy Oak in 1966 and renamed the E.O. Hunt tree in 1986. In 1979, it was named the biggest of its kind in Mississippi. Pictured here are campers at Camp Happy Day climbing its limbs. The site of Camp Happy Day is now the South Mississippi Regional Center. (Courtesy of Mississippi Gulf Coast Community College C.C. "Tex" Hamill Down South Magazine Collection.)

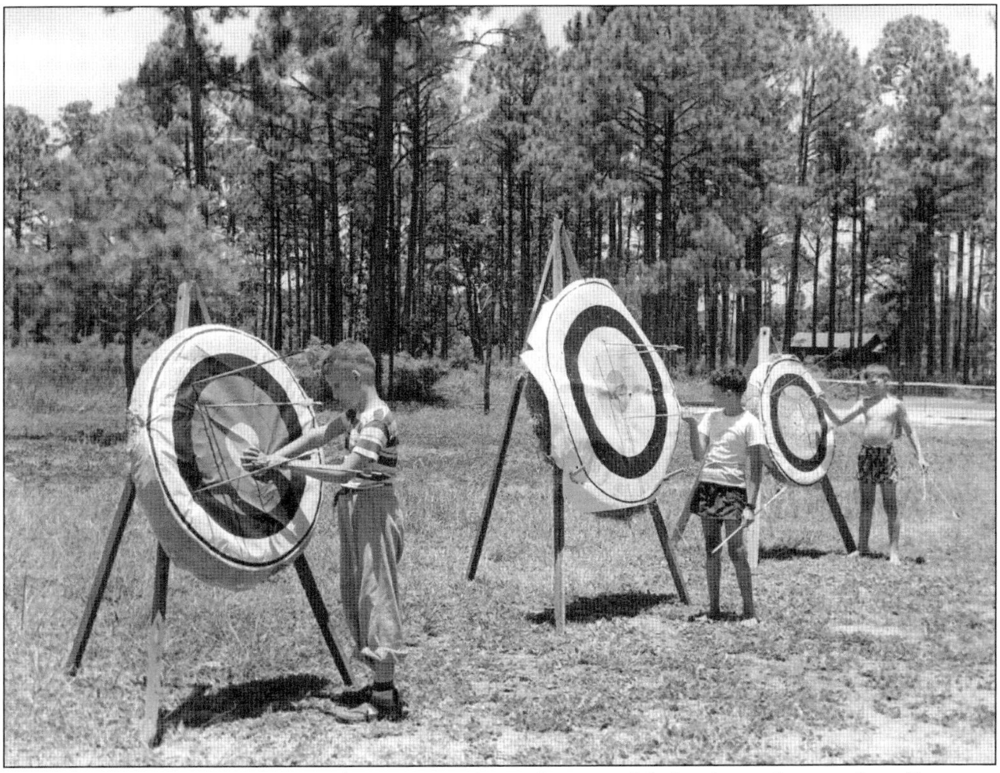

Camp Happy Day campers are learning archery. Boys could also learn how to handle guns, particularly rifles. The camp brochure indicates that some activities, such as archery and shooting, were reserved for boys only, while other activities, such as swimming and horseback riding, could be enjoyed by both boys and girls. (Courtesy of Mississippi Gulf Coast Community College C.C. "Tex" Hamill Down South Magazine Collection.)

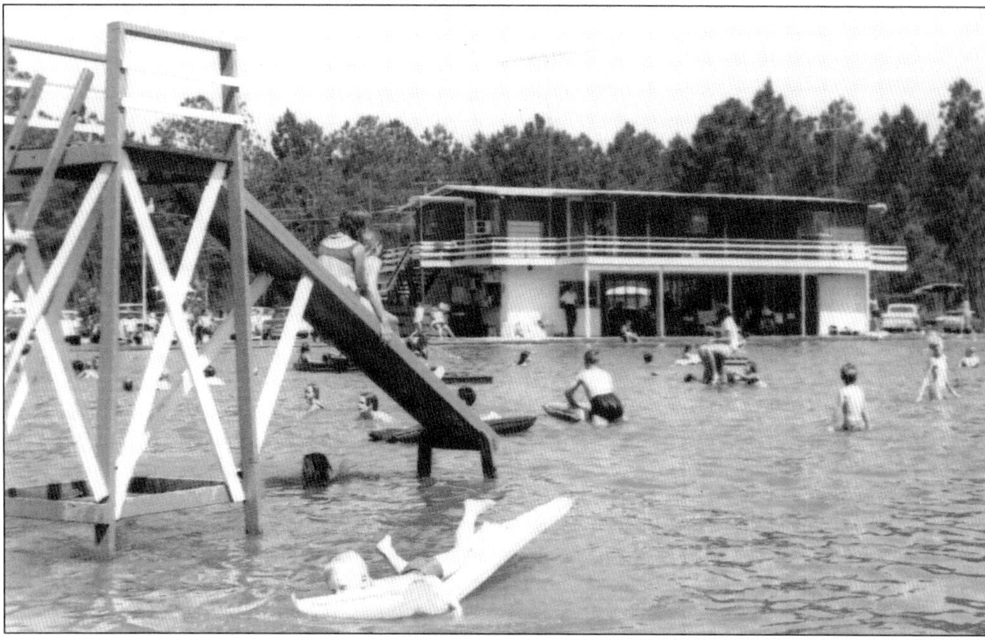

Camp Happy Acres was located on Beatline Road between Daughtery Road and Twenty-eighth Street. The camp was owned by Maxine and Erwin "Smitty" Smith and operated during the late 1960s. There was a man-made lake for swimming and diving, a tall slide in the water (much taller than the one shown in this photograph), and even a zip line. The building on the Camp Happy Acres property contained a concession area, changing rooms, and other amenities. The owners' home was on the second floor. (Courtesy of Mississippi Gulf Coast Community College C.C. "Tex" Hamill Down South Magazine Collection.)

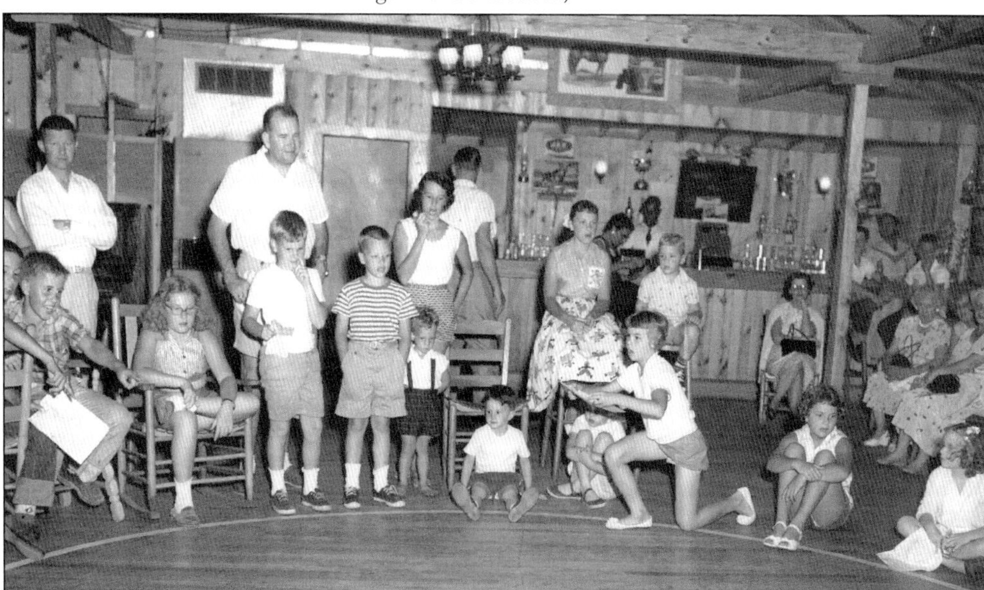

This 1958 photograph shows exciting turtle races at the Holiday Inn's Ye Old Fashioned Pub. Alligator races were also held. (Courtesy of Mississippi Gulf Coast Community College C.C. "Tex" Hamill Down South Magazine Collection.)

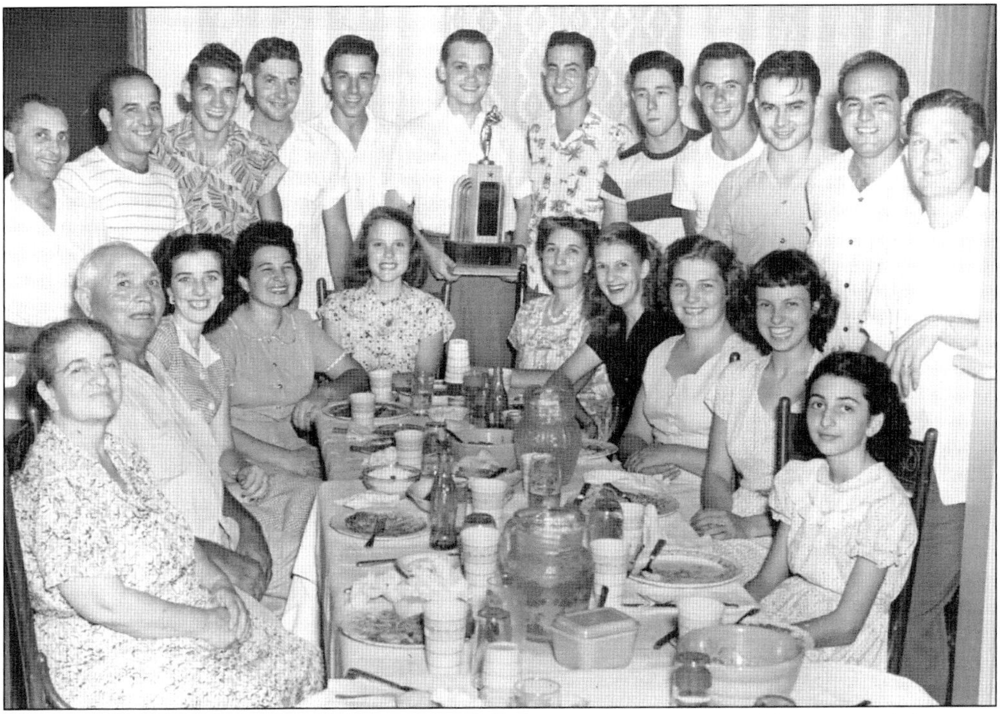

This local baseball team was sponsored by Wilkerson's Grocery Store. The name of the team was not recorded, but baseball and other sports were—and still are—very popular in Long Beach. The seated people in the photograph are probably members of the Wilkerson family or family members of the players. (Courtesy of Mississippi Gulf Coast Community College Dixie Press Collection.)

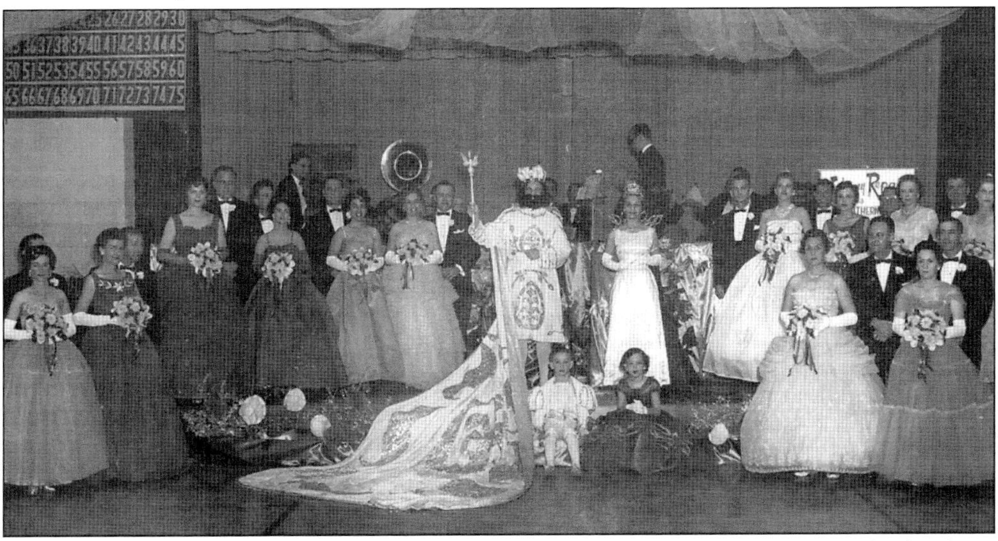

The first Mardi Gras ball was organized in 1961 by the St. Thomas Mothers' Club. The first king and queen were named King Scott and Queen Rosalie, in honor of the first two names for Long Beach—Rosalie and Scott's Station. Odelle Saucier was King Scott I, and Lorraine Hebert was Queen Rosalie. Bill Newton was Grand Duke, and Denise Gaddy was Grand Duchess. (Courtesy of Long Beach Historical Society Archives.)

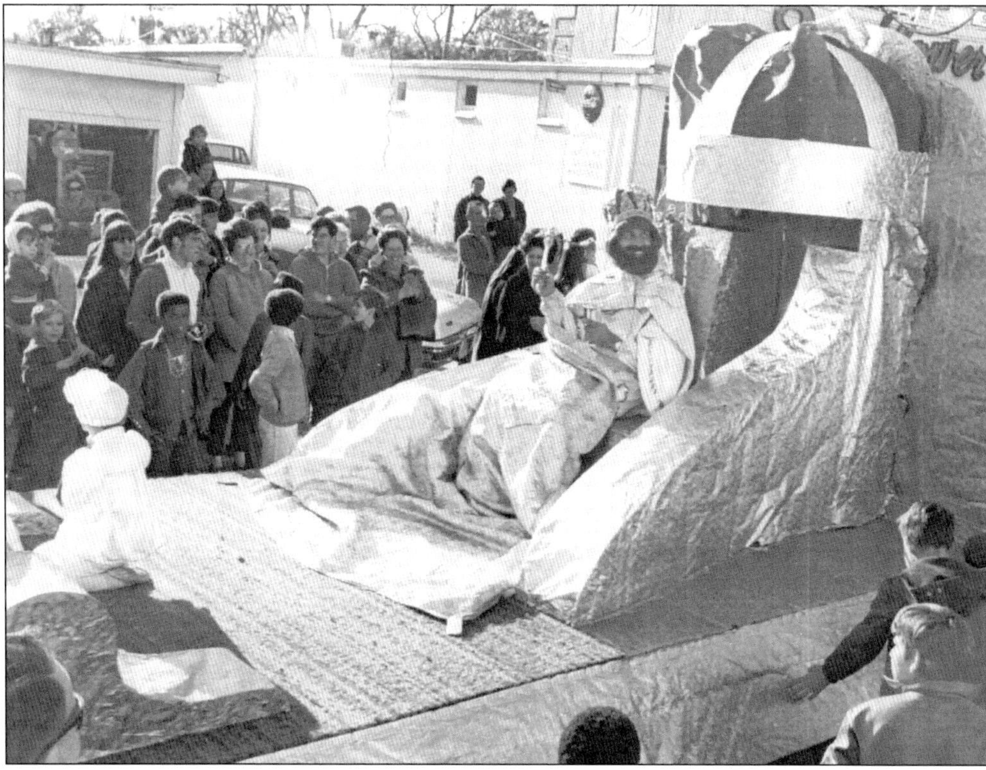

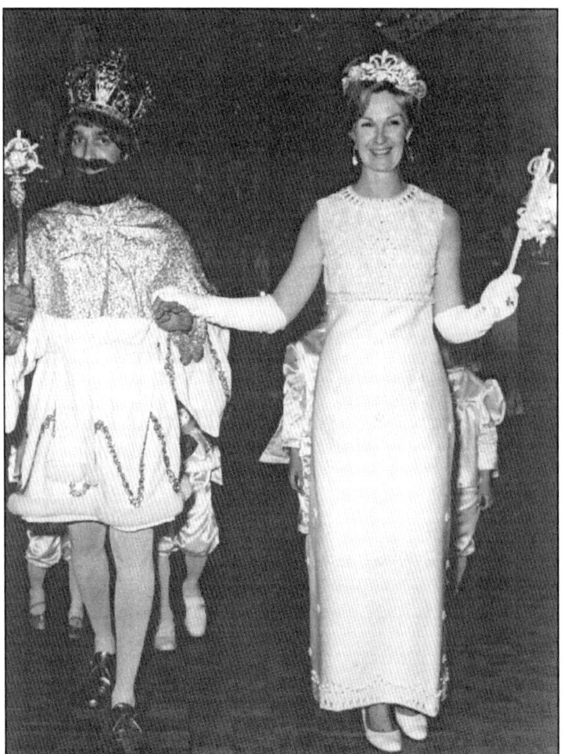

The first Mardi Gras parade was organized by the Carnival Association of Long Beach in 1971. This was also the first year that a Mardi Gras doubloon was produced. A wooden doubloon was used because there were difficulties getting metal ones. After that time, regular aluminum doubloons were used to throw to the crowds. Danny Hansen, King Scott XI, is on his way to give a king's toast to his queen, Earline Dubuisson Selensky. (Courtesy of Beth Hansen.)

Here are the 1971 Mardi Gras king and queen, Danny Hansen Sr. as King Scott XI and Earline Dubuisson Selensky as Queen Rosalie. (Courtesy of Beth Hansen.)

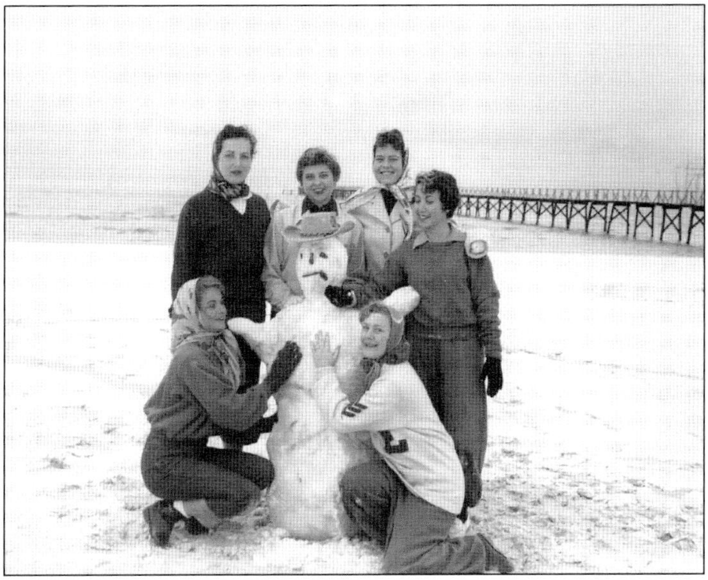

When a rare snowfall occurs in southern Mississippi, everyone takes advantage of the short time before the snow melts to throw snowballs and build snowmen. A snowman on the beach is an unusual sight. No one in this photograph is identified. (Courtesy of Mississippi Gulf Coast Community College Dixie Press Collection.)

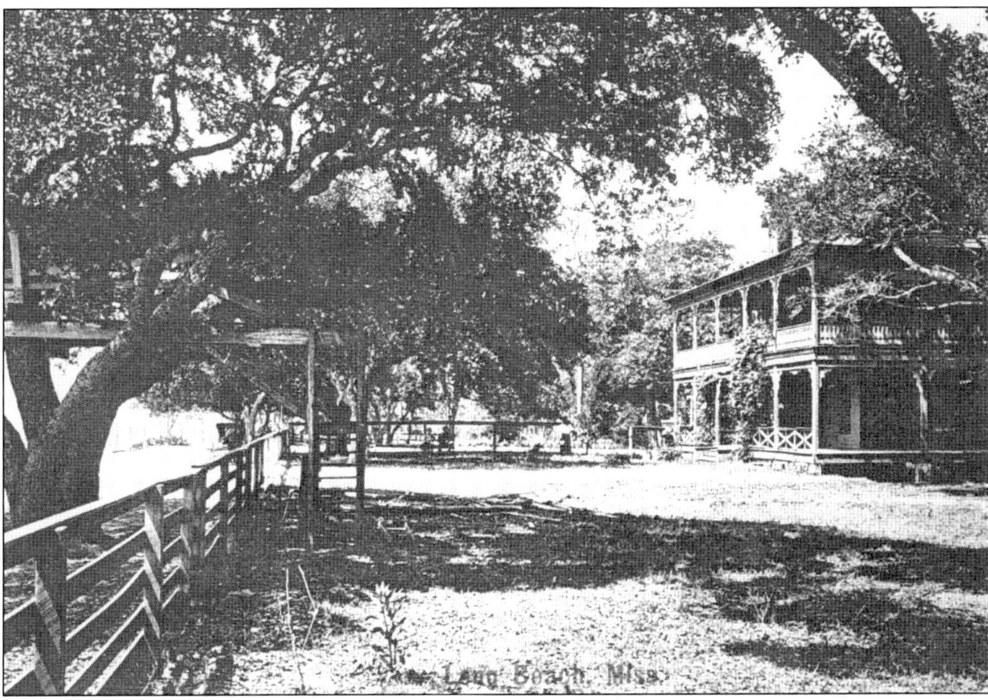

The Brown Hotel was the first hotel in town. It was opened in 1888 by brothers Nathan and Henry Brown, who moved to Long Beach from St. Louis, Missouri. Located on Highway 90 just west of Nicholson Avenue, the Brown Hotel could accommodate up to 50 guests at one time, and there was a long pier with bathing pavilions at the end that extended into the Mississippi Sound. One visitor reported in 1907 after a stay at the Brown Hotel that there were many amenities, and "the table is one of the finest in the section under the capable administration of Capt. John H. Graham, one of the oldest hotel men on the Gulf coast." The hotel was sold as a private residence in 1900 to J.R. and Nellie Nevers, who later reopened it as the Live Oak Hotel. Today, there is a vacant lot on the site. (Courtesy of Paul Jermyn.)

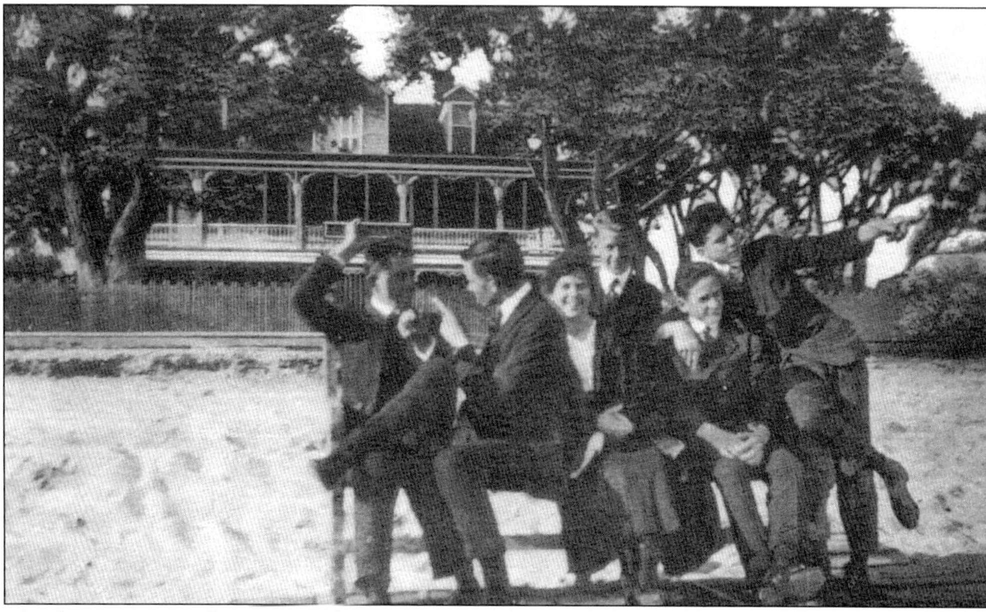

This happy group of young people is spending a nice day on the beach across from the Live Oak Hotel around 1917. The Live Oak, originally the Brown Hotel, had been a private residence before being converted into another hotel. (Courtesy of Paul Jermyn.)

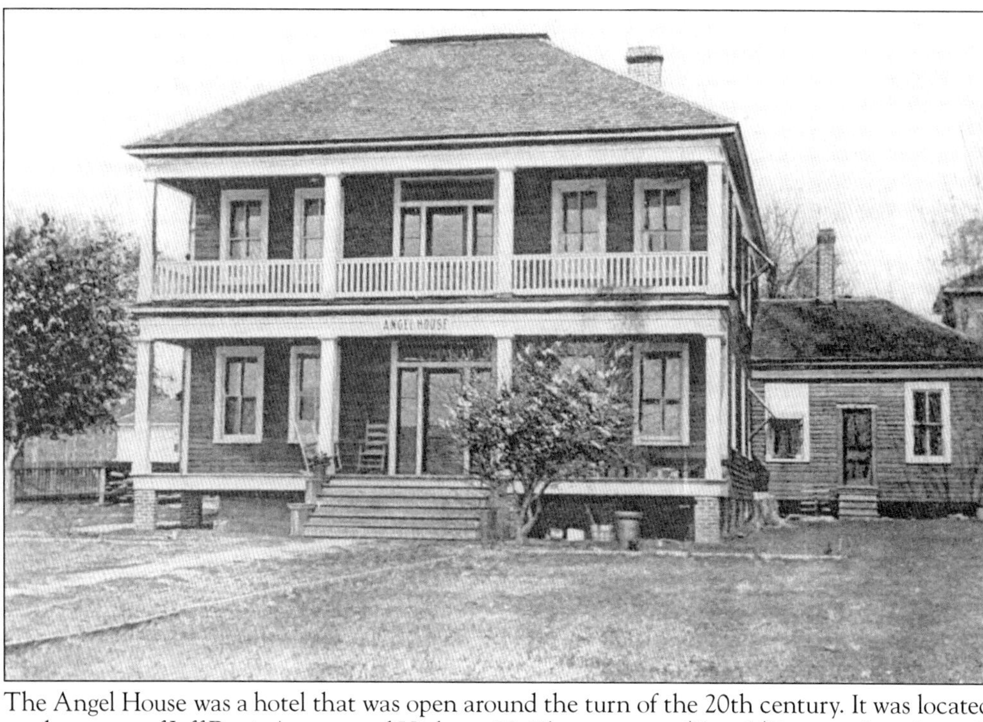

The Angel House was a hotel that was open around the turn of the 20th century. It was located on the corner of Jeff Davis Avenue and Highway 90. The rates were $6 and $7 per week with meals included. Many visitors took the Louisville & Nashville train ($1 round-trip fare) over from New Orleans to spend a day or two. During dinner hour on Sundays there was live piano music. Later, the National Food Store was at this site until Hurricane Camille. (Courtesy of Paul Jermyn.)

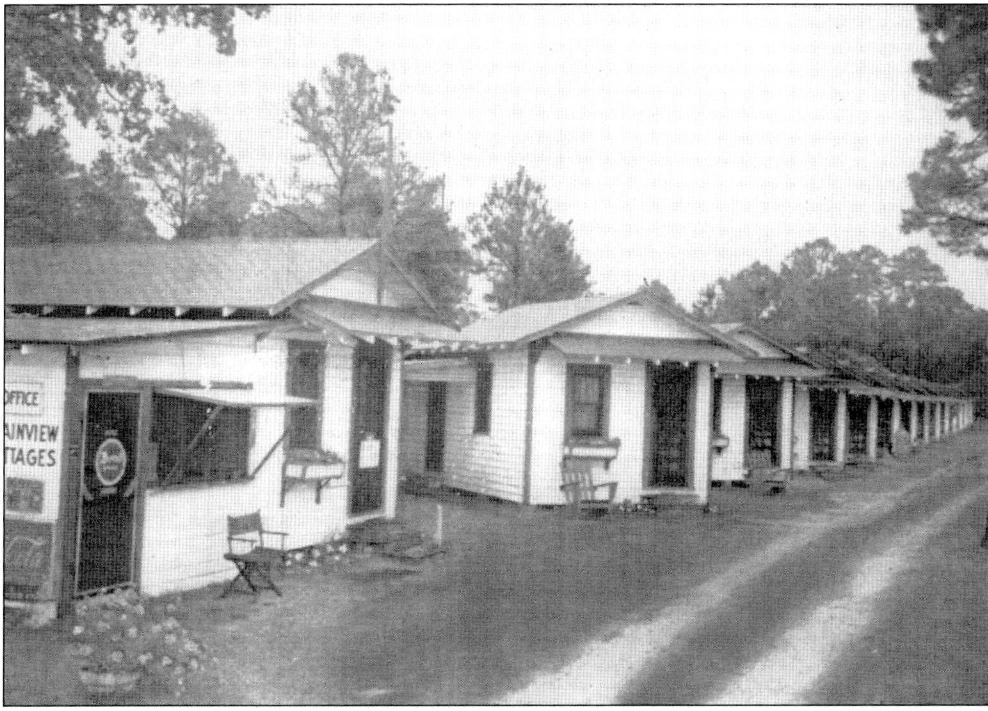

The Plainview Tourist Camp was located near Marcie Drive. The cottages offered "all modern conveniences," including a car shed, gas, and electricity. The cottages, the owner's home, and a next-door restaurant were destroyed in the 1947 hurricane. During the hurricane, restaurant owner Harry Kaletsch and his family barely survived when the storm surge destroyed the building. (Courtesy of Paul Jermyn.)

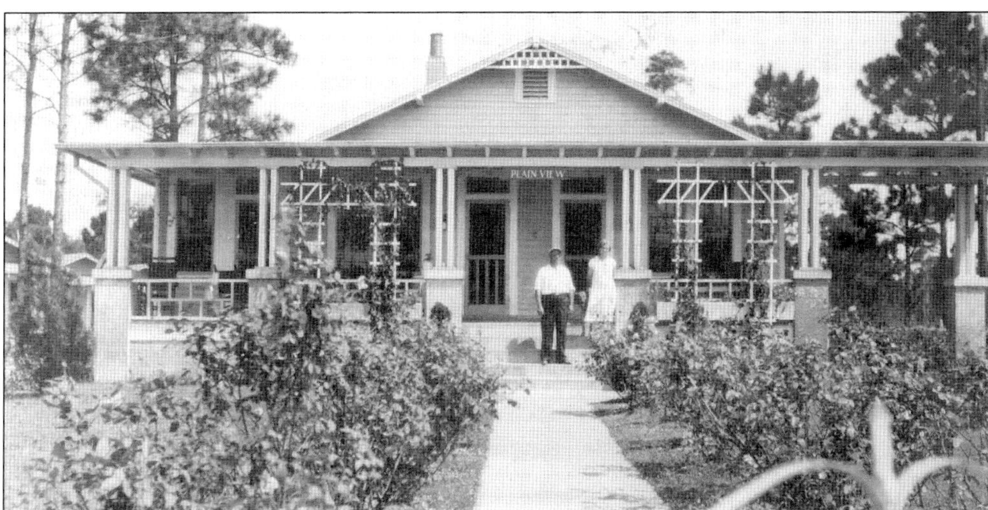

Plainview was the name given to the home of the owners of the Plainview Tourist Camp. It was fairly common for the owners of tourist camps and cottages to live nearby, since most were family-run businesses. The home was destroyed in the 1947 hurricane, along with the cottages and restaurant. (Courtesy of the Mary Ellen Alexander Collection.)

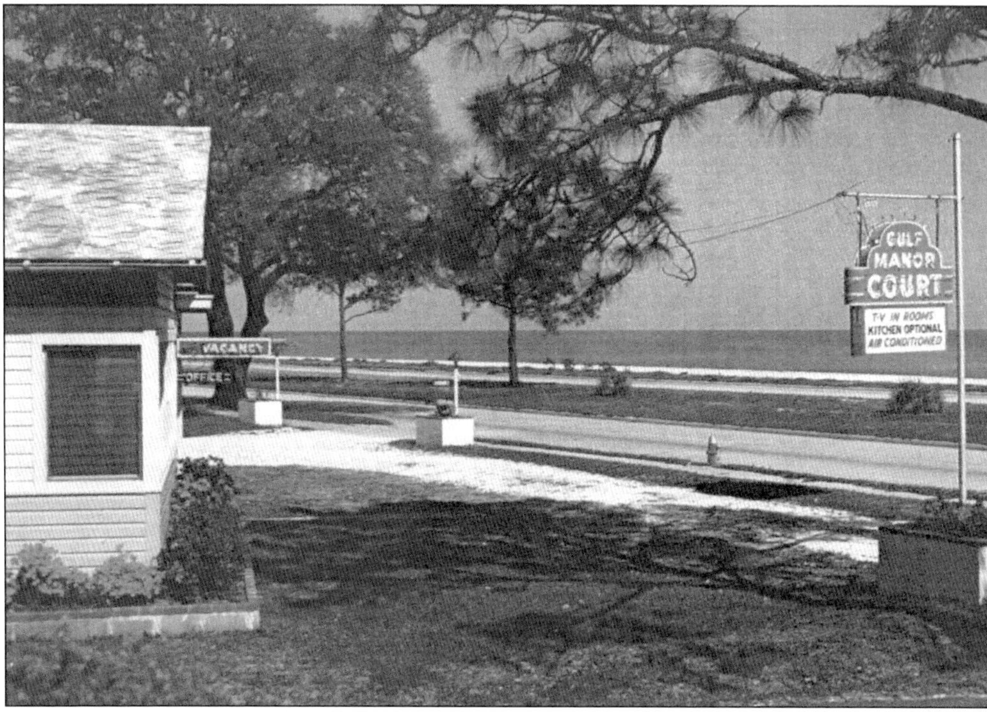

The Gulf Manor Court was located across from the beach. Some of the units were housekeeping cottages, and the court had a pool and a television lounge. (Courtesy of Paul Jermyn.)

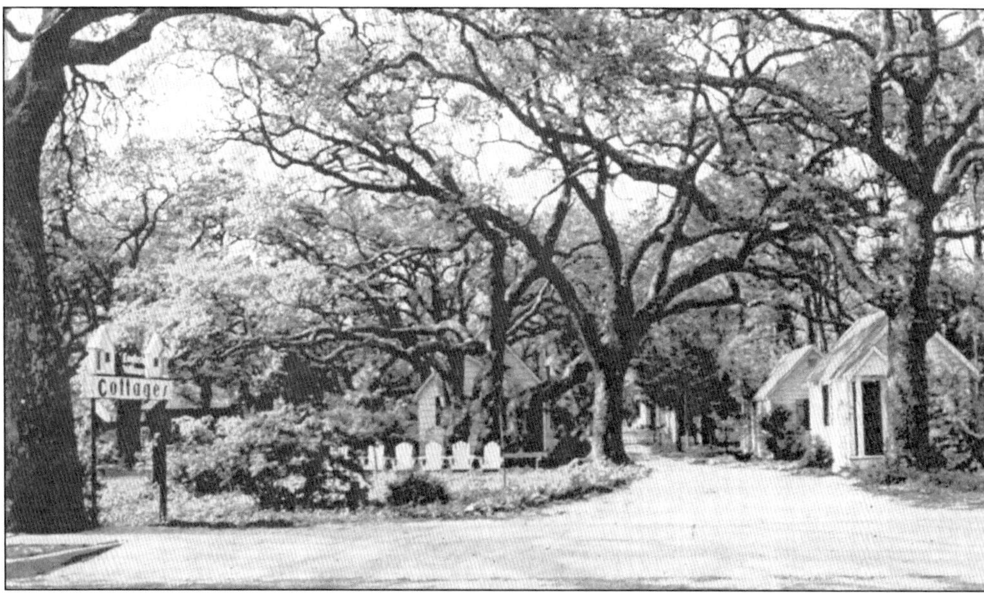

English Village Court was located at what is now called English Village Drive. The amenities here included tile baths, vented wall heat, and kitchenettes. There was also a private pier. According to a postcard that advertises the court, daily rates ranged from $5 for a single bedroom and $10 for a two-bedroom unit. It also had weekly rates. The owners also boasted that they were "in a quiet residential section near everything of interest." The court was owned by Hugh and Ineta Campbell, and it was destroyed by Hurricane Camille in 1969. (Courtesy of Paul Jermyn.)

The Pine Lodge Motor Court and Restaurant had a heated swimming pool and a fishing pier. There was a telephone and television in each room, and each unit was air-conditioned. Some had kitchenettes, and there was "filtered deep well water." This motor court was located at Beach Boulevard and Richards Avenue. (Courtesy of Paul Jermyn.)

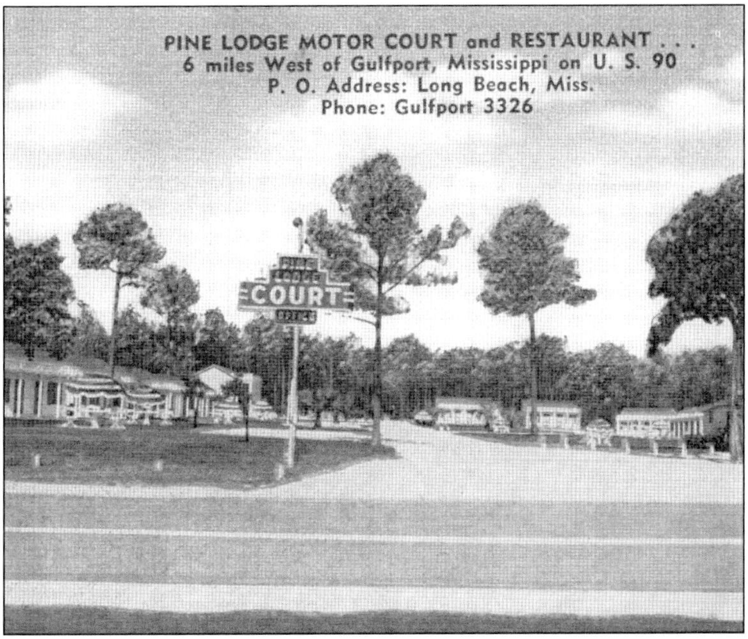

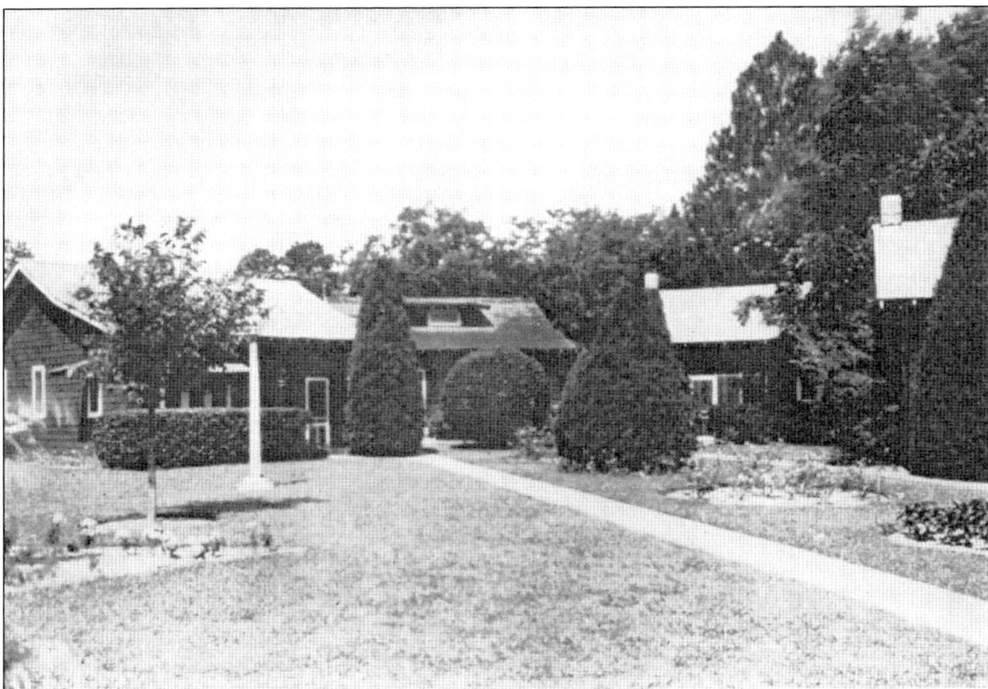

MONROE COTTAGES—U. S. HIGHWAY 90—LONG BEACH, MISS.

Monroe Court (also known as Monroe Cottages) was built in the 1930s by Jay and Ethel Monroe. The cottages were located at 502 Mason Avenue, one block from the beach. The grounds were well landscaped, and the owners catered to permanent residents as well as tourists. It has been reported by some that John Dillinger spent some time as a resident at Monroe Court. The court was destroyed by Hurricane Camille. (Courtesy of Paul Jermyn.)

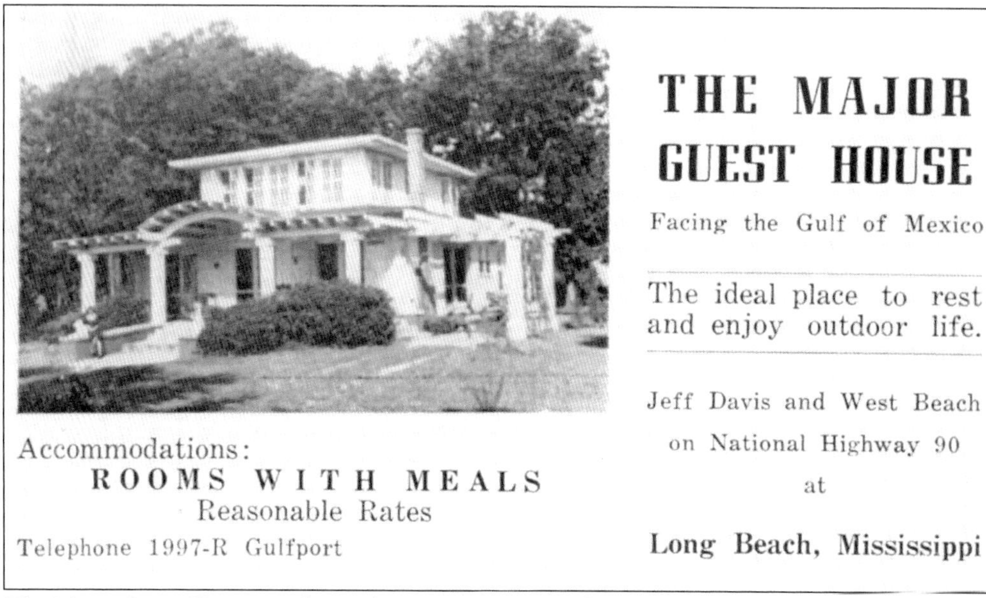

The Major Guest House was located at 106 West Beach Boulevard. The 1947 city directory lists Sidney and Myrtle Major as the residents at that address. Not much is known about the Major House, but since it appears to be a single building instead of units or separate cottages, it was possibly a bed-and-breakfast rather than a hotel or motor court. (Courtesy of Paul Jermyn.)

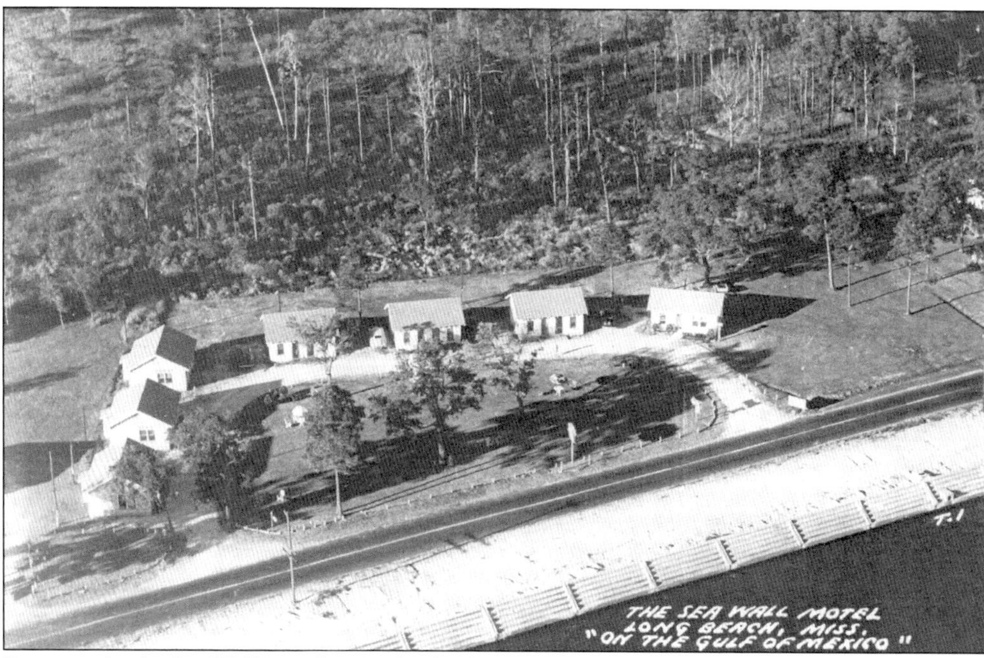

Surprisingly, the Sea Wall Motel seemed to be the only business in Long Beach that took advantage of the draw of the historical seawall name to promote the business. Advertising as a "beautiful spot . . . facing the gulf," the motel was destroyed by Hurricane Camille. (Courtesy of Long Beach Historical Society Archives.)

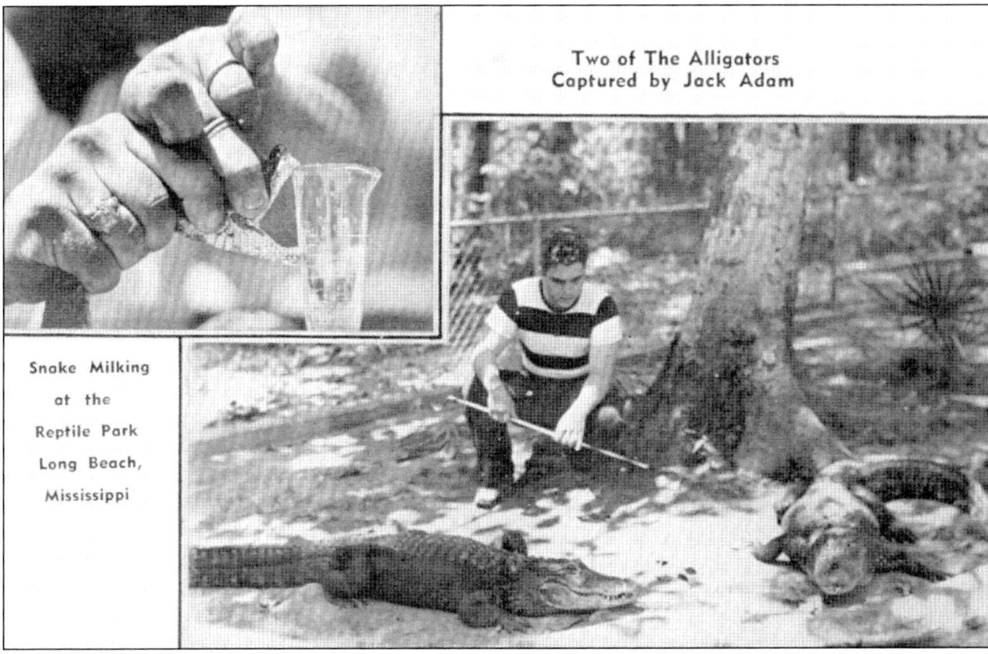

This postcard shows some of the draws at Jack Adam's Reptile Park. Not much is known about this attraction, but some sources say that it was located on White Harbor Road near the beach and closed sometime during the early 1970s. Adam later moved to Mesa, Arizona, and opened another reptile-themed park there. (Courtesy of Paul Jermyn.)

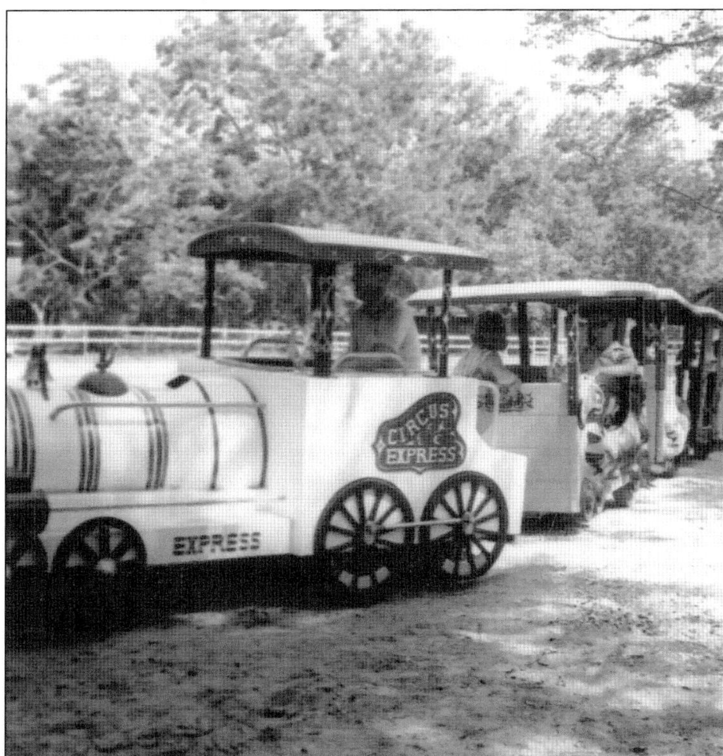

Animal Kingdom was owned by Jack W. Riley and two partners. Opened in 1968, it was located at Beatline Road and Railroad Street (at White Harbor Road). This site was the former home of Camp Happy Day. There was a pool where swimming courses were taught by the Red Cross. Visitors could tour the kingdom on this tour train. (Courtesy of Mississippi Gulf Coast Community College C.C. "Tex" Hamill Down South Magazine Collection.)

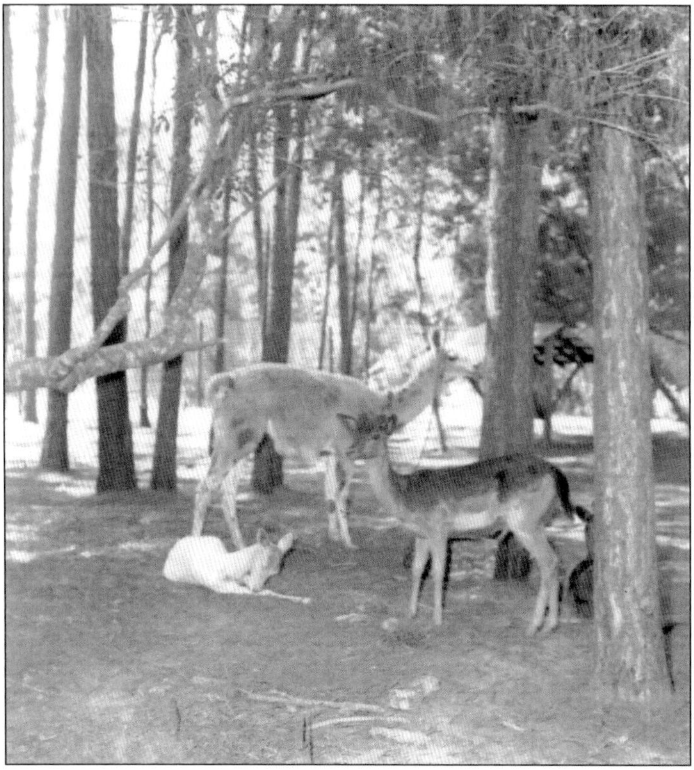

Some of the many animals that were available for visitors to observe, feed, and pet included these deer. There was also a spider monkey that some said had the run of the property. (Courtesy of Mississippi Gulf Coast Community College C.C. "Tex" Hamill Down South Magazine Collection.)

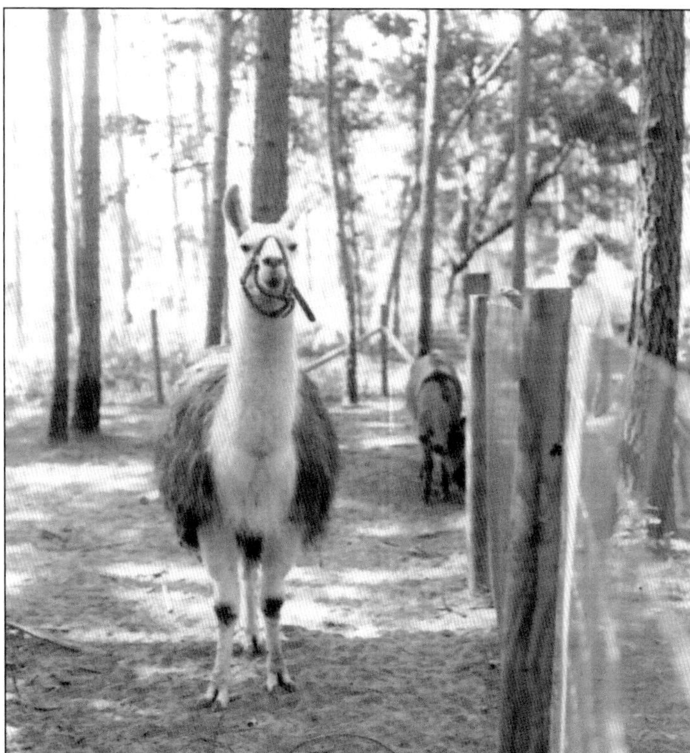

There were several llamas at the Animal Kingdom. Visitors were allowed to pet and feed the llamas, which were sometimes spotted napping under the E.O. Hunt oak tree. (Courtesy of Mississippi Gulf Coast Community College C.C. "Tex" Hamill Down South Magazine Collection.)

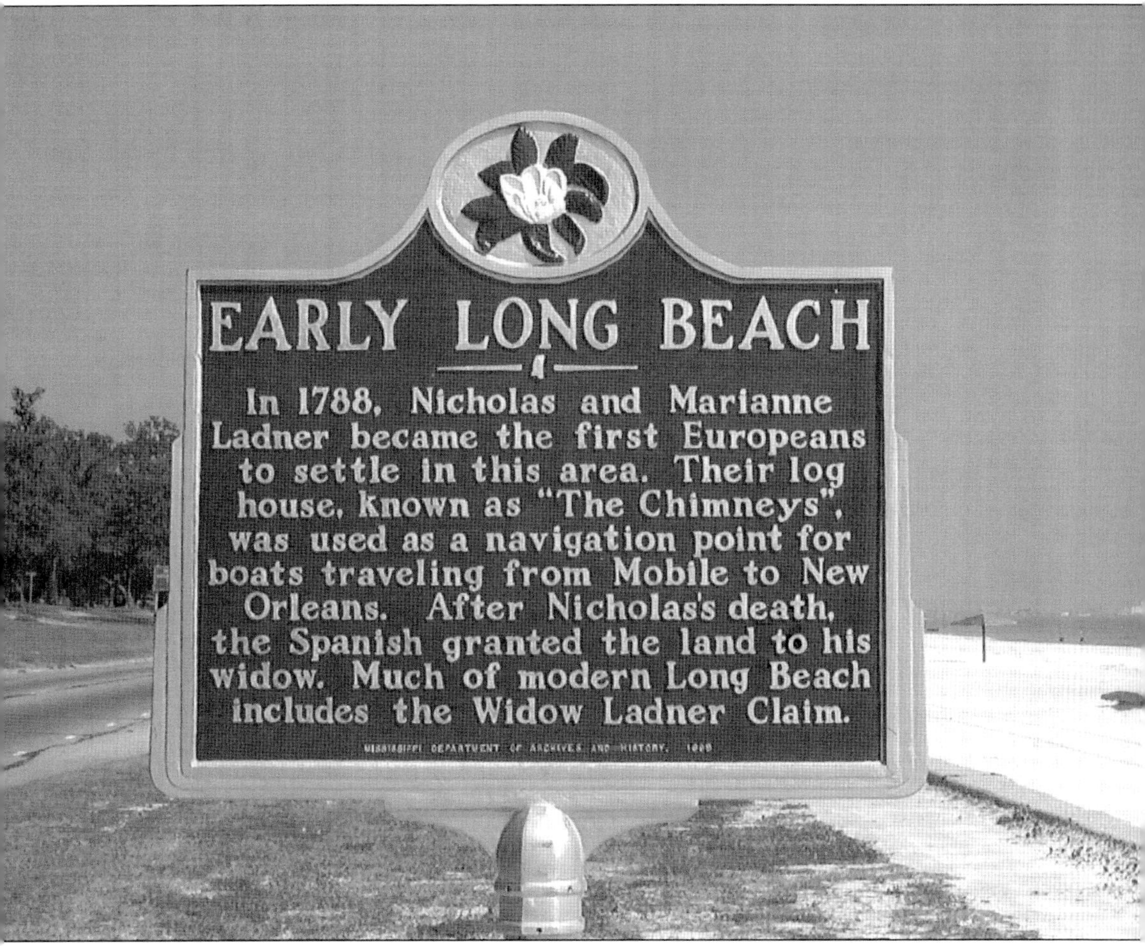

This historical marker was placed on the beach near the first settled area in Long Beach—the place known as the Chimneys. This marker is one of two installed by the Mississippi Department of Archives and History. The Long Beach Historical Society has placed 15 markers throughout the city, commemorating important events and places in Long Beach history. (Courtesy of the Mary Ellen Alexander Collection.)